Mathematics and the Elementary Teacher

4th edition

Mathematics and the Elementary Teacher

RICHARD W. COPELAND
Florida Atlantic University

Macmillan Publishing Co., Inc.
New York
Collier Macmillan Publishers
London

Earlier edition copyright © 1976
by the W. B. Saunders Company.

Macmillan Publishing Co., Inc.
866 Third Avenue, New York, New York 10022

Collier Macmillan Canada, Ltd.

Library of Congress Cataloging in Publication Data

Copeland, Richard W
  Mathematics and the elementary teacher.
  Includes bibliographies and index.
  1. Mathematics—Study and teaching (Elementary)
I. Title.
QA135.5C596   1981   372.7   80-19585
ISBN 0-02-324830-0

Printing: 1 2 3 4 5 6 7 8   Year: 2 3 4 5 6 7 8

PREFACE

The fourth edition of *Mathematics and the Elementary Teacher* is being published by Macmillan Publishing Co., Inc. The first three editions of this book were published by W. B. Saunders, which has now merged with Holt, Rinehart and Winston, Inc.

The relation of this book to *How Children Learn Mathematics,* 3rd Ed., published by Macmillan in 1979, should be clarified. *How Children Learn Mathematics* is an application of Piaget's ideas to mathematics education and is most useful to students who already have some background in teaching mathematics to children. *Mathematics and the Elementary Teacher* is broader in context as applied to methods of teaching and may be more appropriate for a first course in mathematics education. It does use Piaget's ideas as a base but also considers the views of other well-known psychologists.

Changes in this edition include adopting a more basic format, one that fits more closely to what teachers teach in the elementary school. There is less emphasis on theory and peripheral topics.

In reference to specific changes, classification and ordinal and cardinal numbers are considered together in a single chapter.

Each operation—addition, subtraction, multiplication, and division—is treated as a separate chapter. There are new sections on error patterns and diagnoses in each of these chapters. Common fractions are the subject of two chapters, one for the operations of addition and subtraction and the other for the operations of multiplication and division.

There is a new chapter on using the pocket calculator in the classroom. There is also a new chapter on exceptional children because the mainstreaming process will involve all elementary school teachers in working with these children.

It is hoped that this book will continue to meet the needs of both preservice and inservice elementary school teachers as they help children discover mathematics.

R. W. C.

CONTENTS

_____Mathematics and the Elementary Teacher_____

1

HOW DO CHILDREN DEVELOP MATHEMATICAL CONCEPTS ?

How does a youngster "learn" mathematics? Are his mental processes the same as those of an adult? Can we by a process of segmenting knowledge into simpler and simpler form come to a point where any child can understand it? This last question poses a premise that has sometimes been used as a basis for determining the level at which mathematics can be introduced to children. Mathematical content has been moved farther and farther down in the elementary grades on the assumption that proper procedure or "system" is all that is necessary.

Objecting to such a line of thought, the developmental psychologist holds that a child is a developing organism and does not learn like a miniature adult. There are a number of limitations to his ability to solve problems. He may be unable to reverse a thought process, he has an egocentric outlook, he is unable to generalize, he needs concrete materials. Each of these ideas will be discussed later in the text.

How then should mathematics be taught? Can it be taught by "show and tell" as are the colors? For example, "This is red."; or in math, "This is three."

An old Abbott and Costello comedy sequence begins with Costello holding a banana in each hand. Holding up one hand, he says, "One banana"; holding up the other hand, he says, "Two bananas." Putting his hands together, he says, "Three bananas." This could be teaching math by the "show and tell" method.

THE BEHAVIORISTS AND DEVELOPMENTAL PSYCHOLOGISTS

Such questions as those above point up sharp distinctions between two schools of thought on how children learn mathematics. One school of thought is that of the **behaviorists**. Their premise is, "Provide the proper conditioning and you can get human beings to behave in almost any way you want." Hence the name "behaviorists." Two-well known psychologists representing this school are B. F. Skinner and Robert Gagné.

A very different school of thought is that of the **developmental psychologists**. A well-known representative of this school is Jean Piaget.

These two schools of thought will be compared in terms of various factors related to the educational process such as readiness, motivation and reward, what should be taught, and how it should be taught.

Readiness

Do children have to reach a certain point of development before they are "ready" or able to understand a mathematical concept such as addition?

The behaviorist (Skinner) is less concerned with readiness than the developmental psychologist (Piaget), because the behaviorist considers education largely an external process—that is, a process developed by the teacher or programmer. Teaching, according to the behaviorist, is something done *to* the child. It is a process through which the child is put to obtain certain desired results or behaviors.

The educational process devised by the behaviorists involves looking at what is to be taught (addition, for example), isolating all the necessary components and then placing them in a chain or sequence for the learner to follow. In isolating all the component elements, the premise is that there is no room for error. The child misses no necessary step and consequently should not fail if the program has been devised correctly. Thus, the program is built outside the child and he is a response mechanism. If the program has been built properly by the teacher, there should be no readiness problem. The assumption, of course, is that the child can be taught logical processes at any stage of development.

In contrast to this line of thought, the developmental psychologist

HOW CHILDREN DEVELOP MATHEMATICAL CONCEPTS

holds that the mental processes of the child must be taken into account. He believes that the child cannot learn the same content as the adult, and there are developmental stages in the ability of the child to think logically or mathematically. These stages as described by Piaget will be looked at in more detail later in this chapter and also in other chapters as they relate to specific mathematical content.

To cite just one example of a readiness problem at this point, consider the concept of addition. If the typical six-year-old is shown a picture of 2 daisies and 7 roses, he can identify that they are a set of flowers and that some are daisies and some are roses, but he cannot successfully answer the question whether there are more roses or more flowers.

The behaviorist might argue that it is the teaching process that is lacking. The developmentalist would claim that addition as a process cannot be understood by the average six-year-old because he lacks at least two logical constructs—one being **reversibility of thought** and the other the **inclusion relation**. These constructs cannot be taught by external means alone. The child's mind is not an empty box to be filled as the teacher sees fit.

A second familiar logical concept is **conservation of number.** Do the following two rows contain the same number of objects?

Children of five or six years usually say that the top row contains more, even if they count and find five in both rows. Piaget calls this readiness problem "non-conservation of number" and maintains that such children do not have the necessary intellectual processes to realize what a number such as "five" means.

Learning theorists have conducted many experimental studies to determine whether or not such concepts as conservation, transitivity, or multiple classification can be taught earlier by external reinforcement than Piaget's "developmental stage" approach would indicate.

As is so often the problem with experimental research, the results are contradictory. There are many qualifying factors. Some studies conclude that conservation, for example, can be taught earlier (Sigel, 1966; Bruner, 1964; Beilin, 1965; Brainerd, 1969; Peters, 1970). Others find that it cannot (Wohlwill, 1960; Almy, 1966; Mermelstein, 1967; Langer, 1970; Kuhn, 1972). Procedures that have been used in an attempt to induce earlier learning include: (1) verbal rule instruction

Six-year-old thinks spread out set has more, even after counting.

(Beilin); (2) cognitive conflict (Smedslund); and (3) language activation (Bruner).[1]

Piaget does not believe that acceleration, *even if it were possible,* would be desirable—believing that this is an optimum time dictated by the child's development (at least as far as logico-mathematical thought structures are concerned).

What Is To Be Taught

The behaviorist position is more traditional on what is to be taught. You teach subject matter, content, or answers. The trend "back to basics" usually aligns itself with the behaviorist school.

[1] For description of these procedures see E. Mermelstein and E. Myer: "Conservation Training Techniques and Their Effects on Different Populations." *Child Development,* **40**:471, 1969.

HOW CHILDREN DEVELOP MATHEMATICAL CONCEPTS

The developmentalist is not so concerned with subject matter, basic facts, skills, or answers per se as with the process of understanding the concepts or operations involved. For example, when being taught the basic addition facts such as 3 + 2, does the child understand addition as a concept? Or has he just learned to give the answer "Five" when he is asked "What is 3 + 2?" Can the child use the concept of addition in a situation that requires it?

Being able to use addition as needed because its meaning is understood is quite different from being able to give the right answer. The behaviorists are product or answer oriented, as revealed in their familiar behavioral objectives for addition:

"Given any two single digit addends, the child will respond with the correct sum."

But being able to say "Five" when one sees "3 + 2" is simply a memory or recall bit of knowledge. Most five and six-year-olds can respond correctly "Five" and yet, when shown a set of 3 candies and a set of 2 candies and another set of 5 candies, will say that there is more in this set (5) than in these sets (3 and 2). See p. 56.

How Math Should Be Taught

One controversy centers on the question of how much and what kind of guidance should be provided to students. Those favoring learning by discovery or invention (Piaget and Bruner) advocate maximum opportunity for physical exploration by the student. Solutions for problems and generalizations result from the student's own action on his environment, and from his own mental operations.

Those preferring **guided learning** (Gagné and Skinner) emphasize the importance of carefully sequenced instructional experiences (information processing) through maximum guidance by teacher or instructional material. Basic **associations** of facts are stressed.

The term **association** refers to the familiar stimulus-response or S→R mechanism: Control the stimulus to obtain the desired response. It is a psychology applied to teaching rats, with positive reinforcement of cheese for right responses and electric shocks for wrong responses. The reward or positive reinforcement for the child is praise, a good grade or a gold star. The reward then is external, that is, provided by the teacher.

The procedure for Gagné is to begin with a task analysis—what do you want the learner to be able to do? The capability must be stated **specifically** and **behaviorally**. It can be conceived as a terminal behavior and placed at the top of what will become a pyramid-like network.

capability

The question, then, is "What do we first need to know?" Suppose it is *a* and *b*.

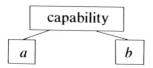

But in order to perform task *a* you must be able to perform tasks *c* and *d*. And before you can perform *b* you must perform tasks *e, f,* and *g*.

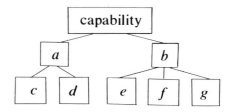

Hence a pyramid or hierarchy is built. If the capability with which we began is "problem solving," the learner must first know **principles**. But to understand certain principles he must know specific **concepts**, and prerequisite for the concepts are particular **associations** or facts. This analysis ends up, according to Shulman, with classically or operantly conditioned responses $(S \rightarrow R)$.[2]

Upon completing the map of prerequisites, Gagné would administer pretests to determine what has already been mastered and what precisely still needs to be learned. This model is conducive to "programming" and programmed materials as a method of teaching. A very tight teaching program or package develops.

Piaget characterizes this procedure in which the mind can be likened to an empty box as follows:

In more or less close connection with the Pavlovian school of Soviet reflexology American psychology has evolved a certain number of theories of learning based on the stimulus-response view . . . the most recent of the great Americal learning theorists, Skinner, the author of some remarkable experiments with pigeons . . . convinced of the inaccessible nature of the intermediate variables [the

---

[2] Lee S. Shulman. "Psychological Controversies in the Teaching of Science and Mathematics." *The Formative Years, Principles of Early Childhood Education.* Edited by Stanley Coopersmith and Ronald Feldman. San Francisco: Albion Publishing Co., 1974, p. 174.

HOW CHILDREN DEVELOP MATHEMATICAL CONCEPTS

mind] decided to confine his attention to stimuli or inputs that could be varied at will and to observable responses, or outputs, and then to take account only of the direct relationships between them, ignoring the interval connections. This "empty box" conception of the organism, as it has been called, thus deliberately thumbs its nose at all kinds of mental life, and confines itself solely to behavior in its most material aspects.[3]

In contrast to carefully controlled associations of stimuli to responses, Piaget uses the terms **assimilation** and **accommodation** to name the mental operations by which understanding is acquired. The child must **assimilate** new data into the concepts he has formed and accommodate data that does not fit. He assimilates easily a new bird into his concept of birds but must accommodate to other concepts such as a butterfly seen for the first time.

Logical processes such as mathematics must be based on the psychological structures available to the child. These structures change as the child matures physiologically and neurologically and as the child has the necessary experiences in the physical world. These experiences must involve actions performed on objects and communication with other people such as the teacher and other children.

Contrasting Objectives

The decision for the teacher, then, is based on her philosophy of education as spelled out in her **objectives**. Shulman maintains that the objectives of Bruner and Gagné are not the same—Bruner's (and Piaget's) being *processes* that allow the learner to handle new problems effectively as he faces them, and Gagné's being *product* in terms of mastering a specific organized body of subject matter.[4]

As described by Gagné:

> To be an effective problem solver, the individual must somehow have acquired masses of structurally organized knowledge. Such knowledge is made up of content principles . . . even if "strategies" or "styles" of thinking could be taught, and while if is possible that they could, they would not provide the individual with the basic firmament of thought which is subject matter knowledge.[5]

Piaget, in contrast, comments on the teaching machine and subject

[3] Jean Piaget: *Science of Education and the Psychology of the Child.* New York: The Viking Press, Inc., 1971, p. 76.
[4] Shulman, *op. cit.,* p. 1974.
[5] Robert Gagné: *Conditions of Learning.* New York: Holt, Rinehart and Winston, 1965, p. 170.

matter method as follows:

> In cases where it is a matter of acquiring a set body of learning as in the teaching of languages, the machine does seem to be accepted as of undeniable service. In cases where the idea is to reinvent a sequence of reasoning, however, as in mathematics, though the machine does not exclude either comprehension or reasoning on the student's part, it does channel them in an unfortunate way and excludes the possibility of initiative.[6]

But,

> These machines have performed at least one great service for us, which is to demonstrate beyond all possible doubt the mechanical character of the schoolmaster's function as it is concerned by traditional teaching methods: if the ideal of that method is merely to elicit correct repetition of what has been correctly transmitted, then it goes without saying that a machine can fulfill those conditions correctly.[7]

Bruner's position is between that of Piaget and Gagné. Inhelder, a main writing associate of Piaget's, summarizes Piaget's "confrontation" with Bruner as follows:

> . . . we agree that information-processing techniques are of great importance in the study of cognitive development. However, it seems necessary to emphasize that information-processing techniques have several aspects of which Bruner and his co-workers have studied only some.

> Information-processing techniques seem to consist, on the one hand, of selection, of storage, and of retrieval of relevant cues. On the other hand, these techniques imply transformation of information and its coordination. The later is our fundamental concern.

> To us, transformation of information implies assimilatory and accommodatory processes which, unless coordinated, produce deformation of information. Our experiments seem to show that whereas selection, storage, and retrieval can be learned in procedures, coordination cannot.[8]

An example is the ability to order or seriate a set of sticks, each slightly different in length. Even if the child is shown 10 sticks, arranged in order by length, he is unable to recall later (as by drawing) what he saw because he does not have the intellectual operations to coordinate the necessary data.[9] His drawings are a deformation of the ordered set of sticks that he saw (see drawing p. 29.)

[6] Piaget, *op. cit.,* p. 78.
[7] Piaget, *op. cit,* p. 77.
[8] B. Inhelder: Comment. *American Psychologist,* 21:160, 1966.
[9] Jean Piaget and Barbel Inhelder: *Memory and Intelligence.* New York: Basic Books, Inc., Publishers, 1973, p. 31.

Math Drill and Practice

The behaviorist then takes the content to be taught, divides it into components, and chains the components together in a logical sequence (connectionism). If a child misses any component, he goes back or repeats the sequence leading to that component. Thus, repetition is the correctional mode. The premise is that if he repeats it, sooner or later he will remember it. Thus the procedure is the familiar "drill and practice."

The developmentalist holds that drill and practice will not necessarily teach the concept involved. Also, there will be little if any transfer to a new problem situation requiring use of the same concept. The behaviorist responds that he expects little transfer.

The developmentalist holds that to correct errors children must first understand the logical or mathematical concept involved. This involves more than repetition. The child must explore the situation for himself using physical or concrete materials. He must structure for himself the necessary concept. To understand addition, for example, the child should put sets of objects together, noting their number before and after they are put together. He should separate and reassemble the objects. Even this will not be enough without the necessary readiness factors.

Piaget calls addition and subtraction one reversible logical system and states that one cannot be understood without the other. Just repeating orally or in writing that "three plus two is five" does not master the concept involved.

The developmentalist views the job of the teacher as the provision of both the necessary physical materials for the children and the questions that help the children structure for themselves the concept involved.

Practice is necessary for immediate recall of the basic addition facts and it should be required, but not at the expense of understanding, which should come first. There are many good games for drill and practice such as a modification of bingo called "Addo" for memorizing the basic addition facts.

Transfer of Training

The transfer of what has been learned in one problem situation to other problem situations is very important if one is to be an effective citizen.

Gagné is a conservative on matters of transfer. He believes that for an element which has been learned in one sequence to be transferred to another situation it must be applied directly as it was learned. Transference occurs when specific identical (or highly similar) elements already learned occur in some new sequence.

Bruner and Piaget, in contrast, subscribe to the broadest theories of transfer of training—hence the emphasis on process. Broad transfer is necessary in understanding mathematics because such cognitive structures as seriation, conservation, commutativity, and transitivity (each to be discussed later) are basic parts of many math problems.

Motivation

The behaviorist considers motivation to be an external thing applied by the teacher in terms of reward (positive reinforcement). The reward is traditionally a good grade, a gold star, or some type of praise or approval.

Piaget considers motivation to be more of an internal thing. There is an intrinsic need to know in the mind of the learner if the problem under study is seen as relevant or worth knowing (to the learner). And this, of course, is a challenge to the teacher—relating what is to be taught to something the learner sees as worth knowing.

STAGES OF INTELLECTUAL DEVELOPMENT

The logical structure of the child's mind is not the same as that of the adult, and it does not reach the adult stage of operation until 11 or 12 years of age, according to Piaget. If this is true, instructional procedures for the child of less than 11 or 12 years must be planned on the basis of the level of development of the child.

Piaget finds four basic stages of development in children. The first is a **sensorimotor stage** lasting until approximately two years of age. The second is a **preoperational stage** lasting from two until approximately seven years of age. The third is a **concrete operational stage** lasting on an average from seven to 11 or 12 years of age. Finally there is a **formal operational stage**, which is an adult level of thinking.

It is necessary that the teacher understand these stages if she bases her instructional program on the stage of development of each child in her class.[10] Children at different stages cannot learn the same content. They cannot learn about number, for example, until they reach the concrete operational stage. Piagetian diagnostic tests are not difficult to use and will be discussed in later chapters as the various mathematical ideas are introduced.

The **concrete operational** stage marks a beginning of certain types of logical thought in children. Thinking logically is necessary to understand number. The transition from pre-logical to logical thought can be tested easily. The most pervasive concept, used by Piaget as a basis for this test, is the idea of **conservation** or **invariance**. It is a logical concept. Applying it as a test of conservation of number, the child is shown two sets of objects and asked if there are more objects in one set than in the other, or if the sets are the same.

The configuration of one set is then changed—for example, one set may be spread out—and the question repeated.

The child at the **preoperational** level usually thinks there are more in the spread-out set. Sensory impressions are the basis for his answer. It looks like more since the objects cover a larger space. At the concrete operational level the child can use the "logic" that if there was the same

[10] For further study see Richard W. Copeland: *How Children Learn Mathematics: Teaching Implications of Piaget's Research,* 3d ed. New York: Macmillan Publishing Co. Inc., 1979.

number there is still the same number. Number is conserved, or invariant, as the shape or arrangement of the set of objects is changed.

Usually between six and seven years of age the child will reach the **concrete operational** level of thought as far as number is concerned. It is then that he can begin to learn about number in other than a rote fashion. At the preoperational level the child may "count" the number of objects in each set, five, for example, and still tell you there are "more" in the spread-out set. It is obvious that the number 5 means little at this point of development. Many children in the first grade are still at this level, so that what passes as instruction in arithmetic may be wasted.

The child at the concrete operational level should have concrete objects as a basis for abstracting mathematical ideas; hence the name "concrete operational level of thought." As the child manipulates objects he is at some point able to disengage the mathematical idea or structure involved. It is necessary for the child of four to eleven to begin learning about abstract mathematics inductively by using objects in the physical world. It is not sufficient to "tell" or "explain" or "show." The child should derive the mathematics from the objects himself. This idea cannot be overemphasized because most of us are used to being "told" or having something "explained." According to Piaget, "Words are probably not a shortcut to understanding; the level of understanding seems to modify the words that are used rather than vice-versa."[11]

The basic cause of failure in school is often this lack of sufficient concrete experiences:

> . . . mathematics is taught as if it were only a question of truths that are accessible exclusively through an abstract language . . . of symbols. Mathematics is, first of all and most importantly, actions exercised on things [counting objects, measuring objects, handling and manipulating objects] , and the [mental] operations themselves are more actions, . . . imagined instead of being materially executed. Without a doubt it is necessary to reach abstraction, . . . but abstraction is only a sort of trickery and deflection of the mind if it doesn't constitute the crowning stage of a series of previously uninterruped concrete actions. The true cause of failure in formal education is therefore essentially the fact that one begins with language (accompanied by drawings) instead of beginning with real and material action.[12]

While seven has been given as an average age of the development of **conservation of number,** it is an average age and this understanding may

[11] Eleanor Duckworth: "Piaget Rediscovered." *Readings in Science Education for the Elementary School,* edited by E. Victor and M. Lerner. New York: Macmillan Publishing Co., Inc., 1967, p. 319.
[12] Jean Piaget: *To Understand is to Invent.* New York: Grossman Publishers, 1973, pp. 103–104.

Brian, age six, at preoperational level for conservation of quantity. He thinks there is "more" in the tall glass, even though he thought the amount was the same before the liquid was poured from the other tall glass into the wide container.

occur at five and one half years for one child and at eight years for another.

Piaget cautions that when an age is specified it should be considered in the following context:

The age of seven is a relative one in a double sense. In our research we say that a problem is solved by children of a certain age when three-quarters of the children of this age respond correctly. As a result, to say that a question is solved at seven years old means that already one-half of the six-year-olds can solve it, and a third of the five-year-olds, etc. So, it's essentially relative to a statistical convention. Secondly, it's relative to the society in which one is working. We did our work in Geneva and the ages that I quote are the ages we found there. I know that in certain societies, for instance in Martinique, where our experiments have been done by Monique Laurendeau and Father Pinard, we have found a systematic delay of three or four years. Consequently the age at which those problems are solved is also relative to the society in question. What is important about these stages is the order of the succession. The mean chronological age is variable.[13]

[13] Ceclia B. Laratelli: "Aspects of Piaget's Theory That Have Implications for Teacher Education. Selected Readings." *The Formative Years, Principles of Early Childhood Education.* Edited by Stanley Coopersmith and Ronald Feldman. San Francisco: Albion Publishing Co., 1974, p. 158.

At approximately 11 or 12 years of age the child supposedly moves to the fourth and last stage, the **formal operational** level of thought, at which time he can reason or consider at the abstract level without having to resort to the physical world. It is a hypothetical-deductive thought level. At this time it is possible to begin formal mathematics with some premise arbitrarily chosen and then to reason in deductive logical steps at the abstract or symbol level. Such a level of thought, however, is not characteristic of the elementary school child, who should have first-hand experiences with objects as ground work for understanding mathematics.

In teaching the child of 11 or 12 years of age or over, two questions should be considered. First, if most children are formal operational at 11 or 12, do they still need experiences with concrete materials to understand mathematical ideas? It is the writer's opinion that they do—at least for certain ideas. Nondecimal base ideas such as base five are understood better by college students when they have the opportunity to work with manipulative materials designed to represent base five ideas. Also, many college students never had the benefit of concrete materials as a basis for passing through the concrete operations stage while they were in elementary or secondary school.

The second consideration is whether Piaget has identified too early an age—that is, 11 or 12—as being the age at which most children reach the formal operational level. Some recent studies indicate that only 50 per cent of college freshmen were functioning completely at the concrete operational level, with fewer than 25 per cent fully formal operational in their thought.[14]

KNOWLEDGE IN TERMS OF HEREDITY AND ENVIRONMENT

Knowledge to Piaget is not simply a copy of the external environment. Neither is it preformed inside the subject as some interpreters of development would have it. Instead, a set of intellectual structures are progressively constructed by continuous interaction of the learner and the physical world. It is on this last point that Piaget is furthest removed from the majority of psychologists and common sense.[15]

[14]J. Dudley Herron. "Piaget for Chemists." *Journal of Chemical Education,* March 1975, p. 146.
[15]Jean Piaget: Piaget's Theory. *Manual of Child Psychology.* 3rd ed. Edited by L. Carmichael. New York: John Wiley & Sons, 1973, p. 703.

Knowledge is constantly linked with actions or operations, that is, with transformations—joining together, separating, putting into one to one correspondence.

The relation between the learner and objects in the physical world is in no way determined beforehand and, what is more important, is not stable. Knowledge, at its origins, neither arises from the environment nor the learner but from interaction between the two.[16]

Thus Piaget, while developmentally oriented, does not look at knowledge as a predetermined unfolding interior process. Neither does he fit with the "common sense" approach of intelligence as a copy, file, and retrieval system.

INDIVIDUALIZATION OR SOCIALIZATION

Present trends are toward the individualization of instruction. Some of the best known commercial "individualized" programs, however, lean toward a paper and pencil type approach rather than a math lab approach.

Even where a program is experience-centered, should it be entirely individualized? Piaget thinks not.

> When I say "active" I mean it in two senses. One is acting on material things. But the other means doing things in social collaboration, in a group effort. This leads to a critical frame of mind, where children must communicate with each other. This is an essential factor in intellectual development.[17]

Group problem solving and discussion are one means of raising questions and setting natural conflict forces in motion to determine which solutions are right, and why. This often necessitates a cognitive reorganization of the participant—in determining why he was wrong, for example.

It is important to realize that whereas the preoperational child is egocentric and considers his viewpoint the only one, the concrete operational child is able to assimilate differences in viewpoint and to alter his concepts accordingly.

Thus social interaction with other children is important. A clash of convictions causes an awareness of other points of view which may need to be reconciled, thus helping a child out of his egocentricity.

[16] *Ibid.*, p. 704.
[17] R. E. Ripple and V. N. Rockcastle: *Piaget Rediscovered.* Ithaca, N.Y.: Cornell University Press, 1964, p. 4.

The teaching of mathematics has always presented a somewhat paradoxical problem. There exists, in fact, a certain category of students . . . quite intelligent . . . capable of demonstrating above-average intelligence in other fields, who always fail, more or less systematically, in mathematics . . . it is difficult to conceive how students who are well endowed when it comes to the . . . utilization of . . . logico-mathematical structures can find themselves [so] handicapped in the comprehension of . . . what is to be derived from such structures [that is, mathematics].[18]

This problem is usually answered in terms of certain students having an "aptitude" for or being "good" in mathematics. In contradiction to this assumption it is Piaget's conclusion that mathematics involves

a technical language comprising a very particular form of symbolism. . . . So the so-called aptitude for mathematics may very well be a function of the student's comprehension of that language itself, as opposed to that of the [mathematical] structures it describes. . . . Moreover, since everyting is connected in an entirely deductive discipline [such as mathematics], failure or lack of comprehension of any single link in the chain of reasoning causes the student to be unable to understand what follows.[19]

The central problem of mathematics teaching then becomes one of relating the particular logic sequence being taught to the psychological or intellectual structures available to the child. And this, of course, is what mathematics educators in this country have just begun to do.

MATHEMATICIANS AND LANGUAGE

Goethe, in *Maximen und Reflexionen*, said that "Mathematicians are like Frenchmen: whatever you say to them they translate into their own language and forthwith it is something entirely different."[20]

When Poincaré was at the height of his powers as a creator of mathematics he took a battery of Binet intelligence tests and did so poorly he was rated an imbecile.[21]

David Hilbert (1862–1943), one of the greatest mathematicians of

---

[18]Jean Piaget: *Science of Education and the Psychology of the Child.* New York: The Viking Press, Inc., 1971, p. 44.

[19]*Ibid.,* pp. 44–45.

[20]Howard W. Eves: *Mathematical Circles Squared, A Third Collection of Mathematical Stories and Anecdotes.* Boston: Prindle, Weber & Schmidt, 1972, p. 102.

[21]*Ibid.,* p. 98.

recent times, astonished his associates at mathematical gatherings because he was so slow at comprehending new ideas. To understand an idea he had to work it out himself from the beginning.

Hilbert confessed that whenever he read or was told something in mathematics, he found it very difficult, if not almost impossible, to understand the explanation. He had to seize the thing, get to the bottom of it, chew on it, and work it out on his own—usually in a new and much simpler way.[22]

The same idea is described by Piaget when he says that "Words are probably not a shortcut to understanding; the level of understanding seems to modify the language that is used rather than vice-versa."[23]

THE ROLE OF EXPERIENCE IN TEACHING

It is almost a cliché to say that in order to learn a student must "experience" and in so doing must be "active." This is in contrast to traditional procedures of "imparting" knowledge by the verbal means of "telling" or "explaining," or by the visual means of "showing" as via a "demonstration."

Assuming that the beginning teacher has come to believe that the traditional method is not good and should be replaced by an "experience" or "activity" curriculum, she may still err in terms of the quality of the activity or experience. Activity or experience per se is not enough. Being active involves investigating problem situations, posing possible solutions, looking for cause-effect relations, noting results of various actions, and being able to make generalizations.

As described by Piaget, the learner in being active "must transform things and find the structure of his own actions on the objects."[24]

Playing in the sandpile may be meaningless, mathematically speaking. On the other hand, the child may find that her sandbucket full of sand can be poured into a shallow tray and exactly fill that, too, even though she may have thought that her bucket held more sand. She may then try to resolve this perceptual conflict with some kind of logical thought process.

---

[22] *Ibid.*, p. 128.
[23] Eleanor Duckworth: "Piaget Rediscovered." *Readings in Science Education for the Elementary School,* edited by E. Victor and M. Lerner. New York: Macmillan Publishing Co., Inc., 1967, p. 319.
[24] R. E. Ripple and V. N. Rockcastle: *Piaget Rediscovered.* Ithaca, N.Y.: Cornell University Press, 1964, p. 4.

Similarly, a favorite example of a mathematician concerns one of his first arithmetical experiences of counting a row of pebbles he had laid out from left to right and then being surprised to find he got the same number counting from right to left. This commutative property of number was not in the pebbles (they could have been candies) but in the actions of the learner on the pebbles as he counted.

Active learning should involve more than what has been advocated by Pestalozzi, Froebel, Montessori, and Isaacs. Montessori materials are based on adult psychology. For example, making cylinders fit into holes, seriating colors, etc., are activities, but they provide a very structured or limited type of environment. The emphasis is more on sensory training than on intellectual development.

What makes an active method "active" is not the external action, or what a person "does" or how he "performs," but the mental elaborations or constructs that he is able to make from the external actions he has performed. Can he apply these mental constructs to a similar problem in another context? In other words, can he generalize?

A CONTRAST IN PHILOSOPHY

Present trends toward specificity in the form of performance or behavioral objectives are often so highly structured that the teacher is told how to select the lesson, what to do next, what questions to ask, what answers to get, and what replies to give. Most teaching as presently practiced would probably conform more closely to the behaviorist school than to the developmental, in part at least because the behaviorist procedure is simpler and easier to use. It is easier to tell the kids what to do—to "show and tell" using a "program"—than to allow them freedom and time to explore as a basis for understanding.

The teacher must, of course, be aware that many parents (and some educators) consider mathematics essentially computation based on memorized addition and multiplication "facts." If these "number facts" and successful "computation" are your teaching objectives, then Gagné and Skinner procedures may be the best method. However, when you come to the pages of "word problems" in the textbook which really test application and generalization, the stimuli or road signs such as "add" are not readily apparent; thus, finding the appropriate response for a solution of the problem becomes very difficult.

In contrast, the student who has developed some working procedures and processes on his own may tackle these word problems with more confidence and success.

Piaget holds that neither mathematics nor science is a set body of knowledge to be "taught." Instead, they are processes of reasoning within frameworks that we call mathematics and science. His work would make a strong stand for a flexible curriculum, particularly at the elementary school level, which would provide many occasions for developing the mind. Facts and skills would be by-products rather than end products. The emphasis would be on intelligence—being able to use facts and skills in a larger context, to apply them to the environment.

EXERCISE

1. Consult the *Educational Index, Eric, Child Development Abstracts, Psychological Research Abstracts,* etc., under topic heading—Piaget or Conservation or Transitivity. Describe relevant studies on acceleration of learning.
2. Discuss the advisability of acceleration.
3. Identify so-called mathematical experiences or problems that are essentially linguistic rather than mathematical or operational in character. (For additional information see "Socialization to Number," p. 37 and "Understanding Time," p. 252.)
4. Would you agree with Piaget's position on aptitude for mathematics? Why?
5. Describe a mathematics program of instruction based on the philosophy of Piaget as contrasted to one based on the philosophy of Gagné. Describe in terms of (1) objectives, (2) methods and materials, and (3) evaluation.
   The following references will be helpful:
   (a) **Jerome S. Bruner:** *The Process of Education.* Cambridge, Massachusetts: Harvard University Press, 1962.
   (b) **Jerome S. Bruner:** *Toward a Theory of Instruction.* Cambridge, Massachusetts: Harvard University Press, 1964.
   (c) **Robert M. Gagné:** *The Conditions of Learning.* New York: Holt, Rinehart and Winston, 1965.
   (d) **Jean Piaget:** *Science of Education and the Psychology of the Child.* New York: The Viking Press, Inc., 1971.

INDIVIDUAL TERM PROJECTS

Demonstrate or describe one of the following topics or subtopics when the related chapter is discussed in class. Use manipulative materials and visual aids where possible. Related written report optional.

1. Chapter 2, Classification, Ordinal Number and Cardinal Number:
   (a) J. Piaget, *The Early Growth of Logic in the Child,* pp. 60–74 (*all* and *some*)
   (b) J. Piaget, *The Early Growth of Logic in the Child,* pp. 101–110 (class inclusion)
   (c) J. Piaget, *The Child's Conception of Number,* pp. 99–114 (ordinal number)
   (d) J. Piaget, *The Child's Conception of Number,* pp. 41–61 (cardinal number)
   (e) Demonstrate and evaluate how number is introduced to children in kindergarten and first grade books.
2. Chapter 3, Addition:
   (a) Describe how the basic addition facts are introduced to children.
   (b) J. Piaget, *The Child's Conception of Number,* pp. 162–182 (class inclusion)
   (c) J. Piaget, *The Child's Conception of Number,* pp. 185–190 (readiness for addition)
   (d) Demonstrate procedures for introducing renaming in addition to children.
3. Chapter 4, Subtraction:
   (a) J. Piaget, *The Child's Conception of Number,* pp. 190–195 (equating quantities)
   (b) Demonstrate with manipulative materials procedures for introducing renaming in subtraction to children, including 3-digit numerals with zeros in the minuend.
4. Chapter 5, Multiplication:
   (a) Demonstrate how to introduce the single-digit multiplication facts to children.
   (b) Demonstrate and rationalize placement of numerals in the conventional algorism for multiplication using the problem $\times\ \frac{32}{14}$
5. Chapter 6, Division:
   (a) Demonstrate the conventional algorism for long division using manipulative materials.
6. Chapter 8, Fractional Numbers—Introduction, Addition, Subtraction:
   (a) Demonstrate introduction of fractions to children.
   (b) Demonstrate the introduction of addition of unlike fractions to children (see fifth grade math books).
7. Chapter 9, Fractional Numbers—Multiplication and Division:
   (a) Demonstrate introduction of multiplication of fractions to children.
   (b) Demonstrate introduction of division of fractions to children.
8. Chapter 10, Decimal Fractions and Per Cent:
   (a) Demonstrate introduction of multiplication and division of decimal fractions to children.
9. Chapter 11, Problem Solving:
   (a) Report on procedures that may help children in solving word problems and estimating in mathematics.
10. Chapter 12, The Calculator in the Classroom:
    (a) Investigate and report on research relative to the proper use of the pocket calculator in an elementary school math class.
11. Chapter 14, Time:
    (a) Report on children's understandings of age as described in Chapter 9 of Piaget's *The Child's Conception of Time.*

    (b) Report on readiness for measuring time as described in Piaget's *The Child's Conception of Time,* pp. 177–195.
12. Chapter 15, Geometry:
    (a) Describe the geometry presently taught in grades K–3. (See children's math books.)
    (b) Describe the geometry presently taught in grades 4–6.
13. Chapter 16, Measurement:
    (a) Describe measurement as presently taught in grades 1–6. (See children's math books.)
    (b) Describe readiness for measurement as studied in Piaget's *The Child's Conception of Geometry, either*: pp. 30–63 *or* pp. 91–103.
14. Special Topics:
    (a) Mathematics education for the exceptional child.
    (b) Famous mathematicians—Archimedes and Gauss.
    (c) Individualized instruction in mathematics—materials and methods.
    (d) Research studies on the ideas of Piaget (see educational index under headings—conservation, classification, seriation, and so on).
    (e) Activities from Piaget's *The Origin of the Idea of Chance in Children* (probability).
    (f) Montessori and mathematics education.

2

CLASSIFICATION, ORDINAL NUMBER, AND CARDINAL NUMBER

CLASSIFICATION

Even before a child can talk, his parents are pointing out and naming objects such as "dog," "horse," "house," and "car." These efforts both encourage the youngster to talk and help him to learn the names of the many objects in the physical world.

As the youngster begins to recognize objects, pointing at them and naming them, he is beginning to discriminate and classify. He recognizes a certain animal as a "horse," another as a "dog." He begins to classify animals as to type or as belonging in a certain set or class. He recognizes one set of animals as "horses" and another set as "dogs." He learns later that both the set of dogs and the set of horses are included in another set, that of "animals." The youngster is beginning to learn about and to classify the objects in his environment.

The concept of "sets" provides a basis for such classification. For example, there are sets of people, which include sets of men, sets of women, sets of boys, sets of girls, sets of blue-eyed boys, sets of red-headed girls, and so on.

A set of boys   A set of girls

22

Psychologically or biologically, the importance of classification is that it removes the need for a "new" adaptation each time a new object is encountered. The child shown a picture of an egret and asked what it is replies that it is "some kind of bird." A student desk is recognized as like a chair but also having a flat surface on which to place books or tablet. If a new object can be classified properly, the same adaptation can be made for it has been made for other members of that class already encountered.

One of the properties of a set in which we are most interested is its **number property**, that is, how many objects it contains. Are there enough pencils for each person to have one? This is one basis for introducing children to number—by relating number to sets of objects. This is the subject of a later section.

Children need experiences involving classifying objects into sets. The most elementary type of classification problem is that of **sorting** or **grouping** objects so that they are alike in some way, such as having the same color. The ability to make a single classification can sometimes be solved by perceptual structures or the child's sense. A child's senses may tell him that an object is "red"; no logic is required.

To determine a child's skill at sorting, one might ask the child to pick out or to sort from a collection of objects those objects that are alike in some way. If there are different shapes, such as squares, circles, and triangles, and different colors, children often sort first by shape rather than by color. As the child performs the task, he should be asked to verbalize what he is doing, or "Why are you putting them together that way?"

As children recognize one object as being different from another, they are beginning to classify objects into sets based on some property or properties. Their ability to discriminate can also be determined by asking them "where" a given object, such as the "square" form, is. They point out or touch the object if they understand. Later, as they begin to talk, they may be asked to "name" an object: for example, "Who or what is that?"

Beginning first with one form such as a triangle, the teacher may place it in front of her and ask the children to pick out from a pile of triangles, squares, and circular shaped objects some that are "like" hers. What is it about these figures that makes them alike? Three edges. The children may then be asked if they know the "name" of the shape. If not, they should be told that it is called a triangle. At the concrete operational stage children may need motor or manipulative experience with objects. They should be allowed to handle and trace with their fingers the outline of various shapes.

A six-year-old classifies by shape.

To obtain a set of logic blocks similar to those shown in the accompanying photo, write for catalogs of companies listed in the footnotes in Chapter 17 on page 316. These may be used to study all the activities listed.

Classification Activities for Children

All around us, then, are things related to other things in some way. In order for us to learn about our world we must understand these relationships. When incoming data are received perceptually (seeing, feeling, hearing an object) we must perform certain mental operations to relate this object properly to other objects.

There are many activities which teachers should identify and use with children in developing classification operations. They include:

1. Identifying properties of objects.
2. Matching or grouping objects by one property.
3. Matching or grouping objects by more than one property.
4. Combining objects to make up subclasses and combining subclasses to make supraclasses.
5. Identifying complements of subsets.

Ray, six, asked whether there are more wooden beads or brown beads, says more brown beads even though all are made of wood. He is unable to relate the larger subclass to the whole class quantitatively (see items 4 and 7).

6. Changing from one criterion for grouping to another.
7. Making comparisons of "all" and "some."
8. Using the idea of intension and extension in hierarchical classification.
9. Realizing an object has simultaneous membership in many classes (intersection and multiple classification).

Kindergarten and first grade activities should involve primarily items 1, 2, 6, and 7 from the above list.[1]

ORDINAL NUMBER

Children need to consider number in terms of both its ordinal and cardinal context. Ordinal number will be considered first.

[1] For a detailed explanation of other activities listed see Richard W. Copeland: *How Children Learn Mathematics*, 3d ed. New York: Macmillan Publishing Co., Inc., 1979, pp. 62–87.

Piaget finds that

There is a very primitive ordering structure in children's thinking, just as primitive as the classification structure . . . the structure of seriation.[2]

Using a set of 10 sticks, with the shortest about 5 centimeters in length and each succeeding one longer by 0.5 centimeter, we can investigate children's understanding of the idea of order.

A four-year-old responds as follows:

"Show me the smallest stick." She points to the right one.

"Now show me a stick a tiny bit bigger." She picks out a big one.

"Show me the biggest." She picks out a big one at random.

"Now try to find the smallest, then one a little bit bigger, then another a little bit bigger." She picks sticks at random.

The interviewer then orders the first 3 sticks to make a staircase and asks the child to continue it. The child picks sticks of any length but

Mark, a bright four and one-half year old, is successful with single seriation.

[2]Jean Piaget: *Genetic Epistemology*. New York: Columbia University Press, 1970, p. 28.

arranges them so their tops do make a staircase outline. (Children at this level, less than four and one-half years of age, do not understand verbal descriptions of mathematical relations such as more than, less than, and taller than.)

Children at the stage 1 or preoperational level cannot coordinate the series. They pick out a little stick and then a big one, another little one and another big one, or they pick sticks in groups of three—a little one, middle-sized one, and big one. There is no overall coordination.

At stage 2, around five years of age, the children are at the end of the preoperational stage. They can now order the whole series but it is a trial and error procedure. They try one stick and then another until they succeed.

At stage 3, from six to seven years of age, the concrete operational level, children have a totally different and systematic way of solving the problem. They first find the smallest stick, then look through the collection for the next smallest, then for the next smallest, and so on until the whole series is built.

These stage 3 children are using the structure or logic of **reversibility** (reciprocity). They realize that each stick is both longer than the preceding one and shorter than the one to follow. They are coordinating the relation "longer than" and the relation "shorter than."

These children are also using the structure or logic of **transitivity**. They realize that if the third stick is longer than the second and the second is longer than the first, then the third must be longer than the first. Thus the whole series is constructed. Understanding the concept of transitivity can be investigated by hiding the first stick and asking the child how the length of the third stick compares with it. Preoperational children will say they do not know because they haven't "seen" them together. Their answers are based only on the perceptual means of "seeing" that one stick is longer.

To be successful in problems of seriation or ordering, it is important to keep in mind the necessary psychological structures of:

1. Reversibility of thought, or ability to order in two directions, such as forward and backward.
2. Transitivity: if B is greater than A and C is greater than B, then C is also greater than A, thus coordinating a series of relations (around seven years of age).
3. The dual relations involved for any given element in determining its position: that it must be larger than the preceding element and yet smaller than the element to follow.

Five-year-olds at stage 2.

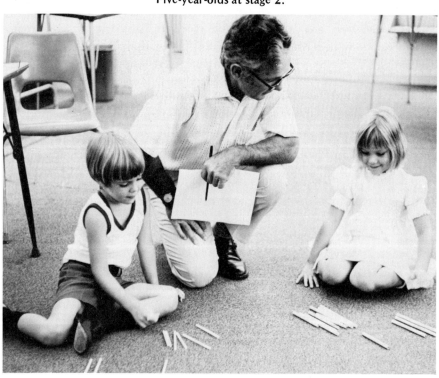

Typical preoperational or stage 2 responses of children[3] are as follows:

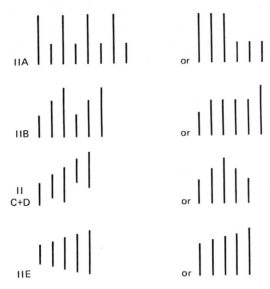

At stage 3, six to seven years of age, the sticks are quickly ordered in a systematic fashion with few errors, quickly corrected. The insertion of additional or "forgotten" sticks is no problem. The child can consider any stick such as *D* as being larger than *C* and smaller than *E*. Also unique to stage 3, the necessary coordination or mental elaboration allows the child to construct the series *in either direction* from smallest to largest or largest to smallest. He is working on a logical or operational level rather than the perceptual level of stage 2, in which the series is slowly built by trial and look.

Serial and Ordinal Correspondence

If children are successful in seriating or arranging a set of sticks in order of length from shortest to longest, can they also make a double seriation—that is, arrange two sets of objects from shortest to longest and make a one to one correspondence between the two sets? Piaget found this is no more difficult for children than constructing a single series.

There is no need for using numbers in making such a double seriation,

---

[3] Jean Piaget and Barbel Inhelder: *Memory and Intelligence.* New York: Basic Books, Inc., Publishers, 1973, p. 29.

but to pick out an object in one row and determine what object "belongs" to it in the other row involves making an **ordinal correspondence**.

For example, with a row of 10 dolls each a different size and a row of 10 balls each a different size, what are the problems of the child in finding the right ball for each doll?

At stage 1, the child cannot make a serial correspondence. At stage 2 the child can, but perceptual methods based on trial and error are used.

At stage 3, the child uses operational or intellectual procedures to solve the problem, but the differences in stage 2 and stage 3 methods are not easy to detect. At stage 3, the correspondence made between dolls and balls is truly an ordinal or numerical one as contrasted to a purely perceptual correspondence in stage 2. The child described in stage 2 has to have the number idea involved called to his attention, and he measures the dolls in pairs side by side before placing them in the series.

The child at stage 3, around seven years of age, considers all the dolls and balls at the same time rather than considering small groups or just pairs. Stage 3 children may not even feel a need to arrange the balls in a series. Some make a direct correspondence—picking out the biggest ball for the biggest doll, then the next largest ball for the next largest doll, and so on.

Relating Ordinal Numbers to Cardinal Numbers (Ordinal and Cardinal Correspondence)

Children must learn to relate the idea of ordinal number to the idea of cardinal number. To determine how many objects are in a set, the objects have to be ordered in some way so that each object is counted once and only once.

Wendy, six, stage 3, can make an ordinal correspondence—can find the "right" stick for each doll.

If, instead of 10 sticks, we use 10 pieces of cardboard such that each is one counting unit longer than the preceding one, and if A is considered 1, then B is 2 times A or $1 + 1$. Similarly, C is 3 A's, D is 4 A's, and so on.

Having asked the child to seriate these pieces of cardboard from shortest to longest, he is asked how many A's in B, in C, and so forth. Instead of using the letters, point to A and say how many of these make one of these (B) and then one of these (C).

Does the child understand this pattern? Ask him how many cards like A it will take to make one like this (pointing at the sixth card, for example). If the child wants to take the A card and measure off on the sixth card to find the answer, he does not see the relation of ordinal to cardinal number. However, if he counts from A to find that the card indicated is the sixth and can then conclude that there must be six A's in it, he realizes the relation of ordinal to cardinal number. If the card is in sixth position (ordinal number), then its cardinal value in terms of A or 1 must be six.[4]

The Number Line

As stated earlier, the number line is a very useful device for helping children in every grade to visualize arithmetical ideas. The number line as illustrated in this discussion is intended to aid in understanding the idea of ordinal numbers. However, it can also be used in teaching the operations of addition, subtraction, multiplication, and division. It is also useful in teaching fractions. The number line will be utilized in the following chapters as each of these ideas is considered.

The number line is a geometric idea, involving as it does the mathematics of position in space. It is symbolized by a line with an arrowhead at one end (for the whole numbers) to indicate that the line extends indefinitely in one direction:

Now, suppose we indicate a point on the line as follows:

[4] For further study see, Richard W. Copeland: *Math Activities for Children.* Columbus, Ohio: Charles E. Merrill Publishing Co., 1979.

This point may be arbitrarily designated by any numeral. If whole numbers are being considered, we may choose to begin with 0:

Another point may be selected at any given distance from 0 and be designated 1:

In so doing we have represented a unit segment such that in naming other points with whole numbers, each numeral should be the same distance from the number which precedes it as 0 is from 1:

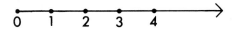

Points are added to the line as needed to illustrate the idea being considered.

Using such a number line the idea of "one" is the line segment from 0 to 1. Do not begin on the line at 1 to represent 1 but move your finger in a loop or hop from 0 to 1 saying "one." College students will sometimes make a loop or hop from 1 to 3 and say this is 3 when of course it is 2.

EXERCISE

1. Develop duplicate sets of concrete materials such as paper cutouts of different shapes or paper cutouts of clothing such as trousers and blouses. Make a wash line or clothesline using paper clips as clothes pins. Test some five to seven-year-olds' ability to "order" by showing them your wash line hung with clothes; ask them to hang out a set of clothes so that their wash line is just like yours. Also see if they can "reverse order" by beginning at the opposite end of the line so that theirs is "backwards" from yours. The concept of reversibility is necessary to understand number.

2. Give each child a set of five paper cutouts of the same shape (for example, squares) in five different colors. Ask them to make a row and compare to each others' rows in terms of how they are alike and different, and to tell you what the difference is.

3. Test some five to seven-year-olds on their ordering ability using the 10 sticks as described on p. 26. Do the children have the concept of transitivity?

4. Test some five to seven-year-olds on their ability to make an ordinal correspondence between objects in two rows (see p. 29).
5. Test some five to seven-year-olds on their ability to relate ordinal and cardinal number (see p. 30).

CARDINAL NUMBER

Children before coming to school may have been socialized to number by learning to memorize a sequence of sounds and say they can "count to twenty," but often they still cannot tell you how many objects there are on the table. Such children are **rote counters** who have not yet mastered the matching or one to one equivalence necessary for "rational" counting.

Parents may think their children have "learned" their numbers when they can "say" the number names in order. This is a point of beginning because we need the names in order to communicate.

As a readiness activity for **rational counting**, children may be asked to match objects in one set with objects in another; for example, they can be asked to put a dress on each doll or a napkin at each table setting.

As they learn the number names in order, these can be matched to the elements in a set to determine the *number* of the set. The operation of matching elements in one set with those in another successfully is called **one to one correspondence**.

1   2   3   4

CLASSIFICATION

Thus, children match the number names in order 1, 2, 3, and so on, to the elements of a set to find "how many" or the cardinal number of the set. There are many activities of this sort in beginning math books.

But suppose a child counts five in one set and counts five in another set which is more spread out, and then says that there are more in the spread-out set. Does this child understand what "five" means? The problem points to the lack of the following concept.

Conservation of Number

To find out just what a five to seven-year-old understands about number, show him a row of objects (seven, for example). Ask him to pick from a pile of objects enough to make another row with just as many.

At stage 1 the child copies the row in terms of end points or length only. He may use more or fewer counters, but his row is the same length. For example, he makes his row below the other using more counters as follows:

Thus, there is no one-to-one correspondence.

At stage 2 children can make a one-to-one correspondence.

However, if one set is transformed in some way, such as by spreading the objects out, there is no lasting equivalence for children in stage 2. These children think the longer row has more.

The child in stage 2, even if he is able to count and find seven in each row, still thinks there are more in the longer row. He does not understand the invariance or conservation of number.

At stage 3 the child has the concept of **lasting equivalence** or **conser-**

Julia, five, has concept of conservation of number.

vation—that is, regardless of how the objects in either row are moved about (transformation), he realizes that the number in the set remains the same (or is invariant).

At stage 3 the child focuses his attention on the transformation (such as spreading the objects apart), and he sees each transformation in terms of another transformation which could negate or reverse the process, such as putting the spread-apart counters back in their original positions (identity). Hence, he concludes logically that the number does not change.

This ability involves the cognitive structure of **reversibility of thought**. Expressed mathematically or algebraically, ^{+}A is negated by ^{-}A.

The stage 2 child, in contrast, does not have this reversibility of thought. He sees only the result of moving one row of objects apart, where the end points are now further apart than the end points of the other row. Perceptual cues are the basis for his answer. Counting does

CLASSIFICATION

not help. The length of the row, rather than the number, is the determining factor.

A child on the verge of moving from stage 2 to stage 3 can be assisted by asking him to count and see if that might help. This produces a conflict situation for the child ready to understand, in that counting tells him one thing and his eyes tell him another; he then resolves the conflict in favor of the logic of number if he is able.

Williams[5] found in testing 96 children between five and one-half and seven years of age that two were in stage 1, 86 in stage 2, and only eight were in stage 3.

Other studies indicate also that not until six and one-half to seven years of age are most children at stage 3, the stage of understanding number. It is obvious that systematic work with number such as beginning addition should not be introduced until the child has been tested and found ready. For many children this will not be before seven years of age.

Socialization to Number

From the study just cited, Williams concluded that for children in the first two stages experiences involving numbers should be limited to objectives of a language arts sort—that is, learning to read, recognize, pronounce, and write the symbols:

> . . . the only realistic goal being a socialization of the children to the culturally accepted number symbols 1, 2, 3, etc. A reservation is that the socialization conclude with the number 10 unless the child shows a desire to go further . . . what occurs in socialization has nothing to do with number.[6]

Only at stage 3 is there the logical thought necessary to understand number as revealed by the conservation, or class inclusion, test.

That this group of children (Williams) was socialized to number was verified by their performance on the Metropolitan Readiness Tests, Form A, especially those questions which revealed only rote knowledge. On these the children did better than could have been expected by chance.

Following are examples of the kind of questions asked which reveal

---

[5] Robert Williams. "Testing for Number Readiness: Application of the Piagetian Theory of the Child's Development of Number." *Journal of Educational Research,* **64** (No. 9):393, 1971.
[6] *Ibid.,* pp. 393-396.

only rote knowledge or socialization:

		Correct N	Correct %	% of Correct Responses Expected by Chance
Q 7.	"In the next row, put a mark on the 4."	94	100	20
Q 8.	"In the box where the ducks are, put a mark on 56."	74	79	25
Q 9.	"See the box where the grapes are. Now write the number 5 in the space beside the grapes."	88	94	0
Q 10.	"Find the box where the flag is. Mark the number that comes next after 8 when you are counting."	76	81	25
Q 25.	"In the box where the book is, write eighty-one."	62	66	0

From Metropolitan Readiness Tests, Form A, Test 5, Numbers. New York: Harcourt, Brace, and World, Inc., 1965.

Testing for Conservation

Siegel and Goldstein found that children of less than four and one-half years of age do not respond correctly to quantitative relational terms such as "more than," "less than," or "the same."[7] Such relational ideas are not meaningful to them at the verbal level.

They also found that most children of less than five years seven months, when asked to establish a quantitative relation between two sets in a conservation task, were found to give a "recency response"— that is, point at or name the last set indicated.[8] Asked if they are the same, or if A has more, or does B have more, the answer given was B.

In testing children for conservation, decisions should be made care-

[7] L. Siegel and A. Goldstein: "Conservation of Number in Young Children: Regency Versus Relational Strategies". *Developmental Psychology*, 1:128, 1969.
[8] *Ibid.*, pp. 128–130.

CLASSIFICATION

fully based on several transformations made for each child. Children should be asked for justification, or why they gave the answers they did, to determine the basis for their answers.

Transformations such as those shown below should be considered in testing for conservation of number. This is in contrast to always placing the objects in two lines or rows, with the transformation being to spread one row of objects out so that it is longer and then asking the child if there are more in that row.

Which has more or are they the same?

Also, work with sets of first smaller and then larger numbers, beginning with sets of 3, 4, or 5, and then trying larger sets of 7 or 8, for example. Stage 2 children may be successful with small sets and unsuccessful with larger ones.

Interview Technique for Conservation of Number[9]

To evaluate children's understanding of conservation an effective interview technique must be mastered. It is not easy. Students and teachers should conduct practice interviews while other members of the class watch and then, after the interview, discuss the order of questions, words used, etc.

[9] For a set of 60 math diagnostic tests, see Richard W. Copeland: *Math Activities for Children.* Columbus, Ohio: Charles E. Merrill Publishing Co., 1979.

As a beginning make a row of objects as Johnny watches.

"Now, Johnny, would you make a row with just as many as mine?" (Show him a pile of counters.)

If Johnny cannot do this—that is, make a one to one correspondence —then stop.

If Johnny can make a one to one correspondence, such as

then spread one row apart:

The question now is really three questions:

1. "Do I have more?" (pointing at one row).
2. "Or do you have more?" (pointing at the other row).
3. "Or do we have the same?"

If Johnny is not sure, ask "Would counting help?"

Finally, the justification question "Why?" to see what logic, if any, he is using.

If he is at stage 3, or concrete operational:

1. His logic may be that of number: "Five in both."
2. His logic may be that of reversibility: "You just spread them apart so I could put them back and it would be the same."

If he is not yet able to solve the problem logically he uses perceptual factors, saying the longer row because "it looks like more" or because "there is one more (extending beyond the end of the other row)." He may even say the shorter row has more. Why? "Because they are closer together."

As a last question, if the child is at stage 1 or 2, ask "Would counting

CLASSIFICATION

help?" If he does not think so, then he is at stage 1. This child may even be able to count correctly but still say there are more in the longer row.

The stage 2 child is transitional. By trial and error or help from the teacher he sometimes gets the right answer. At other times, with larger sets for example, he answers incorrectly, using perceptual factors as the basis for his answer.

Class Inclusion

Conservation of number is not the only logical thought problem for children as they attempt to learn about numbers. The logical thought process of class inclusion must also be present in the mind of the child.

The development of the idea of number as related to the development of classification in the mind of the child is described by Piaget as follows:

> Our hypothesis is that the construction of number goes hand in hand with the development of logic and that a pre-numerical period corresponds to the pre-logical level. . . . Logical and arithmetical operations therefore constitute a single system, . . . the second resulting from generalization and fusion of the first under the complementary heading of "inclusion of classes."[10]

The logic of inclusion of classes may be discussed in qualitative terms as: children include boys, birds include ducks, flowers include roses, and Florida includes Miami. Similarly, inclusion of classes is involved in studying number. The number five as a class includes the classes four, three, two, and one. Understanding "five" involves understanding its relation to its subclasses or subsets 4, 3, 2, and 1, and this involves addition and subtraction.

The head of inclusion of classes is fundamental to understanding number, and yet does not develop in children until around seven years of age. Because it is so important as indicating readiness to understand addition and subtraction it is discussed in more detail in Chapter 3.

Suffice it to say at this point that a child can look at a bunch of flowers containing, for example, 9 roses and 2 daisies and count to tell you there are 11 flowers, 9 roses, and 2 daisies. Yet asked if there are more roses or flowers, the response is roses for most children less than seven years old. They do not yet have the logical construct of class inclusion.

[10] Jean Piaget: *The Child's Conception of Number.* New York: W. W. Norton & Company, Inc., 1965, p. viii.

Learning to Write Number Symbols
or Numerals

If a socialization approach to number is used, children learn to read and write numerals before they really understand number. If they enjoy learning how to make a "six" and to recognize a "six" when they see it, then learning to read and write numbers or how to express numbers symbolically provides activities for the teacher to use with children before they are ready to begin operational work, such as addition or subtraction. These children may also benefit from additional classification or ordering activities.

The **symbols** used to represent the idea or abstraction of "numbers" we call **numerals.**

The Roman numerals by their form gave some indication of how many. For example, "two" was represented by II. But, in our Hindu-Arabic system of notation the symbol now used, such as 2, gives no indication of how many. The symbols presently used have changed from their original form of 2000 years ago. Then they may have been related physically to how many. For example, the numeral 3 could have been three bars, such as $\equiv$, connected with two loops, $\ni$. Similarly, "2" could have been two bars = connected with a diagonal.

Children come to school already counting verbally "in order" as "one, two, three, . . ." Thus, they know the **verbal names** for numbers and also the **order** in which they occur. The sequence of ordinal number is then used correctly before that of cardinal number. The child knows what number name comes after six before he knows how many that number represents.

Knowing the verbal number names allows meaningful communication between the teacher and child as the child learns how to write the number names. Models of the numerals to be copied or written are usually displayed in an order sequence so the child sees what number comes next. The numerals should also be related to the cardinal number they represent, such as placing the numeral 2 and the word "two" by a picture of two objects.

Records can be made of all sorts of numerical data, such as how many children are absent each day. Making a calendar from a blank form may also be of interest. There is also a "social" purpose for the child who enjoys learning how to "make" or write the number symbols he has "heard" so often.

To draw a numeral the child needs to know both where to begin and in what direction to go. In the following diagram the dot indicates at what point to begin and the arrow in which direction to go.

Manuscript

Cursive

While there are variations in the way numerals can be written, the manuscript style of using straight lines and circles is in more general use. The majority of schools teach manuscript rather than cursive writing in the primary grades since many of the children are not ready for the muscular coordination required in cursive writing.

A general rule in writing numerals is to begin at the top and work down. Exceptions to this are the 5 and 8 which end at the top. The teacher can use the blackboard in indicating correct starting points, proportions of the figure, how to proceed, and the place to stop. A good teaching aid for display may be a set of large cards with one numeral drawn on each card. These cards should indicate with a dot the beginning point on the figure and indicate with an arrow the direction in which to go.

The numerals written on the board can be done first with white chalk and then traced with colored chalk by the child. The use of a base line or box may help as a frame of reference. For some numerals a guide line at the top is helpful.

Difficulties in Writing Numerals. A child who draws the numerals incorrectly even when he has the model before him may have perceptual, cognitive, or muscular coordination problems. Some children will have difficulty distinguishing between 6 and 9 and between 2, 3, and 5. They should be asked to point to the numeral on the model that is the same as the one they have drawn to be sure they are not making incorrect associations.

Some children will be helped through the kinesthetic feeling derived from tracing the form of the numeral with their fingers on the model. They should then be allowed to practice the drawing on their own papers.

Some children construct certain numerals in reverse. The teacher should observe constantly, and should correct faulty practice early by calling attention to the starting point and direction. The numeral 3 is reversed most often and looks like an *E*. A reversal pattern that persists may require clinical attention. Diagnosis and treatment usually follow that prescribed for reading reversals.

Writing the numerals in a tray filled with sand may help. According to Piaget to "know" an object is to "act" on it, such as in tracing the outline of a shape—whether it is a geometrical form such as a square or a geometrical form such as a 2. Just looking at the numeral may not be sufficient.

Another reversal problem occurs in expressing numbers with two digits, such as writing 61 to represent 16. To the child this is logical, since in the word "sixteen" the "six" is pronounced first and our writing sequence is left to right. As emphasis is put on the "place value" of our number system with tens written to the left of ones, this reversal problem should disappear. The writer acquired the nickname "left angle" when he asked the teacher why the form ⌐ was called a right rather than left angle.

In the first grade, reinforcement experiences with ordinal numbers may include such activities as completing the following:

The same completion problem might be shown on a number line:

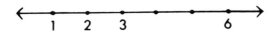

In both cases it is the position of the numerals in the sequence that is important.

PLACE VALUE, ADDITION, AND BASE TEN

In the Hindu-Arabic system of numeration, all numbers are expressed by use of the symbols: 0, 1, 2, 3, 4, 5, 6, 7, 8, 9. The system contains one more than nine different symbols, which we call a **base ten** system of numeration. Using the principles of **place value** and addition in Hindu-Arabic system, any whole number, no matter how large, can be represented by using the numerals 0 to 9.

To help pupils learn how to use place value and base ten in the first grade, they are shown a set of objects such as popsicle sticks:

CLASSIFICATION

and are asked to circle the objects in sets of ten. Then circle each stick that is left:

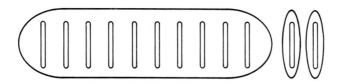

To record the number of these two sets, have the children write in the left-hand box, or the tens column, of the following diagram the numeral that indicates the number of sets of 10 sticks, and in the right box the numeral that represents the number of sets of one stick. In this way the idea is beginning to be established that the position occupied by one numeral in reference to another has a special meaning.

Tens   Ones

1	2

In a similar fashion, in the following example, circle the sets of ten and record the number of sets of ten and the number of sets of one:

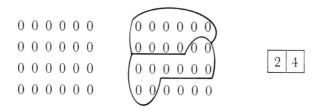

Another concrete way of studying the concept of place value is with containers such as tin cans labeled "tens" and "ones." To represent 24 sticks, the children should put two bundles of 10 sticks in the "tens" can and four sticks in the "ones" can. Later a single stick instead of a bundle of 10 sticks is placed in the tens can to represent 10.

Caution: The idea that ten ones spread out is the same as one ten bunched up presupposes that the child has the concept of conservation of number. Many do not. They see "two" in the tens can, not 2 tens or 20 ones.

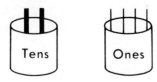

The same type of activity can be developed using a pocket chart, either homemade or obtained commercially:

Hundreds	Tens	Ones
	I I	||||

Using these containers is more concrete than using the abacus in that sets of 10 objects, rather than a single counter, are first used to represent ten.

A device called a counting frame is useful. It too, can be either homemade or obtained commercially.[11] In the illustration which follows, the counting frame "shows" or represents the number 24.

To erase the number from the counting frame, all beads are moved to the left end of the rows. It seems natural to move the beads from left to right in counting, but the procedure may be reserved if that seems more meaningful. The counting frame and the hundred chart to be discussed later help to establish the decimal character of our number system; that is, counting by tens.

It is easy to confuse the counting frame with the abacus. But the beads on the abacus, which is used to teach place value, are arranged in columns, with nine beads to the column, rather than in rows. Also, a single bead on the abacus may represent sets of ten or sets of one hundred.

[11] For further information on classroom aids and how to obtain them, see Chapter 17, p. 316.

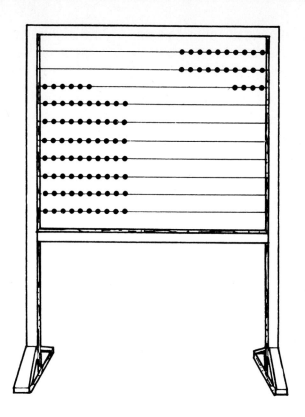

The Abacus

The abacus serves well as a transition toward the abstract in the consideration of the place value concept. Instead of 10 objects being used to represent one set of ten, a single counter is used on a second column. The "place value" refers to the column occupied by the bead.

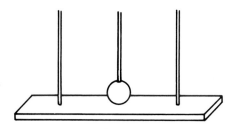

The abacus was used by the Romans to compensate for the principle of place value, which their system of numeration lacked. Neither the

Romans nor the Egyptians had a symbol which performed the function of the 0 in the Hindu-Arabic system. The abacus is still used in the Orient for computing with numbers. In some Chinese laundries in the United States, the counters still have grooves in which beads can be moved back and forth for figuring change. Such a device, which mechanically provides for place value, is a type of abacus. One vestige of the abacus in the West is that we still use the term counter to refer to the tables in stores across which goods and money change hands, even though the beads and grooves have disappeared.

The abacus is well suited to teaching children the concept of place value because it provides concrete materials which children can manipulate. An "open-ended" abacus as shown in the preceding illustration is best to use at first. Later commercial ones like those shown in the following illustrations may be used.

A typical abacus is constructed of wire or wooden rods mounted in columns in a frame, with nine beads or counters on each column.

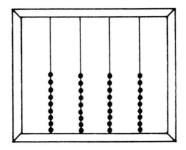

To represent a number from 1 to 9, the appropriate number of beads is moved up in the column on the right. To represent 24, two beads are moved up in the tens column and four beads in the ones column. The numbers 24 and 321 are represented in the following illustrations:

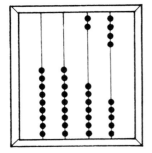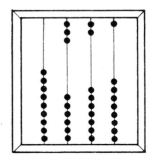

Through such concrete activities the idea is established that the *place* a numeral occupies in relation to other numerals determines the number it represents.

The Hindu-Arabic system of representing numbers involves the principles of **place value, base ten,** and **addition.** For example, consider the number represented by 24. Using the principles of place value we know the 2 has a place value different from that of the 4. Since we are using a base ten system we know that the 2 is sets of ten and that the 4 is sets of one. Using the principle of addition we know that 24 is two sets of ten *plus* four sets of one rather than, for example, 2 multiplied by 4.

After experiences with such concrete materials as pocket charts, counting frames, and abaci, children should represent numbers in expanded notation to reinforce the principles involved.

Hence, 36 should be expressed and verbalized as:

3 tens + 6 ones   and also, in terms of ones, as   30 + 6

Later, the following form will be used:

$$3(10) + 6(1)$$

Using this form also involves the principle of multiplication:

$$(3 \times 10) + (6 \times 1)$$

The Hundred Chart

The hundred chart is also helpful in teaching the pattern of our system of numeration. (See next page.)

Such questions as how are the numerals alike in each column or how are the numerals alike in each row help to establish the idea of the pattern of our base ten system of numeration.

The hundred chart is also of value in readiness activities for developing an understanding of the operations of addition, subtraction, multiplication, and division. Without knowing the addition or multiplication tables, a youngster can solve many problems by counting. For example: How much is 3 plus 5? After locating the numeral 3 on the chart, we count five more places and find that 3 and 5 are 8.

0	1	2	3	4	5	6	7	8	9
10	11	12	13	14	15	16	17	18	19
20	21	22	23	24	25	26	27	28	29
30	31	32	33	34	35	36	37	38	39
40	41	42	43	44	45	46	47	48	49
50	51	52	53	54	55	56	57	58	59
60	61	62	63	64	65	66	67	68	69
70	71	72	73	74	75	76	77	78	79
80	81	82	83	84	85	86	87	88	89
90	91	92	93	94	95	96	97	98	99
100									

THE MEANING OF A MULTIDIGIT NUMERAL

While most errors children make may be characterized as computational, that is, errors in adding, subtracting, multiplying or dividing, the problem is often more basic than that. Children often make computing errors because they do not understand place value.

Since computation is based on understanding place value, place value should be understood thoroughly before beginning computation. Children need practice in representing numbers with sets of objects and also representing sets of objects in terms of their number.

Practice in naming a number in various ways is also necessary background for introducing addition and subtraction problems that require renaming. For example,

$$32 = 3 \text{ tens } 2 \text{ ones} = 2 \text{ tens } \underline{\quad} \text{ ones}$$

Children, to understand the meaning of a multidigit numeral such as 324, need to know not only "place value" but that each numeral

CLASSIFICATION

is the product of its face value and its place value. For example, in 324 the 3 is 3 × 100, the 2 is 2 × 10, and 4 is 4 × 1.

Also the child needs to know that each numeral in a number such as 324 is related to the others by addition.

$$324 = 300 + 20 + 4$$

Expressing both concepts in expanded notation—

$$324 = (3 \times 100) + (2 \times 10) + (4 \times 1)$$

This last type of notation is, of course, not for children in the primary grades. For a more complete study of place values, see Chapter 7, Bases Other Than Ten, which explores nondecimal bases such as base five and several historical systems.

EXERCISES

1. Test some five to seven-year-olds on their understanding of conservation of number using concrete materials such as buttons, blocks, or pieces of candy. Place the children in stages of development as 1, 2, or 3. Discuss implications for teaching.
2. Make a detailed report on the stages of development that you may expect to find as reported in Chapters 2 through 4 of Piaget's *The Child's Conception of Number* (New York: W. W. Norton & Co., 1965).
3. Report on some research studies on conservation of number.
4. Discuss the relevance of the kind of arithmetical activities presently "taught" in first grade.
5. Observe some six-year-olds writing numerals. Note difficulties they have and discuss remedial activities for those who might need it.
6. If any five-year-olds are available, try teaching them how to write a numeral— for example, the numeral that tells how old they are, or how old a brother or sister is.
7. Describe a lesson to introduce the ideas of zero and place value using appropriate manipulative materials.
8. Does Chapter 7, Bases Other Than Ten, help the prospective elementary teacher understand better the problems children have with place value? If so, report on one or more of the topics included therein.

3

ADDITION

"Explicitly teaching operations is probably not a very fruitful form of pedagogy."[1]

ADDITION AS AN OPERATION

In Chapter 2 numbers were studied as members or elements of sets; for example, the set of whole numbers {0, 1, 2, 3, . . .}. **Operations** may be performed on the elements of a set. What you may have learned as the fundamental processes of addition, subtraction, multiplication, and division are **operations**.

Addition as a Binary Operation

Addition is a **binary** operation, which means that it is an operation performed on two elements at a time. Addition is called a binary operation because it assigns to two numbers a third number. To the ordered pair (2, 3) it assigns the number 5. In a problem such as 3 + 2 + 4, the binary operation of addition is performed twice. Two of the numbers are added, and then the third number is added to the sum of the first two. Subtraction, multiplication, and division are also binary operations.

The so-called basic addition facts are learned as number "pairs" from

[1] Jean Piaget as quoted by Eleanor Duckworth in *Learning*, Oct. 1973, p. 24.

0 + 0 to 9 + 9. Thus, there are 100 binary addition facts which children have to learn.

The idea that addition means "to increase" arises from such problems as that concerning the three boys at play being joined by two more boys. But addition should be thought of as related to a "joining" rather than an "increasing" operation. The set of three boys and the set of two boys are both present and simply join each other.

$$000 \quad 00 = 00000$$
$$3 \qquad 2 \qquad 5$$

The question is one of naming the number of the set produced by the union or joining of two sets. Addition is thus associated with the joining of sets or the union of sets.

The idea that if a set of three boys is joined by a set of two boys the result is a set of five boys is referred to as the **union of sets**. The symbol for the union of sets is ∪. This idea may be stated in the following symbolized form, with its relationship to the operation of addition shown under it.

$$\{\text{Tom, Dick, Harry}\} \cup \{\text{Bill, Joe}\} = \{\text{Tom, Dick, Harry, Bill, Joe}\}$$
$$3 \qquad\qquad + \qquad 2 \qquad = \qquad\qquad 5$$

Union is an operation on sets, whereas **addition** is an operation on numbers. Sets are joined, but numbers are added.

Sets may have numbers as members or elements; for example, the sets {1, 2, 3} and {4, 5}. What is the number associated with the union of these two sets?

$$\{1, 2, 3\} \cup \{4, 5\} = \{1, 2, 3, 4, 5\}$$
$$3 \quad + \quad 2 \quad = \quad 5$$

Notation similar to that above is not uncommon in elementary school math materials. Rather than emphasizing notation and definitions, the teacher should introduce addition by having the children join (and separate) sets of objects, noting the result first orally and then in a written sentence.

For example,

$$0\,0\,0\,0 \quad 0\,0\,0 \qquad 0\,0\,0\,0\,0\,0\,0$$
$$4 \quad + \quad 3 \quad = \qquad 7$$

READINESS FOR ADDITION

To understand the concept of addition, the child must be able to make quantitative comparisons between a whole and its parts. For example, shown a set of flowers consisting of nine roses and two daisies, the typical six-year-old can name each of the sets—flowers, daisies, and roses—but asked if there are more roses or more flowers, the response is "roses."[2]

Children under seven years often are unable to consider the whole as a logical class. While the adult can think of 5 as 4 and 1 or 3 and 2, the six-year-old usually cannot. He is limited in two ways. He has not achieved **reversibility** of thought, which allows the adult to think that if $3 + 2 = 5$ then $5 = 3 + 2$. Also, he cannot consider the whole and its parts simultaneously. He is unable to handle the **inclusion relation**. This is why so many first grade teachers struggle in vain to teach addition symbolism.

Tests similar to those developed by Piaget need to be administered to determine when children are ready for formal addition. To test for an understanding of the inclusion relation, Piaget used wooden beads, some brown and some white, but more white. When the wooden beads are formed into sets of brown and white, the child who has not developed sufficiently will respond that there are more white beads than wooden beads:

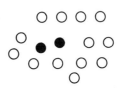

The interview procedure is not easy for the beginner.

"Charles, do you know what these things are?"
"Beads."
"What are they made of?"
"Wood."
"And what color are they?"
"White and brown."
"Are there more white or more wooden beads?"
"More white."
"Are the white ones made of wood?"

[2] For further information see Richard W. Copeland: *How Children Learn Mathematics,* 3d ed. New York: Macmillan Publishing Co., Inc., 1979.

"Yes."

"And are the brown ones made of wood?"

"Yes."

"Then are there more white beads or more wooden beads?"

"More white beads."

This child cannot consider the whole and its parts simultaneously, a process that involves the logic of the inclusion relation and reversibility of thought. He is not yet ready for addition.

Alternate tests may involve considering a set of children containing more boys than girls. The child may respond that there are more boys than children. Similarly, there are more blue bells than flowers for such a youngster if there are more blue bells than daisies.[3]

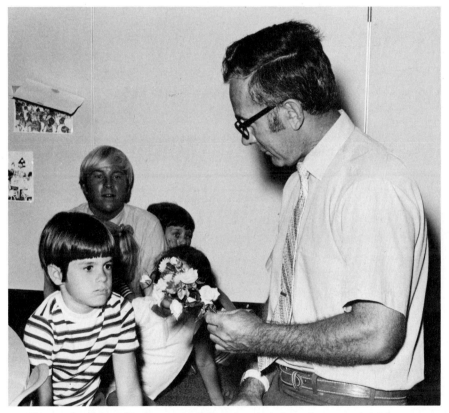

Bryan, six, in considering a set of flowers consisting of roses and daisies, responds that there are more roses than flowers.

[3] Barbel Inhelder and Jean Piaget: *The Early Growth of Logic in the Child.* New York: W. W. Norton & Company, Inc., 1969, Chap. 4.

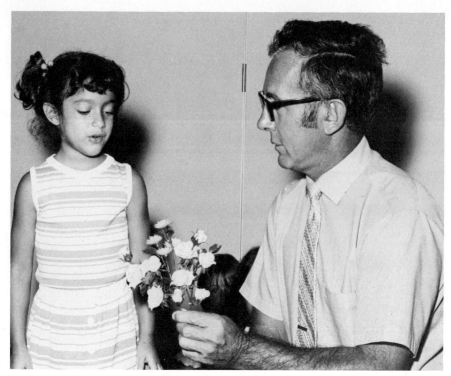

Leslie, a five-year-old working at second grade level, has no difficulty with the inclusive relation.

Reversibility of thought is also necessary. If the brown and white beads came from a wooden set, then logically they can be returned to form a wooden set, and logically the whole will be larger than its parts.

Reversibility of thought is a necessary condition for understanding the **conservation** or **invariance** of number. Children in the six to seven age range often do not have this ability.

Possibly more closely related to understanding addition is the following activity. While children have often memorized the addition facts, and can answer basic addition facts questions such as "What is 4 + 4?" and "What is 1 + 7?", they still fail the following.

The child is told that today he can have this many (lay out four) sweets in the morning and this many (lay out four) in the afternoon, and that tomorrow he may have this many (lay out one) in the morning and this many (lay out seven) in the afternoon. He is asked if he will have the same amount on both days. To illustrate the problem:

○ ○ ○ ○   ○ ○ ○ ○   ○   ○ ○ ○ ○ ○ ○ ○

Children at the nonconservation stage respond that there is more on the second day because of the big lot. Their evaluation is a global one, of the space occupied by the seven, rather than the logic of number. Having such children memorize $4 + 4 = 8$ and $1 + 7 = 8$ has no meaning.

Piaget concludes:

> Addition is a reversible operation. There is therefore no more than a suggestion of it when, at the first stage, the child does not understand that a whole B divided into two parts, A and A', is still the same whole. The operation of addition comes into being when, on the one hand, the addenda are united in a whole, and on the other, this whole is regarded as invariant irrespective of the distribution of its parts.[4]

LEARNING THE BASIC ADDITION FACTS

As the children reach the necessary stage of development—that is, as they acquire reversibility of thought and understand the conservation of number—they are then in position to explore systematically with concrete materials each number class; for instance, five as $1 + 4$, $4 + 1$, $2 + 3$, and $3 + 2$.

Studies of Piaget find that conservation of number and reversibility of thought as a stage of development occurs around seven years of age on the average, but for some it will be at age six and for others at seven and a half. The teacher will have to test each child periodically in order to find out when he has reached this stage of development.

How many addition facts are children expected to learn? From $0 + 0$ to $9 + 9$ there are 100 basic addition facts. These are our basic tools. For addition problems involving addends with two or more digits, we will use a procedure or algorism involving the place-value concept and the commutative and associative properties of addition.

The so-called 100 basic addition facts from $0 + 0$ to $9 + 9$ must be committed to memory. But how should they be taught? Should they be shown to children in some logical pattern such as the "add 1, add 2" approach, shown below? Although this approach is now used less widely, it is shown here for the sake of comparison.

[4]Jean Piaget: *The Child's Conception of Number.* New York: W. W. Norton & Company, Inc., 1965, p. 189.

	1	2	3	4	5	6	7	8	9
Add 1:	+1	+1	+1	+1	+1	+1	+1	+1	+1
	2	3	4	5	6	7	8	9	10

	1	2	3	4	5	6	7	8	9
Add 2:	+2	+2	+2	+2	+2	+2	+2	+2	+2
	3	4	5	6	7	8	9	10	11

The pattern is continued with an "add 3" row, "add 4" row, . . . "add 9" row. In this approach, addition is interpreted only as a counting sequence. Learning such a pattern reminds one of the television comedian who plays a marine private: When asked to recite the eleventh general order, he has to recite the first 10 general orders. Eleven is only known as "coming after 10."

Prospective teachers often describe their approach to teaching a lesson by beginning, "I would show . . .", but showing does not produce understanding. The learner must interpret for himself if he is to understand. Jesse Livermore, a millionaire stock market operator, in analyzing his mistakes once said that he had found that he must follow his own interpretation of facts and not the interpretation of someone else. "They are then my facts, don't you see?"

The child who can look at an idea such as "five" and analyze the idea in terms of its parts and put the parts back together into a meaningful whole is using a procedure that might be characterized as a "whole to parts to whole" analysis. Reversibility of thought is necessary.

The **number family** approach involves studying a number such as 5 in terms of the ways it can be renamed by using two addends. Recall that addition is a binary operation, which means an operation on two numbers, and that addition is associated with the union of two sets.

In exploring ways of renaming 5 as the sum of two addends, begin with a set of 5 objects. Group this into two subsets in as many ways as possible. The following ideas are discovered:

$5 = \square + \triangle$		$\square + \triangle = 5$
$5 = 4 + 1$		$4 + 1 = 5$
$5 = 1 + 4$	also in reverse	$1 + 4 = 5$
$5 = 2 + 3$		$2 + 3 = 5$
$5 = 3 + 2$		$3 + 2 = 5$

The number 5 as an idea is analyzed in terms of any two addends which produce or name 5. These pairs of addends are then considered as a number family.

Since the idea of the empty set does not develop in children until approximately 10 years of age,[5] such addition facts as 5 + 0 and 0 + 5 should possibly be deferred for later study.

Concrete Ways of Learning Addition

Children at the concrete operational stage, having reached the conservation of number and reversibility of thought stage, are ready to explore the basic addition facts using concrete materials. A variety of commercial concrete materials such as the Montessori numerical rods, Cuisenaire rods, Galt Multimat, and mathematical balances are useful. Each of these materials serves as a concrete type of number line in that each counting number can be represented by a different length. (See Chapter 17, p. 316 for sources.)

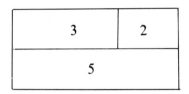

The addition and subtraction facts are explored by pairing rods end to end to equal the length of a third rod. The 5 rod is found to have the same length as the 4 and 1 rods, the 2 and 3 rods, the 3 and 2 rods, and the 1 and 4 rods.

If we begin with a 3 rod and 2 rod placed end to end and find they form a "train" the same length as a 5 rod, this is a concrete approach to **addition**, $3 + 2 = \square$.

If we begin with a 3 rod and a 5 rod and ask what rod with the 3 rod makes a train the same length as the 5 rod, this is a concrete approach to **subtraction** (using the missing addend model), $3 + \square = 5$.

There are basically three types of subtraction problems to be solved in the physical world or at the concrete level:

(1) The additive or missing addend type problem just described, $3 + \square = 5$. For example, if Jane has 3 cents and wants to buy a pencil for 5 cents, how much more does she need? Clerks in

[5] Barbel Inhelder and Jean Piaget: *Early Growth of Logic in the Child.* New York: W. W. Norton & Company, Inc., 1969, p. 146.

stores use this method. If you buy something for 39 cents, and give the clerk a dollar, she solves the subtraction problem to determine your change as 39 + (1 + 10 + 50) = 100.

(2) The take away problem, 5 - 3 = □. If I have 5 cents and spend 3 cents, what is left?

(3) The comparison problem. If Jane is 5 and Bill is 3, what is the difference in their ages?

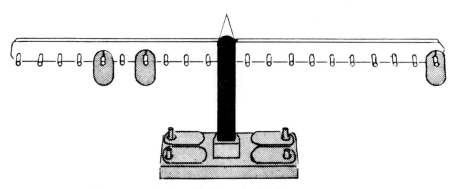

Invicta Mathematical Balance.

The mathematical balance just shown is a most useful device. Since addition is a binary operation, two weights are used on one side of the balance to see what "balances" a single weight on the opposite side. For the "five" class, for example, a single weight is placed on the 5 hook. On the other arm of the balance, the two weights are moved about to see what balances. If one weight is placed on the 2 hook and another on the 3 hook, "balance" is achieved. There is an immediate check of the answer's being correct in that the balance arm is level.

Subtraction problems in the missing addend form, 3 + □ = 5, can be solved by placing a weight on the 3 hook on one arm of the balance and a weight on the 5 hook on the other arm. A third weight must then be placed correctly to balance the arm. For multiplication problems such as 3 × 2 = □, three weights are placed on the 2 hook, and for 3 × 4 = □, three weights are placed on the 4 hook. To balance the 3 × 4, a weight is placed on the 10 hook and another is placed on the 2 hook.

Homemade materials such as popsicle sticks, straws, dried beans, or clothespins can also be used. The child is given five objects, for example, and asked to see how many ways this set of objects can be made to form two sets (since addition is a binary operation).

As these addition facts are developed by the child with the use of concrete materials, he should express the relations in symbol form using number sentences. For example:

○ ○ ○	○ ○	$3 + 2 = 5$
○	○ ○ ○ ○	$1 + 4 = 5$
○ ○	○ ○ ○	$2 + 3 = 5$
○ ○ ○ ○	○	$4 + 1 = 5$

If he has difficulty with the symbol expressions, he may need to return to the concrete materials for additional study. He should not be told that he cannot use concrete materials such as his fingers since he himself will stop using them when he is able.

To understand the meaning of sentences such as $3 + 2 = 5$, they should first be considered as a conventional sentence:

Three boys and two boys are five boys.

then

3 boys and 2 boys are 5 boys.

then

3 and 2 is 5.

and finally

$3 + 2 = 5$

After the number families are discovered and recorded in symbol form, reinforcement or practice will be necessary. This can be done using flash cards, but games such as "addo," which is bingo adapted to the addition facts, are more fun. Spelling bee activities adapted to the addition facts may also have appeal.

The Number Line and Addition

Moving from actual objects toward the abstract, a semi-concrete activity that has meaning for many children is the geometry of the number line. The addition facts for 5 may be expressed on a number line as follows:

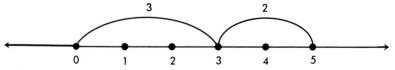

A Tabular Display for the Addition Facts

For systematizing and recording the addition facts, the following table has many advantages. In this table, the addends are displayed at the left and at the top of the table.

+	0	1	2	3	4	5	6	7	8	9
0										
1										
2										
3										
4										
5										
6										
7										
8										
9										

To record or find the sum of 5 + 7, look down the left side of the table to the numeral 5 and then to the right to the column headed by the numeral 7. As each number family is learned, the appropriate facts are recorded until the table is complete as shown in the following illustration.

+	0	1	2	3	4	5	6	7	8	9
0	0	1	2	3	4	5	6	7	8	9
1	1	2	3	4	5	6	7	8	9	10
2	2	3	4	5	6	7	8	9	10	11
3	3	4	5	6	7	8	9	10	11	12
4	4	5	6	7	8	9	10	11	12	13
5	5	6	7	8	9	10	11	12	13	14
6	6	7	8	9	10	11	12	13	14	15
7	7	8	9	10	11	12	13	14	15	16
8	8	9	10	11	12	13	14	15	16	17
9	9	10	11	12	13	14	15	16	17	18

Some of the advantages of this display are:

1. It is compact.
2. It can be used as a reference for subtraction facts as well as addition facts.
3. It familiarizes pupils with a form of display used in other mathematics.
4. It is an aid to understanding the structure and properties of our number system.

In using the above table for subtraction, state the problem in the missing addend form, $4 + \square = 13$. Look down the left side of the table to the number 4, go across to the right to the sum 13, then go up to the top for the unknown addend, 9.

To understand the number family or class of five, not only are there the addition facts such as

$$3 + 2 = \square \qquad \text{and} \qquad 4 + 1 = \square$$

but also the corresponding subtraction facts such as

$$3 + \square = 5 \qquad \text{and} \qquad 4 + \square = 5$$

$$\text{or}$$

$$5 - 3 = \square \qquad \text{and} \qquad 5 - 4 = \square$$

Addition and subtraction are one reversible operation psychologically speaking, according to Piaget, but because of the extent of ideas to be considered for both addition and subtraction they are organized as separate chapters in this book.

THE COMMUTATIVE PROPERTY OF ADDITION

That $4 + 1$ and $1 + 4$ are both names for 5 prompts the question whether this is true for every pair of addends when their order is reversed. If a and b are any two whole numbers, then $a + b = b + a$.

This property of addition, that the changing of the *order* of addends does not change the sum, is referred to as the **commutative** property of addition. This property may seem trite and obvious, but as has been

Checking to see if a row of two "Mickey Mouse" followed by three dwarfs is the same length if the order is reversed. Christy, four and one-half, is successful. Regis, seven, is not.

pointed out, some operations are not commutative. For example, 6 - 3 $\neq$ 3 - 6.

The practical value of the commutative property of addition is that it greatly simplifies learning the 100 basic addition facts, for if 4 + 1 = 5, then 1 + 4 must equal 5. The commutative property is also basic in "checking" addition, by "adding upward" to check problems which were solved by adding downward. The commutative property of addition refers to the *order* of adding. Given a series of addends, one can add in whatever order one chooses.

To appreciate the fact that operations are not always commutative, consider the following illustration from the physical world. Is "put on your socks and then your shoes" a commutative operation? The results are certainly not the same. In making gravy, does flour + water = water + flour? Cooks know that adding flour to water may result in a lumpy mixture.

Teaching the Commutative Property of Addition

Just how difficult is the commutative property for children to learn? How should it be taught? Probably the first thing to say is that you should not begin with a definition, which is the way you may have learned this concept at the college level; for example, for any whole numbers, *a* and *b, a + b = b + a.*

Brown[6] reports that children are not ready for the commutative or associative property until approximately eight years of age, even if you begin to teach it at the concrete level with objects. Simple experiments such as the following can be used to test children's understanding: "I give my doll 4 applies and 2 oranges. Now you give your doll just as much fruit, to be fair, but since she likes oranges better, give her 4 oranges and 2 apples. Do both dolls get the same amount of fruit?

Other variations of this kind of test can involving parking toy cars. First we part seven blue cars (of different sizes) in a row, followed by four yellow cars, and then we put up a parking sign. Then the cars are removed and the child is asked to park the yellow cars first. After the yellow cars and one blue car are parked, the child is stopped and asked to predict if the rest of the blue cars will reach to the parking sign, not reach it, or go past it. (See photos, preceding page, for a similar problem.)

[6]Brown, P. G. "Tests of development in children's understanding of the laws of natural numbers." Master of Education Thesis, University of Manchester, England, 1969.

THE ASSOCIATIVE PROPERTY OF ADDITION

Since addition is a binary operation, when three or more addends are to be added, the addition operation must be performed at least twice. How would one proceed to solve the problem, $3 + 4 + 5$? If the 3 and 4 are added, and their sum then added to 5, this association can be shown with parentheses as follows:

$$3 + 4 + 5$$

$$(3 + 4) + 5$$

$$7 + 5$$

$$12$$

There is another possible association which may be used to solve this problem; that is, the associating of the 4 and 5:

$$3 + 4 + 5$$

$$3 + (4 + 5)$$

$$3 + 9$$

$$12$$

That either procedure, or association by addition, produces the same result for any three whole numbers is a property of whole numbers and addition. This property is called the **associative property of addition** (of whole numbers). Brown's study, cited above, indicates most children are not ready for this type of problem until the second grade at least.

To demonstrate the associative property of addition in a concise form, the two associations are usually shown as follows:

$$\overset{?}{(3 + 4) + 5 = 3 + (4 + 5)}$$

$$\overset{?}{7 + 5 = 3 + 9}$$

$$12 = 12$$

The general case may be stated as follows: for any whole numbers a, b, and c,

$$(a + b) + c = a + (b + c)$$

Whenever three (or more) whole number addends are associated, the choice of **association** does not change the sum. If there were any exceptions, the associative property would not be a property of whole numbers and addition.

It is easy to confuse the associative property with the commutative property, but recall that the commutative property had to do with changing the *order* of the addends. In the equation $(3 + 4) + 5 = 3 + (4 + 5)$ the order of the addends, 3, 4, and 5, is the same on each side of the equation. It is the association or grouping that is different. To say that $4 + 5 = 5 + 4$ or that $3 + 4 + 5 = 3 + 5 + 4$ is, of course, making use of the commutative property of addition because the order of addends is changed. In many addition problems both properties are used, but each property is distinct from the other. There must be at least three addends before the associative property can be used, because there is no choice of association for only two addends. The commutative property *is* involved, however, with only two addends.

To illustrate the use of both the commutative and associative properties of addition, the following problem is developed horizontally with explanations given for each step:

$$6 + 5 + 4$$
$$6 + (5 + 4) \quad \text{associative property of addition}$$
$$6 + (4 + 5) \quad \text{commutative property of addition}$$
$$(6 + 4) + 5 \quad \text{associative property of addition}$$
$$10 + 5 \quad \text{addition performed}$$
$$15 \quad \text{system of numeration (addition and place value)}$$

The associative property of addition is very useful in computation. It enables us to group addends to produce a sum of 10 so that addition is easier. For example, the problem $5 + 3 + 7$ might be solved as $(5 + 3) + 7$ or as $5 + (3 + 7)$. The second form is easier to use since $5 + 10$ is a less difficult sum to recall than $8 + 7$. This property is particularly useful when long columns of numbers are to be added.

Similarly, in working with children, if the sum of $6 + 7$ is forgotten or not known, the number 7 might be renamed in order to "make a ten" and the associative property used as follows:

$$6 + 7$$
$$6 + (4 + 3) \quad \text{7 renamed as } 4 + 3$$
$$(6 + 4) + 3 \quad \text{associative property of addition}$$
$$10 + 3 \quad \text{addition performed}$$
$$13 \quad \text{addition performed}$$

THE ASSOCIATIVE PROPERTY OF ADDITION

Another approach to recalling basic addition combinations is to use the "doubles" combinations, which are easy to remember: for example, $6 + 6$, $7 + 7$, $8 + 8$, and $9 + 9$. In using the "doubles" method and the associative property to solve a problem such as $6 + 7$, we may proceed as follows:

$6 + 7$	
$6 + (6 + 1)$	7 renamed as $6 + 1$ (so the double $6 + 6$ will be obtained)
$(6 + 6) + 1$	associative property of addition
$12 + 1$	addition performed
$(10 + 2) + 1$	system of numeration
$10 + (2 + 1)$	associative property of addition
$10 + 3$	addition of performed
13	system of numeration

Similarly:

$$8 + 9 = 8 + (8 + 1) = (8 + 8) + 1 = 16 + 1 = 17$$

Approximately one third of the 100 basic addition facts can be learned as doubles and "near doubles." Near doubles are addends whose difference is 1. For example, $6 + 7$ and $7 + 6$ are near doubles and each is 1 more than $6 + 6$, and 1 less than $7 + 7$. The "doubles" approach also involves the associative property of addition as illustrated in the preceding example.

To illustrate that the associative property does not hold in every system, Mueller[7] cites the following example from the physical world. Consider three typical elements of refreshment at a ball game—hot dog, mustard, and soft drink.

Does (hot dog + mustard) + soft drink = hot dog + (mustard + soft drink)?

$$\text{good} + \text{good} \neq \text{good} + \text{bad}$$
$$\text{good} \neq \text{bad}$$

[7] Francis J. Mueller: *Arithmetic: Its Structure and Concepts.* Englewood Cliffs, New Jersey: Prentice-Hall, Inc., 1956, p. 50.

The associative property does not hold for "addition" of these elements because different associations produce different results. In cooking, the manner of associating ingredients is also often important. In the world of mathematics as in the physical world, the associative property does not always hold. For the operation of subtraction, for examples, does $(6 - 3) - 2 = 6 - (3 - 2)$?

$$3 - 2 \neq 6 - 1$$

$$1 \neq 5$$

The importance of the associative property will be seen more clearly as renaming in addition and in subtraction are studied later. The associative property is fundamental to these procedures.

EXERCISES

1. Discuss the importance of the ability to classify or to understand the inclusion relation as a basis for meaningful addition. For additional information see *The Early Growth of Logic in the Child* by B. Inhelder and J. Piaget (New York: W. W. Norton & Company, Inc., 1969), Chapter 4; or *How Children Learn Mathematics—Teaching Implications of Piaget's Research*, by Copeland (New York: The Macmillan Publishing Co., Inc., 1979), Chapter 5.
2. What implications are there for teaching addition in Chapters 7 and 8 of *The Child's Conception of Number* by Piaget (New York: W. W. Norton & Company, Inc., 1965)?
3. Use the commutative and associative properties in solving each of the following, giving reasons for each step:
   (a) $3 + 5 + 7$ (b) $8 + 6 + 2 + 4$ (c) $a + x + b + x$
4. If the following sums were forgotten, illustrate how each could be solved by using the associative property of addition:
   (a) $5 + 8 =$ (b) $7 + 9 =$ (c) $6 + 7 =$
5. Using the doubles method and the associative property of addition, solve the following:
   (a) $6 + 7$ (b) $7 + 8$ (c) $8 + 9$ (d) $8 + 7$
6. Develop a lesson plan for the addition facts in the "seven" family. Include provision for concrete materials as a beginning, number line displays, and activities for reinforcement or memorization. Also make an addition table and fill in the addition facts for "seven."
7. Report on the Cuisenaire rods or the Montessori materials as a basis for learning the basic addition and subtraction facts.
8. How many basic addition facts are there for the "eighteen" family? Why?

ADDING NUMBERS SYMBOLIZED WITH TWO OR MORE DIGITS

Having learned the 100 single-digit basic addition facts (0 + 0 to 9 + 9), the child can begin to consider adding larger numbers. To do so he must understand the concepts of place value and base ten. These ideas were discussed in Chapter 2.

Beginning with concrete materials such as popsicle sticks, the sticks are grouped in sets of **tens** and sets of **one**. The number 34, for example, can be represented as three sets of 10 sticks and four sets of one stick.

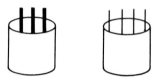

This concrete activity can be followed by symbolizing in expanded form:

$$3 \text{ tens} + 4 \text{ ones or } 3(10) + 4(1) \text{ or } \quad 30 + 4$$

To solve an addition problem, then, such as 13 + 5, how shall we proceed?

At the concrete level the problem may be solved by counting, 14, 15, 16, 17, 18. Another and better procedure is to think of 13 as 10 + 3. We can then use the associative property, associating the "ones," 3 and 5, which is one of our familiar basic addition facts. In symbol form:

13 + 5	
(10 + 3) + 5	13 renamed
10 + (3 + 5)	associative property of addition
10 + 8	elementary addition facts
18	system of numeration (addition and place value)

Solving this problem at the concrete level by beginning first with a set of 13 sticks and a set of 5 sticks, ask the child if grouping his 13 sticks into a set of 10 sticks and 3 sticks would help. If we then join or associate our set of 3 sticks and 5 sticks, what is our result?

$$
\begin{array}{ccc}
10 & + & (3 + 5) \\
10 & + & 8 \quad = 18
\end{array}
$$

Solving the problem vertically, we make use of the associative property by putting "ones" in one column and "tens" in another. Hence, $13 + 5$ is expressed in expanded form vertically as:

$$
\begin{array}{ccc}
\begin{array}{r} 10 + 3 \\ + 5 \\ \hline 10 + 8 \\ 18 \end{array}
& \text{or} &
\begin{array}{r} 1 \text{ ten} + 3 \text{ ones} \\ + 5 \text{ ones} \\ \hline 1 \text{ ten} + 8 \text{ ones} \\ 18 \end{array}
\end{array}
$$

The problem of adding two two-digit numbers is solved in similar fashion: $32 + 24$ expressed vertically in expanded form is:

$$
\begin{array}{ccccc}
\begin{array}{r} 3 \text{ tens} + 2 \text{ ones} \\ + 2 \text{ tens} + 4 \text{ ones} \\ \hline 5 \text{ tens} + 6 \text{ ones} \\ 56 \end{array}
& \text{or} &
\begin{array}{r} 30 + 2 \\ + 20 + 4 \\ \hline 50 + 6 \\ 56 \end{array}
& \text{or} &
\begin{array}{r} 3(10) + 2(1) \\ + 2(10) + 4(1) \\ \hline 5(10) + 6(1) \\ 56 \end{array}
\end{array}
$$

Solving the problem horizontally involves:

$32 + 24$	
$(30 + 2) + (20 + 4)$	addends renamed
$30 + (2 + 20) + 4$	associative property of addition
$30 + (20 + 2) + 4$	commutative property of addition
$(30 + 20) + (2 + 4)$	associative property of addition
$50 + 6$	system of numeration (addition and
56	place value)

Renaming in Addition

The performance of third graders in Florida in 1977 in adding two-digit numbers with renaming was rated as unacceptable by the state assessment program. It is difficult for the adult who has been solving addition problems for years using a familiar method to realize the problem faced by second or third graders considering the renaming or borrowing problem for the first time. (Such difficulty may be better appreciated if the adult solves an addition in base five, a topic to be considered later.)

In approaching a problem such as $\begin{array}{r} 34 \\ + 18 \\ \hline \end{array}$, how shall we proceed? By counting? That works, but it is slow. If we add 4 and 8, the sum is 12.

How shall we fit this in to complete the problem? We can solve the problem without carrying by writing the sum of 4 + 8 as 12 and the sum of 30 + 10 as 40:

$$
\begin{array}{r}
34 \\
+\ 18 \\
\hline
12 \\
40 \\
\hline
52
\end{array}
$$

Beginning at the concrete level, money is most meaningful to children just as it is to adults. How can this same problem be expressed in dimes and pennies?

$$
\begin{array}{l}
3\ \text{dimes} + 4\ \text{pennies} \\
+\ 1\ \text{dime}\ \ + 8\ \text{pennies} \\
\hline
4\ \text{dimes} + 12\ \text{pennies}
\end{array}
$$

A key question that reinforces place value and base ten is: Can this answer be expressed with fewer coins, using dimes and pennies? If we exchange 10 pennies for a dime, the problem can be expressed as:

4 dimes + (1 dime + 2 pennies)

or

(4 dimes + 1 dime) + 2 pennies

5 dimes + 2 pennies

52

Other concrete materials such as the pocket chart, Dienes' Multibase Arithmetic Blocks, or Multimat are useful.

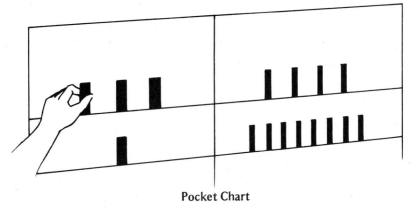

Pocket Chart

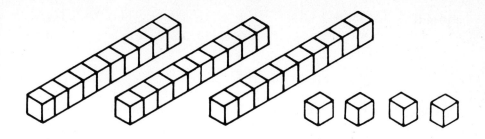

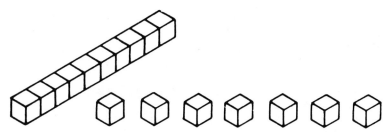

Number Blox, Multimat, or MAB Blocks

Then, without concrete materials and in expanded form notation:

$$
\begin{array}{rl}
3 \text{ tens} + 4 \text{ ones} & \qquad 30 + 4 \\
\underline{1 \text{ ten } + 8 \text{ ones}} & \qquad \underline{10 + 8} \\
4 \text{ tens} + 12 \text{ ones} & \quad\text{or}\quad 40 + 12 \\
4 \text{ tens} + (1 \text{ ten} + 2 \text{ ones}) & \qquad 40 + (10 + 2) \\
(4 \text{ tens} + 1 \text{ ten}) + 2 \text{ ones} & \qquad (40 + 10) + 2 \\
5 \text{ tens} + 2 \text{ ones} & \qquad 50 + 2 \\
52 & \qquad 52
\end{array}
$$

Then, with the familiar form, placing the renamed or carried ten above the tens column

$$
\begin{array}{r}
\overset{1}{3}4 \\
\underline{18} \\
52
\end{array}
$$

And finally, the conventional form with no visual aid except the addends:

$$
\begin{array}{r}
34 \\
\underline{18} \\
52
\end{array}
$$

Adding Numbers Expressed with Three Digits. In introducing the idea of renaming in addition, children should also consider problems involving hundreds. Understanding addition of two-place numbers does not mean that addition of three-place numbers is understood.

The problem $\begin{array}{r} 357 \\ \underline{+268} \end{array}$ can be displayed on a pocket chart as follows:

Hundreds	Tens	Ones
▮▮▮	▮▮▮▮▮	▮▮▮▮▮▮
▮▮	▮▮▮▮▮	▮▮▮▮▮▮

In using the pocket chart the teacher may first have a youngster attempt to represent the addend 357 on the chart (as three sets of 100 cards, five sets of 10 cards, and seven sets of single cards). Underneath this addend the other addend is represented (as two sets of 100 cards, six sets of 10 cards, and eight sets of one card). The sets of one card (8 and 7) are joined and their number 15 renamed as one set of ten and five sets of one. The set of ten is placed in the tens column with the other sets of ten. The sets of ten, $1 + 5 + 6$, are then added, producing 12 sets of ten, which can be renamed as a set of one hundred and two sets of ten. The set of one hundred is placed in the hundred column, and the sets of one hundred, $1 + 3 + 2$, are then added, producing six sets of one hundred. The sum is 6 hundreds + 2 tens + 5 ones, or 625.

In renaming a set of fifteen as one set of ten and five sets of one, the pupil should wrap the set of ten in a rubber band, to indicate that it is one set of ten, as it is placed in the tens column. In renaming the 12 tens as one set of one hundred and two sets of ten, the set of one hundred should also be wrapped with a rubber band as it is placed in the hundreds column.

Possibly more meaningful and convenient are the arithmetic blocks which allow the exchange of 10 longs, or 10 sets of ten, for 1 flat, or one set of one hundred.

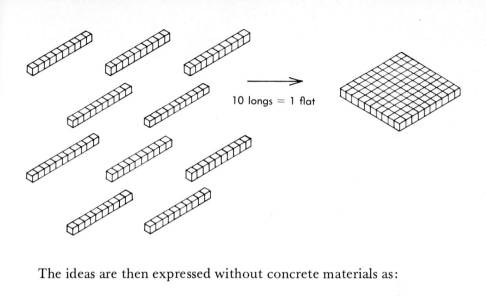

10 longs = 1 flat

The ideas are then expressed without concrete materials as:

3 hundreds	5 tens	7 ones	357
+ 2 hundreds	6 tens	8 ones or	268
5 hundreds	11 tens	15 ones	15 (7 + 8)
or 5 hundreds	12 tens	5 ones	110 (50 + 60)
or 6 hundreds	2 tens	5 ones	500 (300 + 200)
or 625			625

The problem is then considered in the shorter form:

$$\begin{array}{r} \overset{1\ 1}{357} \\ +268 \\ \hline 625 \end{array}$$

using the marks above 5 and 3 to indicate the sets being carried or re-named. As soon as possible, the youngster should be encouraged to dispense with these marks; that is, to perform mentally the process of remembering what is being renamed and to perform the addition in the conventional form:

$$\begin{array}{r} 357 \\ +268 \\ \hline 625 \end{array}$$

Throughout this exploratory development toward the conventional algorism, it is very important that there be a free interchange of ideas and questions. In the first stages of solving a problem with a pocket chart, the children should set the problem up and determine its solution with guidance from the teacher at necessary points. It should not be a "show and tell" performance by the teacher. Even when children suggest procedures that work but do not lead toward the conventional algorism, the procedure should be recognized as another way of solving the problem. Although there may be a number of ways of solving the same problem, it will be obvious after a number of problems are considered that the conventional form is a good one.

EXERCISE

1. Outline a lesson designed to introduce to a class of second or third graders the idea of renaming (carrying) in addition, using the problem $\begin{array}{r} 34 \\ + 18 \end{array}$. Describe in detail how you would use the appropriate concrete material in making the transition from the concrete to the abstract. Do the same with $\begin{array}{r} 342 \\ + 178 \end{array}$.

DIAGNOSING ERROR PATTERNS

Can you diagnose the following common error patterns and suggest a correctional procedure?

Answers

(a)
$\begin{array}{r} 37 \\ +18 \\ \hline 415 \end{array}$
$\begin{array}{r} 79 \\ +9 \\ \hline 718 \end{array}$

(a) Does not rename in addition problems that involve renaming. Draw lines as follows with specification that only one numeral can go in each column.

T	O
3	7
1	8
5	5

(b)   521   385 (with a small 5 above 385)

(b)	521	385
	+134	+576
	655	8116

(b) Child adds from left to right, says 8 plus 7 is 15, writes 1, and carries 5. Needs additional work with place value board.

(c)	26	34
	+3	+5
	11	12

(c) Adds all numbers, 2 + 6 + 3 = 11. Have child represent problem with objects and label place value for recording each sum.

(d)	57	38
	+9	+7
	156	115

(d) The child adds single-digit number in both columns. This child has probably been introduced to multiplication and has the two procedures mixed up. Use prescription similar to those above.

(e)	37	21
	+5	+8
	32	13

(e) Solves as subtraction problem. Ask what the plus sign means.

Instructional Activities to Correct Error Patterns in Addition

1. Use bundles of ten and single sticks to solve problems. Use rule of always grouping 10 single sticks to form 1 set of ten.
2. Use base ten blocks on a place value board. Have a bank at which 10 ones can be traded for 1 ten and 10 tens for 1 hundred.
3. Represent both addends on a counting abacus.
4. Draw frame for problem such as that shown. Use square cutouts with single numerals on them which just fit each column.

H	T	O
	4	9
	7	5

5. Chip trading games beginning with bases less than ten. In a base three game, for example, let 3 blues equal 1 yellow and 3 yellows equal 1 red. Children take terms rolling a die. A child rolling

a 2 gets 2 blues from a child who is the "banker." If on his next turn the same child rolls a 4, he gets 1 yellow and 1 blue from the banker. He now has 1 yellow and 3 blues, which he trades for another yellow; now he has 2 yellows. If he rolls a 3 on his next turn, he can trade his 3 yellows for a red. The winner of the game is the first player to get an agreed-upon score such as 3 reds.

4

SUBTRACTION

INTRODUCING THE BASIC SUBTRACTION FACTS

Addition is introduced to children by joining two sets of objects and relating the numbers of the two sets to the number of the result of joining them. Subtraction, as the inverse of addition, may be thought of as the **separation** of sets. If we separate a set of three from a set of five, what is left? This is the familiar "take-away" model for subtraction.

Stated algebraically,

$$\begin{aligned} \text{if} \quad & a + b = c \\ \text{then} \quad & c - b = a \\ \text{and} \quad & c - a = b \end{aligned}$$

But in introducing this notion to children and using numbers instead of letters,

$$\begin{aligned} \text{if} \quad & 3 + 2 = 5 \\ \text{then} \quad & 5 - 3 = 2 \\ \text{and} \quad & 5 - 2 = 3 \end{aligned}$$

This is sometimes called a triad. Since addition and subtraction are one reversible system both psychologically and logically speaking, as children learn an addition fact such as $3 + 4 = 7$ this should be related to the corresponding subtraction facts as $7 - 3 = 4$ and $7 - 4 = 3$.

Addition was introduced to children using a "number family" approach, that is, children took a set of objects and divided them into two sets in as many ways as possible. (See page 61.) This can also be done concretely by drawing a line vertically down the middle of a sheet of paper and having the children arrange the "family" or set of 5 into two sets and then write the corresponding addition sentences.

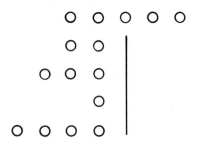

$$O \quad O \quad O \quad O \quad O$$

O O | O O O	2 + 3 = 5
O O O | O O	3 + 2 = 5
O | O O O O	1 + 4 = 5
O O O O | O	4 + 1 = 5

The same display can be used for working out and recording corresponding subtraction facts. One side of the table can be covered or left blank to be filled in. The first problem could be verbalized as 5 −2 is □ or 2 and □ is 5.

The use of the zero facts could also be included as 5 + 0 = 5 and 0 + 5 = 5.

The table used for recording the 100 basic addition facts is also used for subtraction but read in a different way. (See next page.)

For the fact 5 − 2 = □ look down the left column to 2, then across to the right to 5, then up to the top. It is interesting that this procedure really fits the following model better.

$$2 + \square = 5$$

This model for subtraction is called the **missing addend.**

Many students in looking at the expression 2 + □ = 5 consider it to be an addition problem since the plus sign is shown, but addition involves finding the sum. In this expression we have the sum, 5, and are looking for the missing addend, 3.

+	0	1	2	3	4	5	6	7	8	9
0	0	1	2	3	4	5	6	7	8	9
1	1	2	3	4	5	6	7	8	9	10
2	2	3	4	5	6	7	8	9	10	11
3	3	4	5	6	7	8	9	10	11	12
4	4	5	6	7	8	9	10	11	12	13
5	5	6	7	8	9	10	11	12	13	14
6	6	7	8	9	10	11	12	13	14	15
7	7	8	9	10	11	12	13	14	15	16
8	8	9	10	11	12	13	14	15	16	17
9	9	10	11	12	13	14	15	16	17	18

MODELS FOR SUBTRACTION

Two models for subtraction have already been mentioned—the subtract or take-away model, $5 - 3 = \square$, and the missing addend model, $3 + \square = 5$. Introduce only one of these models at a time, but both need to be considered.

In solving word problems we find that some are one type and some the other. For example, "I have five cents and spend two cents. What is left?" This is the subtract or take-away model. But also, "I have two cents and want something that costs five cents, how much more do I need?" This is the missing addend model.

In working out problems at the concrete level, if the subtract model is used for a problem such as $5 - 2 = \square$ five pennies may be displayed. The question then is, should two pennies be displayed also to indicate what is to be taken away? Opinion is divided on this. If two pennies are displayed, sometimes children take away these two pennies and think that solves the problem.

The missing addend model works easily. For the problem $2 + \square = 5$, display two pennies and also five pennies and ask what should be added to the 2 to make 5.

$$0\ 0 + \ ? \ = 0\ 0\ 0\ 0\ 0$$

It is interesting that most subtraction problems solved in stores by clerks use the missing-addend or additive model for subtraction. If we

ething that costs 13 cents and give the clerk 25 cents, the prob-
sually not solved as 25 - 13 but as 13 + □ = 25. It is usually
teps as 13 + 2 + 10.

the missing-addend method also avoids "borrowing," which will
ssed later. For example, when buying something for 65 cents
and giving the clerk one dollar, the problem is solved as 65 cents plus
ten cents plus a quarter. Yet in school most of our time is spent with
the subtract or take-away model and renaming or "borrowing" when
necessary.

Subtraction problems sometimes involve a comparison or difference.
For example, John is nine years old and Bill is seven years old, what is
the difference in their ages? This problem can be solved either by the
subtract method (9 - 7 = □) or the additive method (7 + □ = 9).

READINESS FOR SUBTRACTION

Children have more difficulty with a subtraction problem than with
its corresponding addition fact. For example, 3 + 2 = □ is not as difficult as 3 + □ = 5. Why is this?

In our discussion of readiness for addition a problem was described in
which children could not make a comparison correctly. The problem involved a set of flowers including 9 roses and 2 daisies. Children have difficulty answering the question whether there are more roses or more
flowers.

The problem is that preoperational children, many of whom are in
first grade, do not have reversibility of thought. The children realize
that roses and daisies are flowers, but once they look at the subsets—
roses and daisies—they can only compare roses and daisies. They cannot
compare roses to flowers, which involves reversing a thought process.

Similarly, to solve an addition problem such as 3 + 2 = □ is not as
difficult as a corresponding missing addend subtraction problem such as
3 + □ = 5 because 3 + □ = 5 involves a reversal of thought process. The
child looks at the 3, then to the right to 5, and then has to reverse or
think back to the left to fill in the box. Not being able to do this, many
six-year-olds seeing the 3 and then the 5 put an 8 in the box which, of
course, amounts to saying that 3 + 8 = 5.

This difficulty means that many first graders are not ready for subtraction, and teachers have a hard time "teaching" them except by rote
methods. One teacher was heard to say to children solving missing

addend problems such as 5 + □ = 8 "take the smaller from the larger and put it in the box."

A second readiness problem is that of being able to understand the inclusion relation. Flowers include roses. Therefore, there must be more flowers than roses. But this logical thought process is not available to most children below seven years of age. They cannot consider successfully such problems as "If all the roses died, would there be any flowers left?" or "If all the ducks died, would there be any birds left?"[1]

SUBTRACTING NUMBERS EXPRESSED WITH TWO OR MORE DIGITS

After the single-digit addition facts from 0 + 0 to 9 + 9 have been explored and learned along with the corresponding subtraction facts, the algorism or procedure must be learned for subtracting larger numbers. If the basic subtraction facts are understood, these can be applied within the context of our place-value system by subtracting each number from the number above it, as long as the number in the minuend is larger.

Beginning at the concrete level, such as with money, if we have 68 cents and spend 24 cents, what is left? What operation is necessary?

Each child should solve such problems for himself at the concrete level using sets of objects to represent the number ideas involved. He may, for example, use paper cutouts of dimes and pennies:

	Dimes	Pennies
68	○○○○○○	○○○○○○○○
− 24	○○	○○○○
	○○○○	○○○○

Using symbolism, the following forms (from left to right) can then be explored:

$$
\begin{array}{c}
6 \text{ dimes} + 8 \text{ pennies} \\
- (2 \text{ dimes} + 4 \text{ pennies}) \\
\hline
4 \text{ dimes} + 4 \text{ pennies} \\
44
\end{array}
\quad \text{or} \quad
\begin{array}{c}
60 + 8 \\
- (20 + 4) \\
\hline
40 + 4 \\
44
\end{array}
\quad \text{or} \quad
\begin{array}{c}
68 \\
- 24 \\
\hline
44
\end{array}
$$

[1] See Richard W. Copeland: *How Children Learn Mathematics*, 3d ed. New York: Macmillan Publishing Co., Inc., 1979.

If the same subtraction problem is expressed in additive form, then:

$$4 \text{ pennies} + \square \text{ pennies} = 8 \text{ pennies}$$
$$2 \text{ dimes} + \square \text{ dimes} = 6 \text{ dimes}$$

Renaming in Subtraction

The statewide math assessment program in Florida in 1977 found that only two-thirds of the third graders in the state could solve subtraction problems involving renaming, or could even determine when renaming was necessary.

When a problem such as $\begin{array}{r} 34 \\ -17 \\ \hline \end{array}$ is faced for the first time, how do we solve it, since 7 is larger than 4? Our work with expanded notation and place value may help. Concrete materials may also help. Beginning with wooden blocks as concrete materials, how can 34 and 17 be represented? Thirty-four is shown as 3 longs and 4 units, and 17 as 1 long and 7 units:

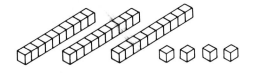

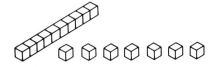

Then, how do we find the difference or subtract 17 from 34? If the children have had sufficient work with concrete materials and the concept of place value, they will suggest renaming the 34, or 3 longs and 4 units, as 2 longs and 14 units. The 7 units can then be subtracted from the 14 units leaving 7 units, and the 1 long can be subtracted from the 2 longs leaving 1 long.

There is often discussion of whether the subtrahend, 17, should be represented at the concrete level, since it is to be subtracted or taken away. It is advisable to represent the subtrahend as a second set and the difference as a third set. The teacher performing subtraction in a non-decimal base, such as base five, at the concrete level will find that displaying the subtrahend helps her. Second, in conventional notation at the symbol level the subtrahend is represented. Also, the subtraction may be considered in an "additive context," such as 7 and □ is 14, or in a difference context, such as: The "difference" between 7 and 14 is □. In such contexts 7 is not taken away but is represented as one addend, with the subtraction problem being that of finding the missing addend.

After experience at the concrete level with simulated money, wooden blocks and pocket charts, the number notation forms are considered. First, the expanded forms:

$$
\begin{array}{ll}
\quad 2 & \\
\;\not{3}\text{ tens}\quad ^{1}4\text{ ones} & \\
\underline{-\;1\text{ ten}\qquad 7\text{ ones}} & \\
\quad 1\text{ ten}\qquad 7\text{ ones, or }17 &
\end{array}
\qquad
\begin{array}{l}
\;20 \\
\not{30}+{}^{1}4 \\
\underline{-\,(10+7)} \\
\;10+7\text{ or }17
\end{array}
$$

Then the form:

$$
\begin{array}{r}
21 \\
\not{3}4 \\
-\,17 \\
\hline
17
\end{array}
$$

And finally, the conventional form:

$$
\begin{array}{r}
34 \\
-\,17 \\
\hline
17
\end{array}
$$

The Terminology of "Renaming," "Borrowing," and "Exchanging"

In a problem such as $\begin{array}{r}34\\-17\\\hline\end{array}$, to subtract 7 from 4 the terminology has been "to **borrow** one" (actually 10 sets of one) from 3. The term **borrow** has been to some extent replaced by **exchange** when solving the problem at the physical level, that is, 1 ten stick is **exchanged** for 10 ones or units. To describe the same notion when the idea is worked out with paper and pencil or at the symbol level, the term is **rename**. The number 3 tens and 4 ones is **renamed** as 2 tens and 14 ones.

Remember that numerals are symbols or names for a number. For example, some symbols for the number idea we call "thirteen" are 13,

6 + 7, 10 + 3, and XIII. The idea that a number has many names and that a number such as 32 or 30 + 2 can be renamed as 20 + 12 or 2 tens + 12 ones is a sound approach mathematically. A number may be named in many ways. In this section we are renaming a number in order to make subtraction easier to perform.

In renaming 32 or 30 + 2 as 20 + 12, we are using the associative property of addition. This may be shown as follows:

$$32$$
$$30 + 2 \qquad \text{system of numeration (addition and place value)}$$
$$(20 + 10) + 2 \qquad \text{addend renamed}$$
$$20 + (10 + 2) \qquad \text{associative property of addition}$$
$$20 + 12 \qquad \text{system of numeration}$$

Thus, exchanging, or renaming (borrowing) in subtraction is based on the associative property of addition. Tens are renamed and associated with ones.

SUBTRACTING NUMBERS EXPRESSED WITH THREE DIGITS

Problems involving the subtraction of three-digit numbers may be treated in the same way as two-digit problems, that is, first solved at the concrete level, then in expanded notation, and finally in the conventional form. First introduce problems involving no renaming.

For problems involving renaming, the notion of changing tens to ones is more familiar to children than changing hundreds to tens. For this reason three-digit subtraction problems need to be considered separately. Some children can visualize changing tens to ones but not hundreds to tens.

To introduce such a problem at the concrete level arithmetic blocks are often used.

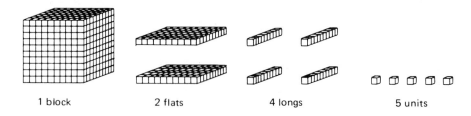

1 block   2 flats   4 longs   5 units

SUBTRACTION

To solve the problem $\dfrac{432}{-247}$ at the concrete level

$$\begin{array}{lll} 4 \text{ flats} & 3 \text{ longs} & 2 \text{ units} \\ -\,(2 \text{ flats} & 4 \text{ longs} & 7 \text{ units}) \end{array}$$

One long (ten) is exchanged for ten units, and 1 flat (hundred) for 10 longs (tens).

After such problems are solved at the concrete level, they are expressed and solved by expanded notation.

$$\begin{array}{ll} 435 & 435 \text{ in expanded form is} \\ -\,247 & 247 \text{ in expanded form is} \end{array} \quad \begin{array}{lll} 4 \text{ hundreds} & 3 \text{ tens} & 5 \text{ ones} \\ -\,(2 \text{ hundreds} & 4 \text{ tens} & 7 \text{ ones}) \end{array}$$

Before subtraction can be performed in this problem, the 3 tens and 5 ones are renamed as 2 tens and 15 ones. In the next step, the four sets of one hundred and the two sets of ten are renamed as three sets of one hundred and 12 sets of ten.

This is shown as

$$\begin{array}{lll} 3 & 12 & 1 \\ \cancel{4} \text{ hundreds} & \cancel{3} \text{ tens} & 5 \text{ ones} \\ -\,(2 \text{ hundreds} & 4 \text{ tens} & 7 \text{ ones}) \end{array}$$

Then the problem is solved in the conventional notation without using the words "hundreds, tens, ones."

$$\begin{array}{rrr} 3 & 12 & 15 \\ \cancel{4} & \cancel{3} & \cancel{5} \\ -\quad 2 & 4 & 7 \end{array}$$

Finally the problem is solved without any writing except for the answer.

EXERCISES

1. Demonstrate with concrete materials how to solve and verbalize the following:

(a) $\dfrac{62}{-15}$ (b) $\dfrac{324}{-178}$ (c) $\dfrac{402}{-135}$

2. A youngster says that for the problem -15, 4 from 5 is 1 and 1 from 3 is 2. How would you help him?

3. Evaluate the advantages of a left to right method of subtraction as described by Ruth Hoppe (*The Arithmetic Teacher*, April, 1975, p. 320).

4. Analyze each of the ten "systematic" errors made by children (from L. S. Cox: Diagnosing and Remediating Systematic Errors in Addition and Subtraction. *The Arithmetic Teacher*, Feb., 1975, p. 152).

SUBTRACTION ALGORISMS

There are four basic algorisms that are in fairly wide use today for solving subtraction problems. Because of the highly mobile pupil population, it is important that the teacher be familiar with each. If a pupil is having difficulty, he should be asked to verbalize the problem so that the teacher can determine which algorism he is using.

The Subtract-Renaming and
Additive-Renaming Methods

The most familiar algorism, that of **subtract-renaming**, might be verbalized as follows:

$$
\begin{array}{r}
423 \\
-165 \\
\hline
258
\end{array}
\qquad
\begin{array}{l}
\text{5 from 13 is 8} \\
\text{6 from 11 is 5} \\
\text{1 from 3 is 2}
\end{array}
$$

In labeling this the subtract-renaming method, it is "subtract" in that we subtract 5 "from" 13. It is "renaming" in that we have to rename the 23 as 10 and 13 in order to substract 5.

The algorism in additive or missing-addend form might be verbalized as follows:

$$
\begin{array}{r}
423 \\
-165 \\
\hline
258
\end{array}
\qquad
\begin{array}{l}
\text{5 and } \square \text{ is 13} \\
\text{6 and } \square \text{ is 11} \\
\text{1 and } \square \text{ is 3}
\end{array}
$$

It is an "additive" or missing addend form in that we begin with the known addend 5 and verbalize as 5 and $\square$ is 13.

Both the subtract and additive models just described use the same procedure for solving a problem in which the minuend (upper number) is smaller than the subtrahend (lower number). This is called "borrowing" or "renaming."

The Subtract-Equal Addition and Additive-Equal Addition Methods

The next two algorisms do not use the familiar renaming (borrowing) idea when a number in the subtrahend is larger than the one above it in the minuend. The procedure is based on the principle that adding the same number to both the minuend and subtrahend in a subtraction problem does not change the problem as far as the answer is concerned.

For example,

$$
\begin{array}{cc}
6 & 6 + 10 = 16 \\
\underline{-2} & 2 + 10 = \underline{-12} \\
4 & 4
\end{array}
$$

For a problem such as $\begin{array}{r}32\\-17\end{array}$, 10 ones are arbitrarily added to the 2 ones, so that the first subtraction, 7 from 12, can be performed. To compensate for this arbitrary addition of 10 ones to the minuend, 1 ten is added to the next column in the subtrahend.

$$
\begin{array}{r}
3 \, {}^{1}2 \\
-{}^{2}\cancel{1} \ 7
\end{array}
$$

The second subtraction is then 2 tens from 3 tens. Each time an addition has to be made in the minuend, a compensating addition is made in the subtrahend in the next column. This technique is called the **equal addition** or **compensation** method.

Verbalizing, using the subtract (from) model,

$$
\begin{array}{r}
{}^{1\,1}423 \\
{}^{2\,7}\underline{-165} \\
258
\end{array}
$$

5 from 13 is 8
7 from 12 is 5
2 from 4 is 2

In this model the numbers become one larger in the subtrahend rather than one smaller in the minuend.

The method is easy to demonstrate at the concrete level. 10 ones are added to the 3 ones and then a balancing or equal addition is made by adding 1 ten to the 6 tens. Since the second column involves adding 10 tens to the 2 tens to make 12 tens, an equal addition is made in the third column by adding 1 hundred to the 1 hundred.

Using the additive or missing-addend form, 5 and $\square$ = 13, and the equal addition method for handling numbers that are smaller in the minuend than in the subtrahend,

$$
\begin{array}{ll}
423 & \text{5 and } \square = 13 \\
- \ 165 & \text{7 and } \square = 12 \\
\hline
258 & \text{2 and } \square = 4
\end{array}
$$

This method has been used widely in the Northeastern United States and by recent immigrants to the United States.

The "equal addition" method is a better method when there are zeros in the minuend, since the zeros are not changed to nines, a process that often causes difficulty. For example;

$$
\begin{array}{ll}
3002 & \text{5 and } \square = 12 \\
- \ 1685 & \text{9 and } \square = 10 \\
\hline
1317 & \text{7 and } \square = 10 \\
& \text{2 and } \square = 3
\end{array}
$$

The Complementary Method

A fifth method, the complementary method of subtraction, is used in Europe today and might be used for enrichment. It is easy to learn in rote form but more difficult to rationalize. The first number in the subtrahend is subtracted from 10, and the result is added to the number above it in the minuend. Each of the other numbers in the subtrahend is subtracted from 9, and the result added to the number above it in the minuend.

For the problem $\dfrac{423}{- \ 165}$, the rote procedure is as follows:

$$
\begin{array}{ll}
423 & \text{5 from 10 is 5, and } 5 + 3 = 8 \\
9\,9\,10 & \text{6 from 9 is 3, and } 3 + 2 = 5 \\
-165 & \text{1 from 9 is 8, and } 8 + 4 = 12 \\
\hline
\cancel{1}258 & \text{finally, cross out the last digit to the left as shown.}
\end{array}
$$

The rationale for the complementary method is based on the idea of the complement of a number. The complement of any number is the difference between that number and the next higher power of 10. For example, the complement of 7 is (10 - 7) or 3, the complement of 73 is (100 - 73) or 27, the complement of 850 is (1000 - 850) or 150. To subtract a number by the complementary method, we add its complement instead. For example, subtracting 65 from a number is the same as adding its complement 35 to the number and then subtracting 100. Another name for - 65 is (35 - 100):

$$
\begin{array}{cc}
82 & 82 \\
-65 & (+\ 35\ -\ 100) \\
\hline
 & 117\ -\ 100\ =\ 17
\end{array}
$$

Scratching out the last digit to the left in the following example is the same as subtracting 100:

$$
\begin{array}{cc}
82 & 82 \\
-65 & +35 \\
\hline
 & \cancel{1}17
\end{array}
$$

The rote procedure in which the first number in the subtrahend is subtracted from 10 and all others from 9 before the result is added to the number above in the minuend is one way of obtaining the complement of the subtrahend.

Some problems may involve renaming when the complements are added. For example:

$$
\begin{array}{l}
888 \\
-655 \\
\hline
\cancel{1}233
\end{array}
$$

5 from 10 is 5 and 5 + 8 = 13; write the 3 and carry 1 (as in normal addition). In the second step, 5 from 9 is 4 and 4 + 8 = 12 plus the 1 carried is 13; write the 3 and carry 1. Finally in the third step, 6 from 9 is 3 and 3 + 8 = 11 plus the 1 carried is 12; write the 12 and scratch out the last digit to the left.

The complementary method is easy to perform because it involves subtractions from 10 and 9 only. It does not, however, provide practice for the other subtraction combinations and is more difficult to rationalize.

Note. In verbalizing the subtraction problems described above, the terms **minuend** and **subtrahend** were used because there were enough new ideas to consider without changing these words. But these terms

are being replaced with the term **sum** for minuend and the term **addend**
for subtrahend. For the problem $\begin{array}{r} 23 \\ -\ 7 \end{array}$ 23 is the sum, 7 the addend, and
the answer we are looking for is the missing addend. This of course is
the missing addend model of subtraction.

EXERCISES

1. Solve each of the following by the different algorithms described:

   (a) $\begin{array}{r} 64 \\ -\ 28 \end{array}$ (b) $\begin{array}{r} 427 \\ -\ 145 \end{array}$ (c) $\begin{array}{r} 8015 \\ -\ 2568 \end{array}$

2. Rationalize with concrete materials
   (a) the equal addition method of subtraction
   (b) the complementary method of subtraction

ERROR PATTERNS IN SUBTRACTION

Can You Diagnose Them?

Answers

(a) $\begin{array}{r} 48 \\ -3 \\ \hline 15 \end{array}$ $\begin{array}{r} 74 \\ -2 \\ \hline 52 \end{array}$ $\begin{array}{r} 68 \\ -5 \\ \hline 13 \end{array}$

(a) Subtracts single number in sub-trahend from both columns in minuend.

(b) $\begin{array}{r} 53 \\ -48 \\ \hline 10 \end{array}$ $\begin{array}{r} 625 \\ -342 \\ \hline 303 \end{array}$ $\begin{array}{r} 531 \\ -276 \\ \hline 300 \end{array}$

(b) When number in subtrahend is larger than the number above it, the difference is recorded as zero.

(c) $\begin{array}{r} 37 \\ -\ 4 \\ \hline 23 \end{array}$ $\begin{array}{r} 43 \\ -\ 1 \\ \hline 32 \end{array}$ $\begin{array}{r} 85 \\ -\ 3 \\ \hline 72 \end{array}$

(c) "Borrowed" from the tens column when it was unnecessary.

(d) $\begin{array}{r} 32 \\ -\ 6 \\ \hline 34 \end{array}$ $\begin{array}{r} 50 \\ -\ 8 \\ \hline 58 \end{array}$ $\begin{array}{r} 24 \\ -\ 5 \\ \hline 21 \end{array}$

(d) Did not regroup the minuend. Subtracted the smaller from the larger number in each column.

(e)	$\begin{array}{r} 3\ 19 \\ \cancel{49} \\ -\ 11 \\ \hline 218 \end{array}$	$\begin{array}{r} 1\ 18 \\ \cancel{28} \\ -16 \\ \hline 12 \end{array}$	$\begin{array}{r} 7\ 13 \\ \cancel{83} \\ -\ 32 \\ \hline 411 \end{array}$

(e) Renamed the minuend when it was unnecessary. The difference in the ones column is a two-digit number. The two-digit number is placed in the answer.

(f)	$\begin{array}{r} 53 \\ -14 \\ \hline 49 \end{array}$	$\begin{array}{r} 72 \\ -56 \\ \hline 26 \end{array}$	$\begin{array}{r} 45 \\ -19 \\ \hline 36 \end{array}$

(f) Renamed the minuend and correctly subtracted in the ones column. No renaming or borrowing was performed in the tens column.

(g)	$\begin{array}{r} 5\ 13 \\ \cancel{493} \\ -\ 45 \\ \hline 418 \end{array}$	$\begin{array}{r} 2\ 16 \\ \cancel{376} \\ -\ 58 \\ \hline 338 \end{array}$	$\begin{array}{r} 3\ 15 \\ \cancel{265} \\ -\ 39 \\ \hline 206 \end{array}$

(g) Incorrectly renamed the minuend. The renamed number in the tens column is obtained by subtracting the smaller digit from the larger digit in the tens column. Subtraction in the tens column is then performed with this renamed number; e.g., the renamed ten of 493 − 45 is obtained by subtracting 9 − 4 = 5. Five is the renamed number.

Instructional Activities to Correct Error Patterns in Subtraction

1. Before attempting conventional subtraction problems, do some renaming problems with right and wrong names for the child to identify.

   Does 42 = 3 tens 12 ones ?

   Does 342 = 2 hundred 14 tens 12 ones ?

   Be sure child is first familiar with the renaming process.
2. First estimate the answer—will it be more than 100?—less than 100?
3. Represent and solve problems with base ten blocks.
4. Represent and solve problems with popsicle sticks (bundles of hundred, ten, and single sticks).
5. Use place value board.
6. Draw frame so that only one numeral can go in each space.

H	T	O
3	4	2
−	6	8

7. Use real money.
8. Use expanded notation.

$$
\begin{array}{ccc}
2 & 13 & 1 \\
\cancel{3}\ \text{hundred} & \cancel{4}\ \text{tens} & 2\ \text{ones} \\
- & 6\ \text{tens} & 8\ \text{ones} \\
\hline
2\ \text{hundred} & 7\ \text{tens} & 4\ \text{ones}
\end{array}
$$

5

MULTIPLICATION

MULTIPLICATION AS RELATED TO ADDITION

In the Bible there is a statement to the effect "go forth and multiply and replenish the earth." What is multiplication? Why is 3 X 5 = 15?

Because it just is?

Because someone told you?

Because it is like addition?

Because you get 15 by counting?

Because it is a Cartesian product?

Because we simply define it that way?

Most of these answers contain an element of truth. Probably the simplest way to introduce multiplication is as a special case of addition in which the addends are the same. Multiplication is an abbreviated way of representing addition; for example, 5 + 5 + 5 + 5 + 5 + 5 may be expressed as 6 X 5.

As youngsters learn such addition facts as 5 + 5 = 10, which is read as "Five and five is ten," or "Five plus five is ten," the question may be asked, "Two sets of five objects is how many?" This, of course, is a multiplication problem, which may be verbalized as "Two fives is ten" or "Two times five is ten" and symbolized or written as 2 X 5 = 10. In introducing multiplication, both the additive form 5 + 5 = 10 and the multiplicative form 2 X 5 = 10 are written and verbalized to indicate the relationship of multiplication to addition:

5 + 5 = 10   five and five is ten

  or

2 X 5 = 10   two fives is (the same number as) ten, or two times five is equal to ten

Similarly, $5 + 5 + 5 = 15$ and $3 \times 5 = 15$.

The vertical form for expressing addition and multiplication ideas must also be considered, since it is a conventional notation.

$$
\begin{array}{cccc}
& & & 5 \\
5 & 5 & 5 & 5 \\
+5 \text{ or } & \times 2 & +5 \text{ or } & \times 3 \\
\hline
10 & 10 & 15 & 15
\end{array}
$$

Note that in the vertical form the number representing the number of sets of five is written below the number representing the number of elements in each set.

READINESS FOR MULTIPLICATION

Readiness for multiplication is present before readiness for subtraction. No reversibility of thought is necessary to consider the problem $5 + 5$ as 2×5. This is why children have less difficulty with first notions of multiplication than of subtraction.

But since addition and subtraction are one reversible system, logically and psychologically, they should be considered at the same time. The same is true for multiplication and division as one reversible system. The conclusion, readiness-wise, is that a *systematic introduction* to addition and subtraction should be started later and multiplication and division earlier, probably in second grade, if they are to be meaningful for most children.

LEARNING THE BASIC MULTIPLICATION FACTS
(0 X 0 TO 9 X 9)

Multiplication as an operation will be considered in two ways, first as it is introduced to children and then as it is defined in relation to an operation on sets.

The idea of a factor machine, which renames a number such as 12 in terms of its factors, 1×12, 12×1, 3×4, 4×3, 6×2, 2×6, is a relatively new way of learning the basic multiplication facts. This is consistent with the number family approach used to teach addition, examining the whole in terms of its parts (addends in addition and factors in multiplication). The more conventional approach, of course, is that of the multiplication tables.

There is much confusion in interpreting the multiplication tables. From what multiplication table is the expression 3 X 5 = 15 taken, or which of the following does the expression 3 X 5 represent at the concrete level?

XXX   XXX   XXX   XXX   XXX

or

XXXXX   XXXXX   XXXXX

There is little agreement in most classes in answer to this question. And yet the two displays are certainly not the same. If textbooks are consulted, it is found that the statement 3 X 5 = 15 is generally considered as being taken from the fifth multiplication table and is represented by the second display.

To say that the form 3 X 5 = 15 is from the fifth multiplication table is to say that 3 fives is 15 or that three sets of five is a set of fifteen. For those who learned that 3 X 5 = 15 is a set of 3 times 5, it should be said that this is an awkward way of expressing the idea involved. In ordering from the grocery store, one does not say "a dozen eggs times three" or "a pound of sugar times five" but rather "three dozen eggs" or "five pounds of sugar." In normal English usage the number named first represents the **number of sets,** whereas the second number represents the **number of each set** or the "size" of each set. The expression 3 X 5 = 15 is a mathematical sentence and should be read as, "Three sets of five (or three fives or three times five) is fifteen." The verb *is* is used because each expression *is* another name for 15. To say that 3 X 5 is 15 is to say that 3 X 5 is another name for 15.

The fifth multiplication table then is:

1 X 5 = 5	4 X 5 = 20	7 X 5 = 35
2 X 5 = 10	5 X 5 = 25	8 X 5 = 40
3 X 5 = 15	6 X 5 = 30	9 X 5 = 45

In interpreting multiplication in terms of tables, we read the display XXXXX   XXXXX   XXXXX as "three sets of five" and write it as 3 X 5 = 15. Correspondingly, the display XXX   XXX   XXX   XXX   XXX is interpreted as "five sets of three" and is written as 5 X 3 = 15. Thus, the mathematical sentence 5 X 3 = 15 is from the third multiplication table.

It is true that the commutative property holds for multiplication (that is, 5 X 3 = 3 X 5) but in interpreting for children the relationship of multiplication to addition by means of concrete materials, 3 X 5 is not the same as 5 X 3.

Displaying the Basic Multiplication Facts

There are 100 single-digit multiplication facts to learn, from 0 × 0 to 9 × 9, before the conventional algorism for multiplication can be used. These 100 facts are usually organized into tables and memorized. Our present practice is to use one table to display multiplication facts, just as one table is used to display addition facts. As each table is learned, the appropriate row is filled in. The following table has the multiplication facts for zero, one, and two filled in.

x	0	1	2	3	4	5	6	7	8	9
0	0	0	0	0	0	0	0	0	0	0
1	0	1	2	3	4	5	6	7	8	9
2	0	2	4	5	8	10	12	14	16	18
3										
4										
5										
6										
7										
8										
9										

To use the table for the product 2 × 4 = □, look down the left side of the table for the numeral 2, then over to the right to the column headed by the number 4, and the **product 8** will be seen. The numbers 2 and 4 are called **factors** of 8. Any numbers whose product is a number are said to be **factors** of that number.

The table above can be used to solve multiplication problems involving factors expressed with more than one digit. For example, to solve the problem 2 × 78, look in the 2 row under the columns headed by 7 and 8. Finding the numbers 14 and 16, add the two middle digits, 4 + 1. The product is 156.[1]

Beginning at the Concrete Level

As each set of multiplication facts is learned, the pupil should "build" or complete a table of his own similar to the one illustrated. Even

---

[1] For further discussion, see William F. Hullihan, "Multiplication Unlimited." *The Arithmetic Teacher,* May, 1968, p. 460.

MULTIPLICATION

though the multiplication facts displayed in the table should be memorized for later convenience, the introduction to the tables should not be done in rote fashion.

Activities appropriate to introducing a table of multiplication facts include the use of concrete materials such as popsicle sticks. To learn the third multiplication table, for example, consider popsicle sticks in sets of three: One set of three sticks is how many? Three. How may this be written? $1 \times 3 = 3$. How may this answer be read? It may be read as, "One three is three, or one set of three is three, or one times three is three." Then two sets of three sticks is how many? three sets of three sticks? four sets of three sticks? Children may display the appropriate number of sets of three sticks and count to determine the product as necessary.

The Montessori materials for teaching mathematics include a wooden board designed with nine columns and nine depressions in each column in which beads can be placed. The table number being studied is a wooden cut-out numeral placed at the left (4). The numeral at the head of each column represents the number of sets. Three sets of four are displayed in the following illustration as 12 beads in a 3 by 4 array.

4	1	2	3	4	5	6	7	8	9

A display such as

$$\begin{array}{ccc} \bullet & \bullet & \bullet \\ \bullet & \bullet & \bullet \\ \bullet & \bullet & \bullet \\ \bullet & \bullet & \bullet \end{array}$$

is called an **array** or **matrix** and is often used in exploring multiplication facts. How many rows? Four. How many columns? Three. How many altogether? Twelve.

The Montessori Schools have an extensive variety of concrete manipulative materials used to develop mathematical ideas. They are beautifully made, but expensive. It is a more comprehensive set of materials than is found in most schools. The emphasis on concrete manipulative material is important, and the children's work is largely individualized. Critics contend, however, that the materials have to be used in a certain way and that the activities and materials are so structured that correct answers are obtained without a real understanding of the underlying principles. As expressed by Dewey:

> Even the kindergarten and Montessori techniques are so anxious to get intellectual distinctions, without "waste of time," that they tend to ignore—or reduce— the immediate crude handling of the familiar material of experience, and to introduce pupils at once to material which expresses the intellectual distinctions which adults have made. But the first stage of contact with any new material, at whatever age of maturity, must inevitably be of the trial and error sort. An individual must actually try, in play or work, to do something with material in carrying out his own impulsive activity, and then note the interaction of his energy and that of the material employed. This is what happens when a child at first begins to build with blocks, and it is equally what happens when a scientific man in his laboratory begins to experiment with unfamiliar objects.[2]

> [The Montessori] demand is for materials which have already been subjected to the perfecting work of mind .... That such material will control the pupil's operations so as to prevent errors is true. The notion that a pupil operating with such material will somehow absorb the intelligence that went originally to its shaping is fallacious. Only by starting with crude material and subjecting it to purposeful handling will he gain the intelligence embodied in finished material.[3]

Numbers Assigned Length. Concrete **number lines** are useful in exploring the multiplication facts. For example, if a rod is assigned a length of "two," then how long will five rods be?

---

[2] John Dewey: *Democracy and Education: An Introduction To The Philosophy of Education.* New York: The Macmillan Publishing Co., Inc., 1916, p. 181.
[3] *Ibid.,* p. 232.

MULTIPLICATION

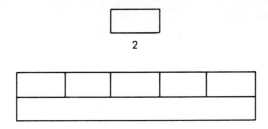

2

Children, using the Cuisenaire rods, line up five 2 rods and find that they are the same length as a 10 rod. A problem such as how many 2 rods are as long as a 10 rod is, of course, a corresponding division problem.

For a problem such as 8 × 2, it is found that eight 2 rods is the same length as a 10 rod and a 6 rod.

Moving toward the abstract, a semi-concrete stage is the drawn number line.

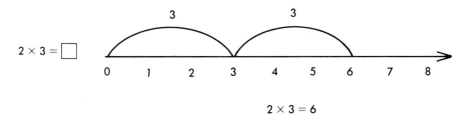

$2 \times 3 = \square$

$$2 \times 3 = 6$$

For an activity-based program, more ideas on teaching multiplication are described in Chapter 17, The Mathematics Laboratory.

Reinforcement. After experimenting with such concrete materials, the results of these activities should be recorded in symbol form as 1 × 3 = 3, 2 × 3 = 6, and so forth, and verbalized appropriately. These facts are then recorded in the 3 row of the multiplication table. After the products have been determined and recorded, they must be committed to memory with such activities as showing flash cards and games.

There are many game activities for reinforcement of the recall of multiplication facts. Multo, a game like bingo, involves calling out two factors such as "3 and 4." If you have a 12 on your card, you place a button on it. We might also build a "factor" machine. If we throw in a 12, what would it throw out? 6 × 2, 3 × 4, 4 × 3, 2 × 6, 1 × 12, and 12 × 1.

The present practice is to learn the multiplication facts systematically in grades three and four, although in some schools these facts are introduced at an earlier level. In any event, as addition facts such as 3 + 3 = 6 are learned, the idea should also be verbalized in multiplicative form as, "Two threes is six" or, "Two sets of three is one set of six." Again, the verb used is *is* because two sets of three *is* another name for a set of six.

Children have difficulty with the empty set and its number property, zero. Since $0 + 0 = 0$, then $2 \times 0 = 0$. And since $2 \times 0 = 0$, if the commutative property holds for multiplication, $0 \times 2 = 0$.

MULTIPLICATION AS A CARTESIAN PRODUCT

The relationship of multiplication to addition is usually introduced to children as a "shortcut" to addition problems in which the addends are the same number. For example, $2 + 2 + 2 = 3 \times 2$.

However, multiplication may represent another physical model. If a girl has a set of three blouses and a set of four skirts, how many different dress combinations consisting of one blouse and one skirt does she have?

$$B = \{\text{blue, yellow, white}\}$$

$$S = \{\text{black, red, green, orange}\}$$

To determine the number of blouse and skirt pairs, a line can be drawn from each blouse to each skirt as follows:

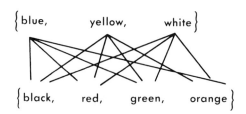

The number of line segments drawn, 12, represents the number of blouse-skirt pairs. It is also the product of the number of blouses, 3, and the number of skirts, 4.

This set of 12 combinations is called the cartesian product of sets B and S. It may be symbolized as $B \times S$, and read as "B cross S."

For any two sets A and B, the cartesian product, A $\times$ B, will be the *set of ordered pairs obtained by pairing each element of A as a first member with each element of B as a second member.*

Multiplication as the cartesian product of two sets is different from the "addition of equal addends" idea as usually introduced to children. The possible pairings of a set of blouses and a set of skirts, for example, is definitely not the "addition of equal addends" interpretation of multiplication, and yet the answer may be obtained by multiplying the number of one set by the number of the other, in this case, 3 × 4 or 12.

A more interesting problem for the college student may be the cartesian product for the possible "dates" or "couples" for a set of three boys and a set of four girls. The cartesian product would be a set containing 12 ordered pairs.

For sets containing numbers as elements such as

$$A = \{1,2,3\}$$
$$B = \{4,5\}$$
$$A \times B = \{(1,4), (1,5), (2,4), (2,5), (3,4), (3,5)\}$$

the number of the set A cross B contains 6 ordered pairs or 6 elements, a fact which may be symbolized as $n(A \times B) = 6$ and read as, "The number associated with A cross B is six."

On the following graph, if each of the coordinates on the x axis $\{1, 2, 3, 4\}$ is graphed with each position on the y axis $\{1, 2, 3\}$, how many positions would be graphed?

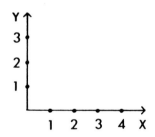

Pairing each x coordinate with each y coordinate would result in 12 points. The coordinates of these points would be as follows:

$$(1, 3)\ (2, 3)\ (3, 3)\ (4, 3)$$
$$(1, 2)\ (2, 2)\ (3, 2)\ (4, 2)$$
$$(1, 1)\ (2, 1)\ (3, 1)\ (4, 1)$$

These points may be graphed as follows:

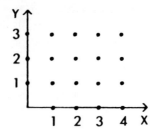

This set of points is a rectangular **array**. If any two sets X and Y (the sets are named with capital letters) are considered and if each element of X is paired with each element of Y, the result will be a product of the number of elements in each set.

For the two sets considered above, $X = \{1, 2, 3, 4\}$ and $Y = \{1, 2, 3\}$, there are 12 ways of matching an element from X with an element from Y. Therefore the number associated with X cross Y is 12.

The procedure of graphing involves the mathematics of both geometry and algebra. This combination is the mathematics of coordinate or analytic geometry. In analytic geometry, lines are conceived of as sets of points. Each point is named by an ordered pair of numbers (x, y), which also locates its position in the plane with respect to the reference axes.

PROPERTIES OF MULTIPLICATION OF WHOLE NUMBERS

The Commutative Property

This property is very useful in learning the basic multiplication facts or tables. Children can explore it by using concrete materials. For example, does 2 X 5 equal 5 X 2?

$$
\begin{array}{ll}
\text{XXXXX \ XXXXX = XXXXXXXXXX} & 2 \times 5 = 10 \\
\text{XX \ XX \ XX \ XX \ XX = XXXXXXXXXX} & 5 \times 2 = 10
\end{array}
$$

The **commutative** property for multiplication of whole numbers is usually stated as follows: For any two whole numbers, a and b

$$a \times b = b \times a$$

Because of the commutative property one can multiply in what-
ever order one chooses. For example, $\times$ $\frac{324}{34856}$ may be rewritten as
$\times$ $\frac{34856}{\quad 324}$, which is the more convenient order. The commutative
property is basic to the conventional check for multiplication problems. Also, a problem such as 4 $\times$ 7 $\times$ 5 is easy to solve mentally if
the 7 and the 5 are first commuted and solved as (4 $\times$ 5) $\times$ 7 = 20 $\times$
7 = 140.

The Associative Property

The associative property does not involve the order of the elements as
does the commutative property. In the expression $3(4 \cdot 5) = (3 \cdot 4) 5$,
the order of the elements is the same. The question is whether associating the 3 with the product of 4 and 5 (that is, $3(4 \cdot 5)$), produces the
same number as associating the product of 3 and 4 with the number 5
(that is, $(3 \cdot 4)5$). Does

$$3 \cdot (4 \cdot 5) = (3 \cdot 4) \cdot 5$$
$$3 \cdot 20 = 12 \cdot 5$$
$$60 = 60$$

That changing the association of factors does not change the product
is called the **associative property** of multiplication of whole numbers.
The general form, for any whole numbers a, b, and c, is usually written
as

$$a(b \cdot c) = (a \cdot b)c$$

In a problem such as $3 \cdot 6 \cdot 5$ then, it is possible (and easier) to perform the multiplication as $3 \cdot (6 \cdot 5)$ rather than as $(3 \cdot 6) \cdot 5$. This
choice of association would not be possible if the associative property
did not hold for multiplication of whole numbers.

The Closure Property

The product of any two whole numbers is a whole number. This
property of multiplication of whole numbers is called the **closure**

property. The whole numbers are said to be "closed" for multiplication because multiplying whole numbers produces a whole number. This is not true in dividing whole numbers. For example, $3 \div 6$ is not a whole number.

The Identity Element

The number 1 is the **identity element for multiplication**; that is multiplying 1 by any whole number or multiplying any whole number by 1 produces that whole number. For any whole number a

$$1 \cdot a = a \cdot 1 = a$$

For example:

$$1 \cdot 3 = 3 \cdot 1 = 3$$

The Distributive Property of Multiplication with Respect to Addition

This property is somewhat more difficult to visualize than those previously studied, but it is very important. Suppose a youngster forgets a product such as 5×9. If one of the factors is renamed and expressed as a sum of smaller numbers, the multiplication may then be performed using the distributive property and simpler multiplication facts:

$$5 \cdot 9$$
$$5 \cdot (6 + 3)$$
$$5 \cdot 6 + 5 \cdot 3$$
$$30 + 15$$
$$45$$

In this example the factor 9 is first renamed as two addends, each of which is then multiplied by the other factor. The products are then added. This method is an application of the distributive property.

The **distributive property** means that an expression such as $5(6 + 3)$ can also be written, and solved, as $5 \cdot 6 + 5 \cdot 3 = 30 + 15 - 45$. In the expression $\overparen{5(6 + 3)}$, the 5 "distributes" over the 6 and the 3 as $5(6) +$

5(3). Similarly, in the sentence $7(5 + 4) = 7 \cdot 5 + 7 \cdot 4$, the factor 7 "distributes" over the addends 5 and 4. More than two addends may be involved. For example, the number $7 \cdot 9$ may also be expressed as follows:

$$7 \cdot 9 = 7(3 + 3 + 3) = 7 \cdot 3 + 7 \cdot 3 + 7 \cdot 3$$

In this example the factor 7 "distributes" over each of three addends. The general case for the distributive property may be stated as follows: For any whole numbers a, b, and c

$$a(b + c) = a \cdot b + a \cdot c$$

or

$$a \cdot b + a \cdot c = a(b + c)$$

The so-called distributive property is actually the distributive property of multiplication with respect to (over) addition. It is the only property we have studied that involves two operations: one operation (multiplication) with respect to another (addition). Although multiplication is distributive with respect to addition, the reverse is not true; that is, addition is not distributive with respect to multiplication. For example, does

$$5 + (6 \cdot 3) \overset{?}{=} (5 + 6) \cdot (5 + 3)$$
$$5 + 18 \neq (11)(8)$$
$$23 \neq 88$$

The distributive property is very useful in solving multiplication problems mentally or when multiplication table facts are forgotten. But even more important, it *is the basis for the algorism we use in multiplication problems.*

Since only the multiplication facts to 9×9 are memorized, a procedure or algorism had to be developed for solving problems involving factors containing two or more digits. The problem 3×17 is not memorized. Then how can it be solved?

$3(17)$	
$3(10 + 7)$	17 renamed
$3 \cdot 10 + 3 \cdot 7$	distributive property
$30 + 21$	multiplication performed
51	addition performed

If this problem is done in vertical form, it is still a two-step problem based on the distributive property, as can be shown with the following unabridged algorism:

$$
\begin{array}{r}
17 \\
\times\ 3 \\
\hline
21 \\
30 \\
\hline
51
\end{array}
\qquad
\begin{array}{l}
(3 \times 7) \\
(3 \times 10)
\end{array}
$$

In the abridged algorism the same thinking is necessary:

$$
\begin{array}{r}
17 \\
\times\ 3 \\
\hline
51
\end{array}
$$

In a problem with a two-digit multiplier such as $\begin{array}{r}34 \\ \times\ 12 \\ \hline\end{array}$, the distributive property is used twice.

$$
\begin{array}{r}
34 \\
\times\ 12 \\
\hline
68 \\
340 \\
\hline
408
\end{array}
\qquad
\begin{array}{l}
2(4 + 30) \\
10(4 + 30)
\end{array}
$$

The distributive property and the single-digit multiplication facts provide the basis for the conventional algorism in multiplication: For any multiplication, each digit of one factor is distributed over the addends in the other factor.

For the problem, 382×465:

$$
\begin{array}{r}
465 \\
\times\ 382 \\
\hline
930 \\
3720 \\
1395 \\
\hline
177630
\end{array}
\qquad
\begin{array}{l}
2(400 + 60 + 5) \\
80(400 + 60 + 5) \\
300(400 + 60 + 5)
\end{array}
$$

MULTIPLICATION

INTRODUCING THE ALGORISM FOR
MULTIPLICATION TO CHILDREN

After children have learned the single-digit multiplication facts from 0 X 0 to 9 X 9 and committed them to memory, it is necessary for them to learn how to adapt these facts to a procedure for solving multiplication problems with factors containing more than a single digit.

The commutative, associative, and distributive properties are all helpful and important in solving multiplication problems. As a word of caution, it is not memorization of words and definitions that is important in teaching children but rather the understanding of how these properties function. The Exercise at the end of this section will reinforce this idea.

A problem such as 3 X 68 is not committed to memory, so how can it be solved? The distributive property just discussed provides a basis for solution, but children should begin at the concrete level in thinking through such problems.

Multiplying Numbers Expressed with
Two or More Digits

Begin with a multiplication problem involving one two-digit factor such as 3 X 23, and in a concrete situation such as, "If you save 23 cents a day, how much will you have at the end of three days?"

Set the problem up at the concrete level with simulated coins of cardboard that each child can use at his seat. Each child should be asked to "show" three sets of two dimes and three pennies. Then ask him to put all the dimes together and all the pennies together to see how much he has.

Dimes	Pennies
0 0	o o o
0 0	o o o
0 0	o o o

Ask the children to verbalize, "three sets of two dimes is *six dimes*" and, "three sets of three pennies is *nine pennies*."

After solving and understanding a number of these problems at the concrete level, the child is ready to consider them in symbol form using expanded notation:

$$\begin{array}{cc} 2 \text{ tens} + 3 \text{ ones} \\ \underline{\times\ 3} \\ 6 \text{ tens} + 9 \text{ ones} \\ \text{or } 69 \end{array} \quad \text{or} \quad \begin{array}{c} 20 + 3 \\ \underline{\times\ 3} \\ 60 + 9 \\ \text{or } 69 \end{array}$$

Another way of expressing the same idea is:

$$\begin{array}{rl} 23 \\ \underline{\times\ 3} \\ 9 & (3 \times 3) \\ \underline{60} & (3 \times 20) \\ 69 \end{array}$$

If the same problem is stated in horizontal form, it could be expressed as:

$$\begin{aligned} 3 \times 23 &= 3(20 + 3) \\ &= 60 + 9 \\ &= 69 \end{aligned}$$

Products Involving Renaming

For a product involving carrying or renaming such as $\begin{array}{r} 24 \\ \underline{\times\ 3} \end{array}$, consider the problem first with concrete materials such as arithmetic blocks or a pocket chart. Represent on the chart as three sets of 2 tens and 4 ones. Verbalizing the problem, "Three sets of four ones is how many? Twelve ones. How can twelve ones be renamed? As one ten and two ones. Let's leave two ones in the ones column and hold the ten for the tens column. Now, three sets of two tens is how many? Six tens. Plus the one ten that we hold makes seven tens for the tens column. The problem $\begin{array}{r} 24 \\ \underline{\times\ 3} \end{array}$, then, is seven tens and two ones or seventy-two."

After solving the problem at the concrete level, consider it again in symbol form using expanded notation.

$$
\begin{array}{r}
2 \text{ tens} + 4 \text{ ones} \\
\times 3 \\
\hline
6 \text{ tens} + 12 \text{ ones} \\
7 \text{ tens} + 2 \text{ ones} \\
\text{or} \\
72
\end{array}
$$

In verbalizing such a problem, do not say, "Three ones times four ones" or "Three ones times two tens" since this is not meaningful. Instead, let the multiplier, 3, represent the number of sets: "Three sets of four ones is □" and, "Three sets of two tens is □"

After using concrete materials and the expanded notation, restate the same problem in the following forms:
First, with a crutch, if necessary:

$$
\begin{array}{r}
1 \\
24 \\
\times 3 \\
\hline
72
\end{array}
$$

And finally in the conventional form:

$$
\begin{array}{r}
24 \\
\times 3 \\
\hline
72
\end{array}
$$

It may be helpful to consider first the problem in unabridged form— that is, in a form that requires no renaming in the multiplication. Consider 24 as 24 ones rather than 2 tens and 4 ones.

$$
\begin{array}{r}
24 \\
\times 3 \\
\hline
12 \\
60 \\
\hline
72
\end{array}
\quad
\begin{array}{l}
\\
\\
(3 \times 4 \text{ ones}) \\
(3 \times 20 \text{ ones})
\end{array}
$$

The accepted algorism, as we can see from the unabridged form, is a shortcut, since part of the problem (carrying or renaming) is done mentally.

The horizontal form for the same problem can be displayed as:

$$3 \times 24 =$$
$$3 \times (20 + 4) =$$
$$(3 \times 20) + (3 \times 4) =$$
$$60 + 12 =$$
$$60 + (10 + 2) =$$
$$(60 + 10) + 2 =$$
$$70 + 2 = 72$$

This form shows clearly both the distributive property and the associative property of addition in performing multiplication.

To introduce a problem involving a two-digit multiplier such as $\frac{37}{\times 12}$, the "addition of equal addends" interpretation of multiplication is still useful. The problem 12×37 can be thought of as 12 sets of 37, which is the same as 10 sets of 37 and two sets of 37 (the distributive property).

This problem should first be considered in unabridged form—that is, with no carrying or renaming during the multiplication:

$$
\begin{array}{rl}
37 & \\
\times\ 12 & \\
\hline
14 & \quad 2 \times 7 \\
60 & \quad 2 \times 30 \\
70 & \quad 10 \times 7 \\
300 & \quad 10 \times 30 \\
\hline
444 &
\end{array}
$$

Another way of solving the problem in unabridged form may be helpful:

$30 + 7$	
$\times\ (10 + 2)$	
$\overline{60 + 14}$	distributive property
$300 + 70$	distributive property
$\overline{300 + 130 + 14}$	addition performed
$300 + (100 + 30) + (10 + 4)$	addends renamed
$(300 + 100) + (30 + 10) + 4$	associative property of addition (used twice)
$400\quad +\quad 40\quad + 4$	addition performed
444	system of numeration

For the conventional abridged algorism, first the product of two sets of 37 is determined:

$$
\begin{array}{r}
37 \\
\times 12 \\
\hline
74 \quad (2 \times 37)
\end{array}
$$

then the product of 10 sets of 37:

$$
\begin{array}{r}
37 \\
\times \ 12 \\
\hline
74 \quad (2 \times 37) \\
370 \quad (10 \times 37)
\end{array}
$$

and then the partial products are added:

$$
\begin{array}{r}
37 \\
\times \ 12 \\
\hline
74 \\
370 \\
\hline
444
\end{array}
$$

The product of the step, 10×37 or 370, in the conventional algorism does not show the 0, but it does show the 3 in the hundreds place and the 7 in the tens place, with the ones place empty. This is the basis of the rote rule "drop over one," which is used in determining the second partial product.

After the product 2×37 is determined, the 1 in the tens place is considered. Do not tell the children to "drop over one space." This is actually a 10 and not 1 and therefore the second product is $\begin{array}{r} 37 \\ \times \ 10 \end{array}$. Ten sets of 7 ones is 70 ones or 7 tens, and therefore the 7 must be placed in the tens column.

In verbalizing this kind of multiplication problem, students often say, "One ten times seven ones," and express the next step as, "One ten times three tens," which has little if any meaning at the concrete level. The problem read with the multiplier representing the numbers of sets, "Ten sets of seven ones," or 10×7, is more meaningful. The last step is then verbalized as, "Ten sets of thirty ones is three hundred ones" or, "Ten sets of three tens is thirty tens or three hundred."

ERROR PATTERNS IN MULTIPLICATION

Can You Diagnose Them?

Answers

1. (a)   34   (b)   25
       X 6   X 7
     304   355

1. Adds before multiplying in second step.

2. (a)   36   (b)   35
       X23   X24
     108   140
      72   70
     180   210

2. In second partial product, multiplies by 2 rather than 20 which the 2 represents.

3. (a)   35   (b)   28
       X24   X53
     140   84
     610   1040
     750   1124

3. In second partial product, does not carry.

4. (a)   253   (b)   485
       X 6   X 7
   1318   2975

4. In regrouping, always carries "one" as in addition problems.

5. (a)   25   (b)   87
       X 6   X 5
      50   115

5. Does second step like an addition problem.

6. (a) 132   (b)   132
       X 7   X 6
     924   1512

6. In second multiplication step, reverses digits to be carried and written.

In second step of (b)—
$3 \times 6 = 18$, $18 + 1 = 19$, write 1, carry 9

In third step—
$1 \times 6 = 6$, $6 + 9 = 15$

Remediation Procedures

Represent and work through problem using manipulative materials such as base ten blocks or popsicle sticks. Verbalize step by step as described on pp. 110–113.

EXERCISES

1. Develop a lesson for introducing the multiplication algorism using concrete materials. Solve 3 × 24 using concrete materials and verbalize each step.

2. A youngster solving the problem $\begin{array}{r} 24 \\ \times\ 3 \\ \hline \end{array}$ says "3 × 4 is 12 so I write 2 and carry 1. Then 3 × 3 is 9." How would you help him?

3. Differentiate between the commutative and associative properties of multiplication.

4. Show with specific examples how the commutative property of multiplication may speed the solution of a multiplication problem.

5. Indicate how the associative property might be useful in solving the following:
   (a) 5 · 5 · 12   (b) 8 · 6 · 5

6. Solve the following by using the distributive property:
   (a) 6 × 9   (b) 8 × 7   (c) 9 × 9

7. A teacher displays eight counters as:

   XXXX   XXXX

   and then as:

   XX   XX   XX   XX

   Which property is she demonstrating?

8. Which of the following will require the use of the associative property of multiplication for its solution:
   (a) 5 × 7 × 8   (b) (5 + 6) × (8 + 3)   (c) 3(11 + 8) + 12

9. Which of the following will require the use of the distributive property:
   (a) 6 × 5   (b) 5 × 9 × 7   (c) 3(5 + 6)   (d) 12 × 32

10. What property is used in each of the following:
    (a) Renaming in addition
    (b) Renaming in multiplication

11. Demonstrate the four multiplication steps in the following problem. Use concrete materials and verbalize each step.

$$\begin{array}{r} 32 \\ \times 13 \\ \hline \end{array}$$

DIVISION

Division as an algorism is more difficult for children to understand than are addition, subtraction, or multiplication. The conventional algorism for division works from left to right instead of from right to left as do the algorisms for the other basic operations. Answers are written at the top rather than the bottom, and there are the problems of remainders and trial quotients.

DIVISION AS THE INVERSE OF MULTIPLICATION

Subtraction has been referred to as the inverse of addition. Division is the **inverse** of multiplication. To use a specific example: $6 \div 3 = 2$ if and only if $3 \times 2 = 6$.

The following general form is preferred by many mathematicians:

$$a \div b = c \quad \text{if and only if} \quad b \times c = a$$

This notation has a rigor at the abstract level but is not understood by children at the concrete operational level. Division should be introduced to children in terms of object manipulation in the physical world.

DIVISION APPLIED TO THE PHYSICAL WORLD

Which of the following displays is described by $6 \div 3 = \square$?

116

$$XXXXXX \quad = \quad XXX \quad XXX$$

or

$$XXXXXX \quad = \quad XX \quad XX \quad XX$$

The difficulty in answering this question is indicative of the confusion about division. When $6 \div 3 = 2$ is verbalized as, "Six divided by three is two," it is not at all clear to children what this represents in the physical world. They are familiar with the dividing of a pie or a cake into servings, the dividing or sharing of toys among their playmates, the line that divides a highway into left and right lanes, and the dividing of a group into teams or sides for games. Clarity in interpreting division in the physical world is dependent on the choice of verbalization. To say, "Six divided by three is two" is not clear enough, nor does it help children visualize the two possible meanings described in the next section.

Partitive and Measurement Division

Multiplication may be related to combining or joining sets (e.g., three sets of two is a set of six). Division as the inverse of multiplication may be related to the dividing or separating of sets. If $6 \div 3 = \square$ is interpreted as a set of six objects divided or separated into sets of three objects, how many sets are produced? Two. This idea may be illustrated as follows:

$$XXXXXX \quad = \quad XXX \quad XXX$$

This interpretation of division is **measurement division**; that is, the divisor represents the unit of measure; How many sets of three in a set of six? This idea may be shown on the number line as follows:

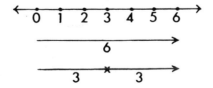

The same sentence $6 \div 3 = 2$ may also represent another concept called **partitive division**. This is a concept in which the divisor (3) represents the number of sets into which the dividend (6) is divided or partitioned: A set of six divided or separated equally into three sets produces how many in each set?

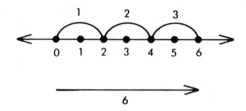

Note that in **partitive division** the divisor represents the *number of sets,* whereas in **measurement division** the divisor represents the *number of each set.*

The partitive interpretation is more closely related to the division of our early experiences; children often divide things among themselves. For example, if six oranges are to be divided among three children, how many will each receive? Or if a set of six oranges is to be divided or separated into three sets, how many oranges will be in each set? Note that the divisor represents the number of sets to be produced. In contrast, in measurement division the divisor is the number of each set or the unit of measure. The same sentence, 6 ÷ 3 = 2, interpreted as measurement division, might be, "How many sets of three oranges are there in a set of six oranges, or if we have six oranges and give three to each child, how many children will receive oranges?"

Summarizing, in **measurement division** the divisor represents the *number of each set* and the quotient represents the *number of sets.* In **partitive division** the divisor represents the *number of sets* and the quotient represents the *number of each set.*

Thus, 6 ÷ 3 = □ interpreted as partitive division is:

A set of six objects divided or separated equally into three sets produces how many objects in each set? (2)

$$000000 = 00 \quad 00 \quad 00$$

whereas, 6 ÷ 3 = □ interpreted as measurement division is:

A set of six objects divided or separated into sets of three objects produces how many sets? (2)

$$000000 = 000 \quad 000$$

DIVISION

If children are to learn to interpret division in the physical world, it is important that teachers make this distinction. The expression "six divided by three" does not help a youngster to visualize the operation of division. However, "six divided or separated into sets of three" or "six divided or separated into three sets" does convey a meaningful idea. In a sentence such as $6 \div 3 = 2$, the idea should not be verbalized as partitive division if it actually represents measurement division, and vice versa.

The same number line displays or concrete representations for $6 \div 3 = 2$ can be used for $6 \div 2 = 3$, but what was partitive division when the divisor was 3 becomes measurement division when the divisor is 2 and vice versa. The verbalization of the problem identifies the meaning.

Money often helps clarify number problems. Using the numbers 8 and 2, make up a division problem for both the measurement and partitive concepts of division.

Measurement: Eight pennies divided into sets of two pennies produces how many sets? Or, if we have eight pennies and give two to each child, how many children get pennies?

Partitive: Eight pennies divided into two equal sets produces how many in each set? Or, if we divide eight pennies equally between two children, how many pennies does each child get?

Consider a problem involving larger numbers. Suppose that a school has 600 students and 30 classrooms. How many students will be in each class if each class has the same number of students? Stated mathematically, $600 \div 30 = 20$. Which interpretation of division is represented in this statement? This is partitive division since the divisor, 30, represents the number of different sets into which the students will be divided, and the quotient, 20, is the number of students in each set or classroom.

Using the same numbers, 600 and 30, consider a word problem involving the measurement interpretation of division. If 600 students are divided into sets of 30, how many classrooms will be needed? In this example the divisor 30 is a unit of measure or the number of each set, rather than the number of different sets as in the preceding example.

Measurement division is related to the idea of repeated subtraction. For example, how many five-cent stamps can one buy with 20 cents? Even though one did not know the appropriate division fact, one might solve the problem by subtracting as follows:

$$
\begin{array}{ll}
20 & \\
\underline{-5} & 1 \\
15 & \\
\underline{-5} & 2 \\
10 & \\
\underline{-5} & 3 \\
5 & \\
\underline{-5} & 4 \\
0 & \\
\end{array}
$$

There are then four sets of five in a set of twenty or $20 \div 5 = 4$.

EXERCISES

1. Illustrate with concrete materials and verbalize the following facts, using the measurement interpretion of division:
   (a) $8 \div 4 = \square$ (b) $12 \div 3 = \square$ (c) $10 \div 2 = \square$
2. Verbalize and illustrate each part of problem 1, using the partitive interpretation of division. Let the number 12 in (b) be inches of ribbon for pledge ties.
3. Make up a word problem for each part of problem 1, using first the measurement and then the partitive interpretation for division.
4. Write division equations for

and verbalize using both partitive and measurement forms.
5. What is wrong with the following word problems, which were submitted by students?
   (a) If you had eight apples and gave four to Mary and four to John, how many apples did you have?
   (b) If 12 boys were in a classroom and only three boys could wash their hands at a time, then how many trips were made to the washroom?

INTRODUCING THE BASIC DIVISION FACTS

Psychologically speaking, Piaget finds children ready for the operation of multiplication, and its inverse, division, at approximately the same

120

time that they are ready for addition and subtraction. However, the practice has been to introduce multiplication and division some two years later. But as the addition facts such as 3 + 3 are learned, the problem can also be verbalized as a multiplication problem: two times three is six.

When multiplication is introduced it should be related to its inverse, division, since psychologically speaking the two operations form one reversible system.

Youngsters should first work with concrete materials in learning the basic multiplication facts. A display such as

$$000 \quad 000 \quad 000 \quad 000 = 000000000000$$

may be represented by 4 X 3 = 12. The sentence 4 X 3 = 12, or four sets of three is a set of twelve, is a fact usually recorded in the third multiplication table. Then if a set of 000000000000 is separated into sets of three, how many sets are there? Children learn to represent this as 12 ÷ 3 = □ and also in the form 3⟌12, both read as how many threes in 12 or how many sets of three in a set of twelve. This is measurement division.

The coat hanger and clothespin illustration shows 12 ÷ 3 interpreted both as measurement division and partitive division.

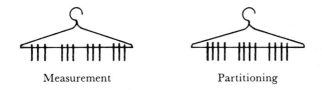

Measurement   Partitioning

The number line also helps to visualize division. For example, 12 ÷ 3 interpreted as measurement division (how many sets of three in 12?):

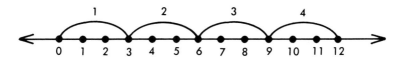

Or interpreted as partitive division (if 12 is divided into three sets, how many are in each set?):

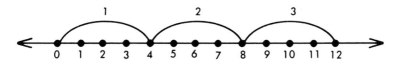

If division is introduced as the inverse of multiplication—that is, as naming the missing factor when one factor and the product are known—then as children learn that $3 \times 9 = 27$ they will also learn to solve such problems as $3 \times \square = 27$ and $\square \times 9 = 27$. Moreover, if division is to be learned as the inverse of multiplication, the table that is developed for the multiplication facts may also be used to reinforce the corresponding division facts.

X	0	1	2	3	4	5	6	7	8	9
0	0	0	0	0	0	0	0	0	0	0
1	0	1	2	3	4	5	6	7	8	9
2	0	2	4	6	8	10	12	14	16	18
3	0	3	6	9	12	15	18	21	24	27
4	0	4	8	12	16	20	24	28	32	36
5	0	5	10	15	20	25	30	35	40	45
6	0	6	12	18	24	30	36	42	48	54
7	0	7	14	21	28	35	42	49	56	63
8	0	8	16	24	32	40	48	56	64	72
9	0	9	18	27	36	45	54	63	72	81

To use this table for solving division problems, such as $4 \times \square = 28$, look down the left side of the table to the factor 4, across to the right to the product 28, and then up to the top of the column containing 28 to obtain the missing factor.

It must be emphasized here that the completed table should be the result of many experiences with concrete and semi-concrete materials. It is a means of classifying in compact form the basic multiplication and division facts as they are discovered or developed by the child himself. The table thus serves only as a compact reference to the basic facts, as an end product rather than a beginning or a device for use in memorizing facts. However, memorizing these facts does require some kind of drill, which should come after the operation and theory are learned, and not before.

DIVISION BY ZERO

The number of people in an unoccupied room is 0. If this set of people is divided into three sets, how many are in each set? Expressed another way:

$$0 \div 3 = 0$$

The reciprocal idea of dividing a number by 0 is not easy to grasp, however. $\dfrac{3}{0}$ is not equal to 0 as can be seen from the following:

First, if $6 \div 3 = 2$
then $\qquad 6 = 3 \cdot 2$ (multiplication as the inverse of division)
Similarly, if $3 \div 0 = 0$
then $\qquad\qquad 3 = 0 \cdot 0$
but $\qquad 0 \cdot 0 = 0$
and $\qquad\qquad 3 \neq 0$

Then what is $\dfrac{3}{0}$ equal to? Let us represent the answers as the number N.

If $3 \div 0 = N$
then $\quad 3 = N \cdot 0 \qquad$ (multiplication as the inverse of division)

But there is no counting number N which can be multiplied by 0 to produce 3. It is, therefore, necessary to say that dividing a number by 0 is undefined. Dividing by 0 has no meaning.

INTRODUCING THE DIVISION ALGORISM

After the single-digit multiplication facts from 0×0 to 9×9 as well as the corresponding division facts have been learned, a procedure or algorism must be developed for solving division problems involving numbers of two or more digits.

The Conventional Algorism

To introduce the long division algorism, a problem such as $3\overline{)63}$, which involves no renaming and no remainder, is considered first. Using concrete materials such as a pocket chart to explore this problem, the dividend 63 could be represented as six sets of 10 ones (each set wrapped with a rubber band) and three sets of one.

Sets of Ten   Set of One

If the measurement interpretation is used with the display above, then the problem is verbalized as, "How many sets of three tens are in six tens? Two. How many sets of three ones are in a set of three ones? One."

Tens   Ones

If the parititive idea of division rather than the measurement idea is used, then the problem $3\overline{)63}$ is interpreted as 63 divided into three equal sets or groups. If the six tens are divided into three equal sets, then, "How many tens are there in each set? Two." Dividing the three ones into three equal sets, "How many ones in each set? One."

Tens   Ones

After the exploratory activities with concrete materials are completed, the problem should be solved in the expanded form of notation:

$$3\overline{)6 \text{ tens} + 3 \text{ ones}}$$

How should the problem be verbalized?

1. "Six tens divided into three equal sets produces how many in each set? Two tens. Then write the two tens above the six tens."
2. "How many of the six tens did you divide? All six. Then write the six below the six tens to indicate that all tens have been divided."
3. "What is left to be divided? Three ones. And if you divide them into three sets? There will be one in each."
4. "Then write the one above the three ones."
5. "And how many of the three ones did you divide? All three. Then write the three below the three ones to indicate that the division is complete."

DIVISION

$$\begin{array}{r} 2 \text{ tens} + 1 \text{ one} \ \ \text{or } 21 \text{ ones} \\ 3\overline{)6 \text{ tens} + 3 \text{ ones}} \\ 6 \text{ tens} \phantom{+ 3 \text{ ones}} \\ \hline 3 \text{ ones} \\ 3 \text{ ones} \\ \hline \end{array}$$

After the expanded form is used to gain a better understanding of place value in division, the abridged or conventional algorism is considered:

$$\begin{array}{r} 21 \\ 3\overline{)63} \\ 6 \\ \hline 3 \\ 3 \\ \hline \end{array}$$

If the student has difficulty in properly placing the digits in the quotient, he does not understand the algorism, and the expanded form or manipulative materials should be considered again.

The short division form $3\overline{)63}^{\,21}$ involves more mental arithmetic than the abridged form. Although short division should not be taught, children who discover it and find they can use it with accuracy should be allowed to do so. Concerning short division, Grossnickle and Brueckner have the following to say.

> All experimental evidence dealing with the long or short form of division proves that the pupil achieves greater accuracy by use of the long form than by use of the short form. . . . No experimental evidence has ever demonstrated that the achievement in division of a group using the short form equals or excels the achievement of a comparable group using the long form.[1]

Renaming the Dividend. In the problem $3\overline{)63}$, the divisor is a factor of each digit of the dividend. In a problem such as $3\overline{)72}$, however, the divisor 3 is not a factor of 7. Such a problem requires the use of the associative property of addition, or the renaming of the dividend. The dividend 72 or 70 + 2 is renamed as 60 + 12. In so doing, 1 ten is renamed as 10 ones and associated with the 2 ones.

The renaming idea may be explored with children by using concrete materials such as popsicle sticks, Multibase Arithmetic Blocks, or pocket

---

[1] Foster E. Grossnickle and Leo J. Brueckner: *Discovering Meanings in Elementary School Mathematics.* New York: Holt, Rinehart and Winston, 1963, pp. 190–191.

charts (see chapter 17). For the problem 3 ⎸72, the divident of 72 is represented on the pocket charts as 7 sets of 10 cards and 2 single cards.

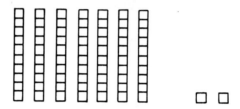

Represented with the Multibase Arithmetic Blocks:

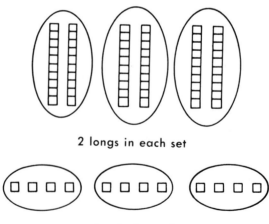

"How many longs can be divided equally into three sets? Six longs."
"And how many will be in each set? Two longs."
"Then what is left to divide? One long and two units."
"Can you divide what is left into three equal sets?"
"Would renaming the long as 10 units help? Yes, that would make twelve units."
"Then how many would be in each set? Four units."

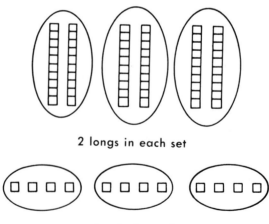

2 longs in each set

4 units in each set

Now consider the same problem in the expanded form of notation without concrete materials:

$$3\overline{\smash{)}7 \text{ tens } 2 \text{ ones}}$$

A verbalization similar to the one just given may be used as the transition is made toward the conventional algorism.

Renaming the dividend 7 tens + 2 ones as 6 tens + 12 ones:

$$3\overline{\smash{)}6 \text{ tens } + 12 \text{ ones}}$$

The problem may also be expressed in terms of "ones" only:

$$3\overline{\smash{)}70 + 2}$$

and then as

$$3\overline{\smash{)}60 + 12}$$

Finally, the problem is considered in the conventional abridged form:

$$
\begin{array}{r}
24 \\
3\overline{\smash{)}72} \\
\underline{6} \\
12 \\
\underline{12}
\end{array}
$$

This conventional algorism is often verbalized in measurement form as, "How many threes are in seven? Two. Then two times three is six. Subtracting six from seven leaves one. Then bring down the two. How many threes in twelve? Four. Four times three is twelve. And there is no remainder." Although this procedure becomes largely a rote procedure for speed in computation, it is important that the pattern and rationale of the long division algorism be understood. This understanding should grow out of the exploratory teaching stage, in which the concrete materials and unabridged algorisms are used.

For division problems involving remainders, two symbol forms are used. The form used first is:

$$
\begin{array}{r}
1 \ \text{R2} \\
3\overline{\smash{)}5} \\
\underline{3} \\
2
\end{array}
$$

Later when fractions are studied in more detail and the fraction is interpreted as an "indicated division," the fractional notation of remainders is used:

$$3 \overline{)5} \; \; 1\tfrac{2}{3}$$
$$\frac{3}{2}$$

Division as Repeated Subtraction

A procedure different from the conventional algorism is now being used to teach long division in many schools. In the conventional algorism the digits of the dividend may be considered separately. For the problem $3\overline{)72}$, recall that the digit 7 was considered first (that is, $7 \div 3$) and then $12 \div 3$.

In the new algorism, division is seen more clearly as a series of repeated subtractions. The dividend is not thought of as tens and ones, with the tens divided and then the ones. Instead the dividend is considered as ones only.

Hence, in considering again the problem $3\overline{)72}$, think of the dividend 72 as 72 ones. The problem may be thought of as how many sets of three are in a set of seventy-two? Are there 10, 20, 30? Since it is easy to multiply by 10 or a multiple of 10, 20 sets of three are used. The numeral 20 is placed in the quotient and multiplied by 3. The product 60 is placed below the 72 and subtracted. The second step, that of dividing 12 by 3, is easily performed, and the result, 4, is placed above the 0 in the ones column. The quotient then is 20 + 4 or 24.

$$
\begin{array}{r}
4 \\
20 \\
3\overline{)72} \\
60 \\
\hline
12 \\
12 \\
\hline
\end{array}
$$

Fewer than 20 sets of three could have been subtracted in the first step. For example, 10 sets of three could have been subtracted twice. This would, of course, involve one more step, but the slower learner might prefer this method.

$$
\begin{array}{r}
24 \\
\underline{4} \\
10 \\
10 \\
3\overline{)72} \\
\underline{30} \\
42 \\
\underline{30} \\
12 \\
\underline{12}
\end{array}
$$

A similar procedure more widely used than the one just described is to locate the partial quotients at the right and add down. The answer is then shown at the bottom.

$$
\begin{array}{r|l}
3\overline{)72} & \\
\underline{60} & 20 \\
12 & \\
\underline{12} & 4 \\
0 & 24
\end{array}
\qquad \text{or} \qquad
\begin{array}{r|l}
3\overline{)72} & \\
\underline{30} & 10 \\
42 & \\
\underline{30} & 10 \\
12 & \\
\underline{12} & 4 \\
0 & 24
\end{array}
$$

Sometimes arithmetic texts use these forms to introduce division because division as repeated subtraction is not difficult to understand. Also, with these forms provision is made for individual differences in ability, since different procedures can be used to solve the same problem. The following examples show three ways that a child might use the same algorism in solving the problem $3\overline{)75}$:

(a)

$$
\begin{array}{r|l}
3\overline{)75} & \\
\underline{15} & 5 \\
60 & \\
\underline{15} & 5 \\
45 & \\
\underline{15} & 5 \\
30 & \\
\underline{15} & 5 \\
15 & \\
\underline{15} & 5 \\
0 & 25
\end{array}
$$

(b)

$$
\begin{array}{r|l}
3\overline{)75} & \\
\underline{30} & 10 \\
45 & \\
\underline{30} & 10 \\
15 & \\
\underline{15} & 5 \\
0 & 25
\end{array}
$$

(c)

$$
\begin{array}{r|l}
3\overline{)75} & \\
\underline{60} & 20 \\
15 & \\
\underline{15} & 5 \\
0 & 25
\end{array}
$$

Any of these procedures may be used to obtain the quotient 25. The more able student learns quickly that the procedure is shortened by subtracting the maximum number of sets of three in each step. This, of course, is basic to the procedure used in the conventional algorism but avoids the problem of too large a trial quotient and having to erase.

Problems involving dividends of three or more digits can be solved in the same manner:

```
 5|7280|            6|1482|
  5000| 1000          1200| 200
  ----               ----
  2280|               282|
  2000| 400           240| 40
  ----                ---
   280|                42|
   250| 50             42|  7
  ----                ---
    30|                 0| 247
    30|    6
  ----  ----
     0| 1456
```

Divisors Expressed With Two or More Digits

The Repeated Subtraction Algorism. Division problems involving divisors containing two or more digits can be solved by using the repeated subtraction algorism:

```
 23|564|              23|564|
   460| 20     or      230| 10
   ---                 ---
   104|                334|
    92|  4             230| 10
   ---                 ---
    12| 24             104|
                        92|  4
                       ---
                        12| 24
```

As divisors and dividends become larger, however, it is questionable whether this procedure is as good as the conventional method.

The Conventional Algorism. The conventional algorism for division involves estimating the largest number that may be placed in the quotient for each step of the problem. The estimated number is a trial quotient because it may prove to be too large or too small. For example, in a problem such as 18|1176, it is difficult to determine the largest number of eighteens in 117 by estimation. The trial quotient may be too large or too small when multiplied by 18, in which case it must be erased and another estimate made.

In some problems it is not difficult to determine the trial quotient; for example, $32\overline{)684}$ or $423\overline{)5642}$. However, in a problems such as $23\overline{)193}$ or $384\overline{)7253}$, it is more difficult. There are two procedures generally used for estimating trial quotients.

Procedure 1—The Apparent Procedure. Divide the first digit of the divisor into the first digit of the dividend unless the digit in the dividend is smaller, in which case the first two digits of the dividend are used. With this procedure the trial quotient may be too large in which case the next smaller whole number is used.

Procedure 2—The Rounding-Off Procedure. This method is used when the second digit of the divisor is 5, 6, 7, 8, or 9. In such cases, $17\overline{)8324}$ for example, the 17 is rounded off to 20, and 2 (the first digit of the rounded off divisor) is divided into 8 (the first digit of the dividend) to determine the trial quotient. For problems in which the first digit of the dividend is less than the rounded off or trial divisor, the first two digits of the dividend are used. For example, the problem $17\overline{)1324}$ would involve rounding off 17 to 20 and dividing 2 into 13. The trial quotient would be 6. This procedure is more likely to produce the correct quotient digit in the first step than Procedure 1. Problems having divisors with three or more digits are treated in a similar manner. For example, $364\overline{)27842}$ would involving round off 364 to 400 and dividing 4 into 27 for the trial quotient. The trial quotient, 6, would be placed over the fourth digit in the dividend since 364 is larger than 278 (the first three digits of the dividend). In this example the trial quotient, 6, is found to be too small, and therefore 7 will have to be used. The correct trial quotient, 7, could have been determined immediately by mentally rounding off both divisor and dividend:

$$364\overline{)27842}$$

rounding off,

$$400\overline{)28000}$$

Dividing the first digit of the divisor into the first two digits of the dividend, $4\overline{)28} = 7$; 7 is therefore the trial quotient.

Procedure 1 is probably the better procedure for introducing the conventional algorism because it is the easier to follow. If a trial quotient is too large, correction involves a decrease by one in the trial quotient. As the pupil develops a better grasp of solving division problems and can visualize what is going on, he should be encouraged to improve his technique of estimating the trial quotient by rounding off the divisors and dividends.

ERROR PATTERNS IN DIVISION—CAN YOU DIAGNOSE THEM?

Answers

1. (a)
```
   231
3)613
```
(b)
```
   242
2)184
```

1. Divides larger number by smaller no matter whether in divisor or dividend.

2. (a)
```
    15
3)153
  150
    3
    3
```
(b)
```
    69
4)384
   36
   24
   24
```

2. Records numerals in answer from right to left as is procedure for addition, subtraction, and multiplication.

3. (a)
```
   84R3
6)4827
  48
   27
   24
    3
```

3. Omits necessary zero in tens place.

4. (a)
```
   570R7
9)4570
  45
   70
   63
    7
```

4. Uses zero in wrong place (ones rather than tens

Remediation Procedures

Work out problems with manipulative materials or place value board. Verbalize each step as the problem is solved concretely. See p. 126. Relate the problem at the concrete level to the conventional written form for division.

Roberts identifies four error categories or "failure strategies"[2] as follows:

1. Wrong operation: The pupil attempts to respond by performing an operation other than the one that is required to solve the problem.
2. Obvious computational error: The pupil applies the correct operation, but his response is based on error in recalling basic number facts.
3. Defective algorithm:[3] The pupil attempts to apply the correct operation but makes errors other than number fact errors in carrying through the necessary steps.
4. Random response: The response shows no discernible relationship to the given problem.

One difficulty with show and tell or highly structured methods of instruction is that the child may generalize incorrectly. For example, children who have learned what "five" is by seeing a certain configuration on a card ⬚ may think that ⬚ is not five. Similarly, △ is a triangle, but ▽ is not a triangle.

EXERCISES

1. What procedure would you use for teaching the elementary division facts? Why?
2. Rationalize the conventional long division algorism by using concrete materials such as a pocket chart for each of the following:
   (a) $2\overline{)46}$ (b) $2\overline{)54}$ (c) $5\overline{)65}$ (d) $6\overline{)112}$ (e) $3\overline{)133}$
3. Solve the following by using the repeated subtraction algorism:
   (a) $5\overline{)60}$ (b) $4\overline{)130}$ (c) $25\overline{)460}$ (d) $327\overline{)7834}$
4. Compare the conventional and the repeated subtraction algorisms for division with respect to their relative effectiveness and ease of understanding.

---

[2] Gerhard H. Roberts: "The Failure Strategies of Third Grade Arithmetic Pupils." *The Arithmetic Teacher,* 15, May 1968, pp. 442–446.

[3] An algorithm is a step-by-step written procedure for determining the result of an arithmetic operation (i.e., a sum, a difference, a product, or a quotient). A variety of algorithms or computational procedures can be used to determine any one missing number; and indeed, at different times and in different parts of the world, many differing but useful algorithms are taught.

BASES OTHER THAN TEN

Teachers sometimes resist working with other bases, feeling that such work is of little value. But it is of value in understanding place value and the structure of our own number system. Teachers are better able to appreciate the problems faced by children learning about place value for the first time. We also begin to see that a base ten system is no better than some others, such as a base eight system. Children enjoy working with nondecimal bases. It is an enrichment activity for the upper elementary grades.

If man had been born with one hand rather than two, he would have probably invented a base five system rather than a base ten system. We can establish a base five system, and for convenience of recognition, use the first Hindu-Arabic numerals: 0, 1, 2, 3, 4. It should be noted that there is no numeral 5, but the set does contain one more than four symbols, and we have to call this system something.

It is necessary to use 0, or some other symbol to represent the same idea, if the principle of place value is to be used in the system. We are tempted to think of base five as being 1, 2, 3, 4, 5, but if it were there would be no placeholder symbol such as 0. Furthermore, if the numeral 0 is included in the set 1, 2, 3, 4, 5, we have six symbols or a base six system.

If we attempt to develop a system in which no placeholder symbol such as 0 is used, then in the five symbol counting set 1, 2, 3, 4, 5, we might proceed to count as follows:

$$1, 2, 3, 4, 5, 5 + 1, 5 + 2, 5 + 3, 5 + 4, 5 + 5, 5 + 5 + 1, \cdots$$

We are then in the same trouble as the Egyptians were. Without a place-value principle or placeholder symbol, we must rely on the principle of repetition, as did the Egyptians. In that case, the numeral 5 would represent only the number 5 regardless of its position with respect to other numerals. As a result, numerals would get large and unwieldy as in the Egyptian and Roman systems.

CONCRETE ACTIVITIES FOR NONDECIMAL BASES

Using our base five set, with the five symbols 0, 1, 2, 3, 4 and with 0 as a place holder, determine and write the number of X's in the following illustration (or use other objects):

$$X \: X \: X \: X \: X \: X \: X \: X \: X \: X \: X \: X \: X$$

One may circle each set of five elements as follows:

$$\boxed{X \: X \: X \: X \: X} \: \boxed{X \: X \: X \: X \: X} \: X \: X \: X$$

and record the number as two sets of five and three sets of one, or as 23_{five}. In the notation 23_{five} the 2 refers to the number of sets of five elements and the 3 to the number of sets of one element; the subscript *five* indicates the base five system.

The numeral 23_{five} should be read "two three," not "twenty-three," since "twenty" means two tens. Similarly, 20_{five} should be read "two zero," not "twenty."

Another approach employing concrete materials is to use pieces of wood in the form of flats, longs, and units.

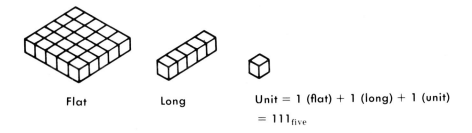

Flat   Long   Unit = 1 (flat) + 1 (long) + 1 (unit)
                                   = 111_{five}

Hence, □□□□□□□□□□□□□ (when represented in base five, this

involves exchanging each set of 5 units for a long) is:

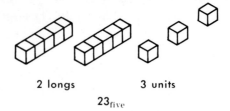

2 longs   3 units

23_{five}

If there were as many as five longs, the five longs would be exchanged for one flat. Hence, 213_{five} at the concrete level is:

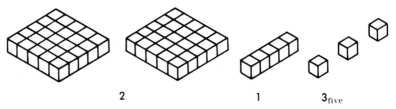

2   1 3_{five}

Moving toward the abstract but still at the concrete level is the abacus. The rule of the game is that not more than four counters can be placed on each spindle.

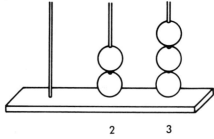

2   3

On the abacus, an object may represent one more than four objects, or five, rather than "one," if it is placed on the second spindle. In this sense, different place values are assigned to objects that are physically exactly alike. The abacus is more abstract than the materials previously described.

For the purposes of comparison, at the semi-concrete level a number line may be used. The points on the number line diagram below are enumerated in both base five and base ten:

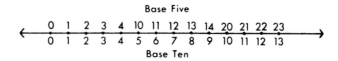

Base Five

0 1 2 3 4 10 11 12 13 14 20 21 22 23
0 1 2 3 4 5 6 7 8 9 10 11 12 13

Base Ten

When we compare the number 23_{five} to its equivalent in the base ten system, 13_{ten}, we find that two sets of five and three sets of one are the same as one set of ten and three sets of one. Thus, the numerals 13_{ten} and 23_{five} are names for the same number. Each system has advantages.

Another way to visualize a nondecimal base such as base five is to imagine the odometer of a car which has only the numerals 0, 1, 2, 3, 4 on each counter. Imagine also that at the start the odometer shows zero mileage or only zeros. As the car begins to move, the counters would turn as follows (read from top down, starting with the left-hand column):

0	24
1	30
2	31
3	32
4	33
10	34
11	40
12	41
13	42
14	43
20	44
21	100
22	101
23	102

This kind of odometer can be made with strips of paper by writing the numerals 0, 1, 2, 3, 4 on each strip and then pasting each strip in the form of a circle:

The strips are then placed on a spindle and turned by hand.

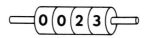

EXPANDED NOTATION

In base five each digit has a place value of a power of five, just as in base ten each digit has a place value of a power of ten. To express 102_{five} in expanded notation, write:

$$1(5^2) + 0(5^1) + 2(5^0)$$

Renaming in base ten, we have:

$$1(25) + 0(5) + 2(1)$$

or

$$25 + 0 + 2 = 27$$

Similarly, in expanded notation 2222_{five} could be written as:

$$2(5^3) + 2(5^2) + 2(5^1) + 2(5^0)$$

and renamed in base ten:

$$2(125) + 2(25) + 2(5) + 2(1)$$

or

$$250 + 50 + 10 + 2 = 312$$

RENAMING NUMBERS

Other Bases to Base Ten

From base five to base ten:

$$234_{five} = \underline{\hspace{2cm}} \text{ (base ten)}$$
$$234_{five} = 2(5^2) + 3(5^1) + 4(5^0)$$
$$= 2(25) + 3(5) + 4(1)$$
$$= 50 + 15 + 4$$
$$= 69$$

From base six to base ten:

$$234_{six} = \underline{\hspace{2cm}} \text{ (base ten)}$$

Expressed in expanded form:

$$
\begin{aligned}
234_{six} &= 2(6^2) + 3(6^1) + 4(6^0) \\
&= 2(36) + 3(6) + 4(1) \\
&= 72 + 18 + 4 \\
&= 94
\end{aligned}
$$

Base Ten to Other Bases

$$329 = \underline{\hspace{2cm}}_{five}$$

To express 329 in base five involves thinking of place value in terms of powers of five rather than powers of ten. Instead of representing 329 as:

$$3(10^2) + 2(10^1) + 9(10^0)$$

we must represent it as:

$$?(5^3) + ?(5^2) + ?(5^1) + ?(5^0)$$

How many sets of 125 are there in 329? Two. Then the numeral 2 goes in the 5^3 (or 125) place. Still to be accounted for is 329 – 250 or 79. How many sets of 5^2 or 25 are there in 79? Three. Then the numeral 3 goes in the 5^2 place. Still to be accounted for is 79 – 75 or 4. How many sets of five are there in 4? Zero. Then 0 goes in the 5^1 place. Finally, how many sets of one are there in 4? Four. Therefore, the numeral 4 goes in the 5^0 place.

The numerals, 2, 3, 0, and 4 may then be assigned place value as follows:

$$\frac{2}{5^3} \ \frac{3}{5^2} \ \frac{0}{5^1} \ \frac{4}{5^0} \text{ or } 2304_{five} = 329_{ten}$$

Some students prefer indicating the place value by drawing lines as shown, and then filling in the number in base five below the numeral, a procedure often used in teaching children the idea of place value in base ten:

125	25	5	1
2	3	0	4

The successive operations used in converting 329 to 2304_{five} may also be shown as follows:

$$\begin{array}{cccc}
2 & 3 & 0 & 4 \\
125\overline{)329} & 25\overline{)79} & 5\overline{)4} & 1\overline{)4} \\
\underline{250} & \underline{75} & & \\
79 & 4 & &
\end{array}$$

BASE TWO

Somewhat more difficult to visualize is a number written in base two, for only two numerals are used, usually 0 and 1. In order to visualize the place value in base two, think again in terms of an odometer. If the odometer had only the symbols 0 and 1 rather than 0 to 9 on each counter, it would register mileage as shown in the Base Two column below. Such an odometer would require many more places to represent numbers.

Base Two	Base Ten
1	1
10	2
11	3
100	4
101	5
110	6
111	7
1000	8

In base two, the numeral 1000 in expanded form is:

$$1(2^3) + 0(2^2) + 0(2^1) + 0(2^0)$$

The numeral 100_{two} is read "one zero zero" and in expanded form would be:

$$1(2^2) + 0(2^1) + 0(2^0)$$

Converting to base ten:

$$4 + 0 + 0 = 4$$

Thus, 100_{two} and 4_{ten} are names for the same number.

Electronic computers use a base two or binary system of numeration. Electricity can be switched on and off very rapidly. Therefore, "on" is equal to 1 and "off" is 1 more. The computer can count and compute—on, off, on, off—thousands of times per second.

BASE TWELVE

If man had had 12 fingers, he would have probably invented another symbol for 1 more than 9 (for example, T), and still another symbol for more than that (for example, E). Our basic numerals would then be

$$0, 1, 2, 3, 4, 5, 6, 7, 8, 9, T, E$$

The principle of place value would not be needed until 1 more than E had to be named, just as we do not use place value in base ten until we have used all the single digits. Using the same principles as in base ten, the numeral after E would be 10, but the symbol 1 represents one set of twelve. Enumerating the points on a number line in base twelve:

0	1	2	3	4	5	6	7	8	9	T	E	10	11	12	13	14	15	16	17	18	19	1T	1E	20	21
0	1	2	3	4	5	6	7	8	9	10	11	12	13	14	15	16	17	18	19	20	21	22	23	24	25

The number 324_{twelve} written in expanded form would be:

$$3(12^2) + 2(12^1) + 4(12^0) \quad \text{or} \quad 3(144) + 2(12) + 4(1)$$

Using a place value chart, 324_{twelve} could be represented as

12^2	12	1
3	2	4

EXERCISES

1. Write in expanded notation:
   (a) 4562_{ten} (b) 4562_{seven} (c) 123_{four} (d) 111_{two}
2. Draw a number line and name points on it in base ten from 0 to 30. Name these same points in bases four, six, two, and twelve.
3. Complete the following:
   (a) 262_{ten} = _____ five   (b) 148_{ten} = _____ eight   (c) 18_{ten} = _____ two
4. Complete the following:
   (a) 432_{six} = _____ ten   (b) 1010_{two} = _____ ten   (c) 567_{twelve} = _____ ten
5. Make up a counting set containing five numerals (but no Hindu-Arabic symbols) and count to the equivalent of 20_{ten} using this set.
6. Count to ten using as a set of symbols $\{X, \circ, \triangle, \square\}$, called X, *circle*, *triangle*; *square*. Let X represent zero.
7. Using two symbols, $\triangle$ and $\square$, with $\triangle$ serving as zero, count to ten.

ADDITION AND SUBTRACTION IN A NONDECIMAL BASE

An appreciation of the difficulty faced by youngsters in learning to add and multiply may be gained by considering the same operations in another base, a base possibly as strange to the elementary teacher as base ten is to children. Base four, for example, involves a system using only four symbols. Teachers often wonder about the usefulness of studying nondecimal bases, just as some of the more traditional teachers do not approve of using concrete "playthings" in teaching number concepts, since number is paper and pencil seat work.

In studying nondecimal bases, the concept of place value is seen in a new light. Place value is not as simple as it appears to be, particularly when you attempt to teach it. Learning about nondecimal systems of numeration has a special significance to teachers. As far as the youngsters are concerned, nondecimal systems are fun and worthwhile from an enrichment standpoint. From the standpoint of utility, electronic computers use nondecimal systems, particularly base two.

Concrete Materials

The importance of beginning with concrete materials to teach unfamiliar number concepts becomes evident as one studies adding in a nondecimal system. Many college students in their first college math course learn or rather manipulate symbols in a nondecimal base but report that these ideas were really not understood until the problems were solved with concrete materials such as the following:

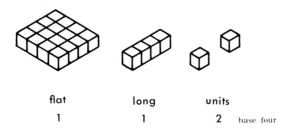

flat	long	units	
1	1	2	base four

Four units make a long, 4 longs make a flat and 4 flats make a block. The rule of the game is to represent the number idea with the smallest number of pieces of wood possible.

Hence, ☐☐☐☐☐☐ becomes ☐☐☐☐ ☐☐

6 units (base ten) = 1 long 2 units (base four)

or

$$6 = 12_{four}$$

Now, for an addition problem, solve $\begin{array}{r} 31_{four} \\ +22_{four} \\ \hline \end{array}$ by first representing with concrete materials:

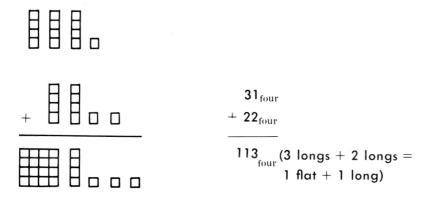

$$\begin{array}{r} 31_{four} \\ +\ 22_{four} \\ \hline 113_{four} \end{array}$$ (3 longs + 2 longs = 1 flat + 1 long)

For a subtraction such as $\begin{array}{r} 33 \\ -12 \\ \hline \end{array}$ first represent with concrete objects, and then solve:

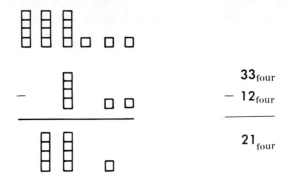

$$33_{\text{four}}$$
$$- \ 12_{\text{four}}$$
$$\overline{\hphantom{-} \ 21}_{\ \text{four}}$$

Verbalizing this problem in additive form: "How many units must be added to the two units to make three units? One unit. Then, how many longs added to one long make three longs? Two longs."

Now, for a subtraction problem that involves renaming:

$$31_{\text{four}}$$
$$- \ \ 3_{\text{four}}$$

To solve such a problem, one of the 3 longs in the minuend must be renamed as 4 units. The subtraction can then be performed:

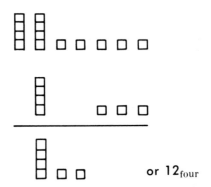

or 12_{four}

Subtraction In a Nondecimal Base

Subtraction in nondecimal bases is considered for several reasons. First, subtraction as the inverse of addition is seen in clearer perspective. Second, the teacher gains a better appreciation of the difficulty faced by youngsters in learning the renaming (borrowing) concept in base ten. Third, it is an enrichment activity for the more able pupils.

In this discussion of nondecimal bases, we will use base five as an illustration, and to solve subtraction problems in base five notation, we will use the table of addition facts for base five. In so doing, we will apply the additive interpretation of subtraction. That is, we will find the missing addend when one addend and the sum are known by looking down the left-hand side of the accompanying table to the known addend, then across to the right to the sum, then to the top of the column above the sum for the missing addend.

+	0	1	2	3	4
0	0	1	2	3	4
1	1	2	3	4	10
2	2	3	4	10	11
3	3	4	10	11	12
4	4	10	11	12	13

For problems involving no renaming, the subtraction facts are the same as in base ten:

$$
\begin{array}{r}
344 \\
-\ 123 \\
\hline
221
\end{array}
\qquad
\begin{array}{l}
3 + \square = 4 \\
2 + \square = 4 \\
1 + \square = 3
\end{array}
$$

However, for a problem involving renaming, it is a set of five that is renamed as five sets of one, not a set of ten renamed as 10 ones. For example

$$
\begin{array}{r}
32_{\text{five}} \\
-\ 13_{\text{five}}
\end{array}
\quad \text{may be expressed in expanded form as} \quad
\begin{array}{r}
3 \text{ fives} + 2 \text{ ones} \\
-\ (1 \text{ five } + 3 \text{ ones})
\end{array}
$$

Renaming:

$$
\begin{array}{r}
2 \qquad\quad 1 \\
-\ \cancel{3} \text{ fives} + \ 2 \text{ ones} \\
-\ (1 \text{ five } + \ 3 \text{ ones})
\end{array}
$$

Using the addition table:

$$3 + \square = 12$$
$$1 + \square = 2$$

$$\begin{array}{r} 32_{\text{five}} \\ - \ 13_{\text{five}} \\ \hline 14_{\text{five}} \end{array}$$

Another example is the problem

$$\begin{array}{r} 312_{\text{five}} \\ - \ 123_{\text{five}} \end{array}$$

which may be expressed in the expanded form as

$$\begin{array}{r} 3(5^2) + 1(5) + 2(1) \\ - \ 1(5^2) + 2(5) + 3(1) \\ \hline \end{array}$$

Renaming:

$$\begin{array}{cccc} 2 & & 10 & 1 \\ \cancel{3}(5^2) + & 1(5) + & 2(1) \\ - \ 1(5^2) + & 2(5) + & 3(1) \\ \hline 1(5^2) + & 3(5) + & 4(1) \end{array}$$

Using the addition table:

$$3 + \square = 12$$
$$2 + \square = 10$$
$$1 + \square = 2$$

$$\begin{array}{r} 312_{\text{five}} \\ - \ 123_{\text{five}} \\ \hline 134_{\text{five}} \end{array}$$

In this problem, since 3 sets of one could not be subtracted from 2 sets of one, the one set of five was associated with the 2 ones and the first step is $3 + \square = 12$. This left zero fives in the second column, so that before the second subtraction could be performed, one of the 3 sets of 5^2 had to be renamed in terms of sets of five as 10.

Problems such as this help the teacher to realize how difficult the so-called borrowing idea can be for the second or third graders if they hope to understand renaming.

To visualize subtraction problems in nondecimal bases such as base five, the number line may be helpful. The problem $3 + \square = 12_{\text{five}}$ may be displayed as:

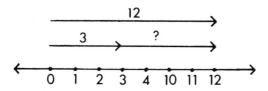

The same problem in the form, $12 - 3 = \square$, may be displayed as:

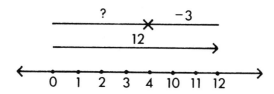

Working at the Symbol Level

To fill in an addition table in base four, we can mentally convert from base ten to base four. For example, in base ten the sum of $3 + 2$ is 5. To convert to base four. "Five is one set of four and one set of one, or one, one base four."

Similarly, in base ten the sum of $3 + 3$ is 6, whereas in base four, 6 is one set of four and two sets of one, or 12, read as "one, two," not "twelve."

+	0	1	2	3
0	0	1	2	3
1	1	2	3	10
2	2	3	10	11
3	3	10	11	12

It is interesting that if we used a base four system for addition, there would be only 16 single-digit addition sums or facts to memorize as contrasted to the 100 single-digit sums we have to learn for base ten.

The addition table for base four may also be shown in the traditional pattern:

$$
\begin{array}{llll}
0 + 0 = 0 & 0 + 1 = 1 & 0 + 2 = 2 & 0 + 3 = 3 \\
1 + 0 = 1 & 1 + 1 = 2 & 1 + 2 = 3 & 1 + 3 = 10 \\
2 + 0 = 2 & 2 + 1 = 3 & 2 + 2 = 10 & 2 + 3 = 11 \\
3 + 0 = 3 & 3 + 1 = 10 & 3 + 2 = 11 & 3 + 3 = 12
\end{array}
$$

Although base four addition would make memorizing the addition facts less laborious, it would have the disadvantage of requiring more digits to represent the same number than does base ten. For example, $64 = 1000_{\text{four}}$.

The addition facts in base four that produce sums of two digits may be rationalized with the number line by enumerating points on the line as follows:

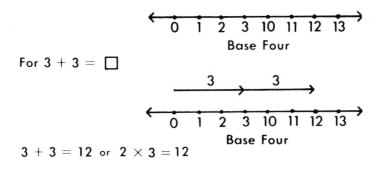

For $3 + 3 = \square$

$3 + 3 = 12$ or $2 \times 3 = 12$

The idea of carrying or renaming in base four involves renaming four sets of one as one set of four. It is sets of four that are being carried in contrast to sets of ten in base ten. The algorism $\begin{array}{r} 231 \\ + 123 \\ \hline \end{array}$ could be solved in rote form as follows:

$\begin{array}{r} 231 \\ + 123 \\ \hline 1020 \end{array}$ $3 + 1 = 10$, write the 0 and carry the 1 (one set of four)
$2 + 3 = 11$, and the 1 carried makes 12, write the 2 and carry 1 (one set of 4^2)
$1 + 2 = 3$ and the 1 carried makes 10 (which is one set of 4^3 and zero sets of 4^2)

The sum 10 in the first step should be read "one, zero" and not "ten" because one, zero is one set of four and zero ones, not one set of ten and zero ones. Likewise, the sum 12 in the second step should be read "one, two" and not "twelve" because 12 is not one set of one hundred and two sets of ten, but one set of 4^2 and two sets of four.

To check such an addition the numbers can be renamed in base ten as follows:

$$231_{four} = 2(4^2) + 3(4) + 1(1) = 32 + 12 + 1 = 45$$
$$123_{four} = 1(4)^2 + 2(4) + 3(1) = 16 + 8 + 3 = \underline{27}$$
$$72$$

Does 72 equal 1020_{four}? Expression 1020_{four} in expanded and converting to base ten:

$$1(4^3) + 0(4^2) + 2(4) + 0(1)$$
$$64 + 0 \quad\quad + 8 \quad + 0$$
$$72$$

Thus, $72 = 1020_{four}$.

Addition and subtraction problems in bases other than ten are now included in some fifth grade material, and multiplication and division problems in other bases are being incorporated in fifth or sixth grade material. Some texts postpone this material to the junior high school level. The grade level at which these ideas are considered depends more on the intelligence and achievement of the pupils and the methods of the teacher than on the grade in which the pupils happen to be. In any case, base five seems to be a favorite starting point, possibly because we can think of each hand as having a set of five fingers.

Youngsters can build their own tables for addition and multiplication for solving problems in nondecimal bases. Teachers who have been using nondecimal systems in their classes report that their pupils are very enthusiastic about such activities.

EXERCISES

1. What is the solution for each of the following additions in base five? The numbers as given are in base five. Solve first with concrete materials. Illustrate your answers on a number line.
   (a) $2 + 2 =$　　(b)　$2 + 3 =$　　(c)　$3 + \square = 11$
   (d) $3 + 4 =$　　(e)　$12 + 4 =$　　(f)　$13 - 4 = \square$

2. The following are expressed in base five. What are the solutions in base five? Solve first with concrete materials.

(a)   13   (b)   34   (c)   44
     +21   +23   +44

3. Each of the following is expressed in base five notation. Perform the subtraction in base five. Solve first with concrete materials.

(a) 432   (b) 341   (c) 4001
    −141   −123   −2342

4. Each of the following is expressed in base five. Rationalize with the aid of a number line.

(a) $3 + \square = 11$ (b) $13 - 4 = \square$ (c) $3 + \square = 13$

5. Make a table for the single digit addition facts in base five, using the numerals 0, 1, 2, 3, and 4.

6. Give an example to illustrate whether each of the following properties holds for base five and the operation of addition.

(a) Commutative   (b) Associative   (c) Identity element

7. In what base is each of the following true? Illustrate your answers on a number line.

(a) $3 + 4 = 10$ (b) $3 + 2 = 11$
(c) $4 + 9 = 11$ (d) $5 + 12 = 20$

8. In what bases were the following subtractions performed?

(a) $11 - 4 = 4$ (b) $13 - 5 = 6$

MULTIPLICATION IN NONDECIMAL BASES

Multiplication can be performed in other bases as readily as in base ten, and the algorism we use may be seen in clearer perspective when applied to a base other than ten. This is worthwhile as an enrichment activity for pupils in the upper elementary grades. It is particularly useful for teacher training, in that new insights in methods of teaching multiplication may be gained.

Multiplication in Base Five

Beginning at a concrete level, how would 3 × 4 in base five be represented? As three sets of four units:

0000   0000   0000

If these objects are grouped in sets of five,

there are two sets of five and 2 ones, which is written as 22_{five}.

For a problem involving a two-digit factor such as 2×14, how should it be represented with concrete materials? As an example, it can be represented as two sets of 1 long and 4 units:

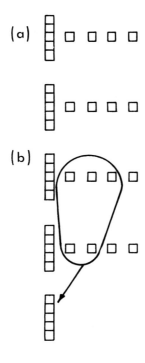

Then two sets of 4 units is 1 long and 3 units or 13, and two sets of 1 long is 2 longs which, with the long "carried," is 3 longs. Hence $(2 \times 14)_{\text{five}} = 33_{\text{five}}$.

Similarly, $(2 \times 24)_{\text{five}} = ?_{\text{five}}$. Represented as two sets of 2 longs and 4 units:

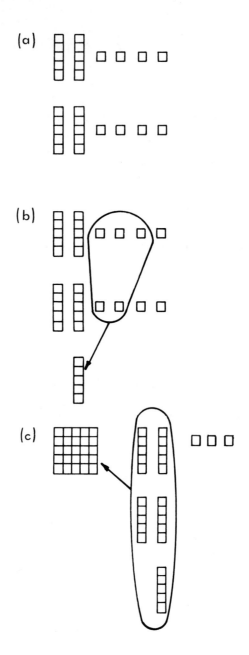

(a)

(b)

(c)

Hence, $(2 \times 24)_{\text{five}} = 1$ flat 0 longs 3 units or 103_{five}.

Moving from the concrete to the semi-concrete, a problem such as 3 × 4 in base five can be developed on the number line as follows:

$$3 \times 4 = 22$$

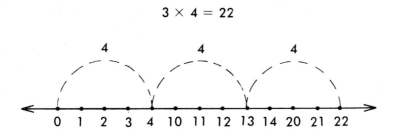

The number 22_{five} represents two sets of five and two sets of one. In expanded notation, $22_{\text{five}} = 2(5) + 2(1)$.

To complete a table such as the following for multiplication in base five, the multiplication can be performed in base ten and then the product renamed in base five. For example, the product 3 × 4 in base ten is 12. How many sets of five are there in 12? There are two sets of five and 2 ones left over. Thus, $12_{\text{ten}} = 22_{\text{five}}$. In other words, to convert a numeral in base ten to another base, divide it by the number of the base, in this case five. Thus, $3 \times 3 = 9_{\text{ten}} = 14_{\text{five}}$ since 9 divided by 5 is one set of five and 4 ones.

A more meaningful approach may be to complete the table using the number line or to solve at the concrete level with base five materials. For example, represent 3 × 4 as three sets of 4 units, which is equal to 2 longs and 2 units.

×	0	1	2	3	4
0	0	0	0	0	0
1	0	1	2	3	4
2	0	2	4	11	13
3	0	3	11	14	22
4	0	4	13	22	31

There are 25 single-digit multiplication facts in base five. Therefore, base five would involve much less memory work in learning the multiplication tables than base ten. The disadvantage, of course, is that more numerals would be required to represent the same numbers. For the purposes of this section, do not try to memorize the multiplication facts in base five; use the table if necessary.

Division in a nondecimal base may give the teacher a better appreciation of how difficult the division algorism is for children. It is also interesting as an enrichment activity for children in grades five or six.

Concrete Level

If the following problem is expressed in base five, how would it be solved?

$$3\overline{)42}_{\text{five}}$$

The number 42_{five} is four sets of five and two sets of one.
Beginning at the concrete level with the Multibase Arithmetic Blocks:

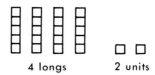

4 longs   2 units

If the partitive concept of division is used, the divisor 3 represents the number of sets into which the 4 longs and 2 units will be divided. The longs can therefore be divided into three equal sets with 1 long in each and 1 long left over:

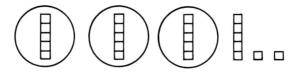

There is then 1 long and 2 units still to be divided. Renaming or exchanging 1 long for the corresponding number of units, we have:

units

Dividing these into three equal sets, there are 2 units in each set and a remainder of 1 unit. The answer is then:

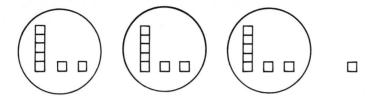

In expanded notation:

$$\begin{array}{r} \text{1 long 2 units R1} \\ \hline 3\overline{)\text{4 longs 2 units}} \end{array}$$

or

$$\begin{array}{r} \text{12 R1} \\ \hline 3\overline{)42}_{\text{five}} \end{array}$$

Symbol Level

Since division is the inverse of multiplication, a table of multiplication facts can be used for the corresponding division facts. By means of the following table of multiplication facts in base five, a problem such as $22 \div 3 = \square_{\text{five}}$ can be solved by thinking of it in terms of the missing factor: $3 \times \square = 22_{\text{five}}$. Look down the left-hand column to the known factor, 3, then to the right to the product, 22, then to the top of that column for the missing factor, 4.

X	0	1	2	3	4
0	0	0	0	0	0
1	0	1	2	3	4
2	0	2	4	11	13
3	0	3	10	14	22
4	0	4	13	22	31

Thus $3 \times 4 = 22_{\text{five}}$ or $22 \div 3 = 4_{\text{five}}$. This is not twenty-two divided by three, but "two two" divided by three; as we learned earlier, *twenty* refers to 2 tens in base ten notation. The "two two" verbalization refers to two sets of five plus 2 ones.

For a problem such as 24 ÷ 4, look down the left side of the table to the known factor, 4, then to the right for the product, 24. Since the numeral 24 is not in that row, the next smallest product, 22, is used. At the top of the column containing 22 is the missing factor, 3. Then $4 \times 3 = 22_{\text{five}}$. Shown in conventional form

$$
\begin{array}{r}
3 \text{ R2} \\
4\overline{)24} \\
22 \\
\hline
2
\end{array}
$$

or $24 \div 4 = 3 \text{ R2}_{\text{five}}$.

For long division problems in base five the same procedure is used as in base ten division. To solve the problem $4\overline{)242}$, the first step is the same as in the problem 24 ÷ 4.

$$
\begin{array}{r}
3 \\
4\overline{)242} \\
22 \\
\hline
2
\end{array}
$$

Next, bring down the 2 in the dividend which has not been divided, and the second step is 22 ÷ 4.

$$
\begin{array}{r}
33 \\
4\overline{)242} \\
22 \\
\hline
22 \\
22
\end{array}
$$

This procedure is a rote process in contrast to the more meaningful concrete approach described in the preceding section, but it is useful in division problems if the divisor contains two or more digits. This is the subject of the next section.

Divisors Expressed With Two or More Digits

For problems in base five with two digits or more in the divisor, such as $32\overline{)242}$, the same techniques are used as in base ten; that is, the first digit in the divisor and the first digit (or the first two digits) in the dividend are used in estimating the first digit in the quotient. In this problem, since the first digit in the divisor, 3, is larger than the first digit in the dividend, 2, the first step is 24 ÷ 3. Since the two-digit divisor is larger than the first two digits in the dividend, the trial quotient is placed over the third digit in the dividend and is multiplied by the divisor 32. Using the base five multiplication table, $32 \times 3 = 201$.

Developing the multiplication in conventional form:

$$
\begin{array}{l}
32 \\
\times 3 \\
\hline
201
\end{array}
\qquad
\begin{array}{l}
\text{3 times 2 is 11, write 1 and carry 1} \\
\text{3 times 3 is 14, plus the 1 carried is} \\
\text{20 (two sets of five and 0 ones)}
\end{array}
$$

$$
\begin{array}{r}
3 \\
32\overline{)242} \\
201 \\
\hline
41
\end{array}
$$

Subtracting in base five, the difference 41 is larger than the divisor, and since our trial quotient is too small, the numeral 4 must be substituted in the quotient. Since $4 \times 32 = 233$ in base five, the conventional division form would be:

$$
\begin{array}{r}
4 \text{ R4} \\
32\overline{)242} \\
233 \\
\hline
4
\end{array}
$$

In the last step, 3 from 12 in base five is 4, (read as, "Three from one two" and not, "Three from twelve" since twelve refers to base ten notation).

Thus, $242 \div 32$ in base five is 4 with a remainder of 4. Such a problem indicates the difficulty faced by children in learning the conventional algorism for division by rote.

EXERCISES

1. Perform the following divisions in base five with concrete materials:
    (a) $13 \div 2$ (b) $4 \div 1$ (c) $31 \div 4$
    (b) $20 \div 4$ (e) $12 \div 2$ (f) $23 \div 3$
2. Illustrate your answers to problem 1 with a number line.
3. Perform the following divisions in base five with concrete materials such as blocks, flats, longs, and units:
    (a) $2\overline{)231}$ (b) $3\overline{)2034}$ (c) $4\overline{)3232}$
4. Perform the following divisions in base five:
    (a) $12\overline{)234}$ (b) $23\overline{)423}$ (c) $42\overline{)3142}$

8

FRACTIONAL NUMBERS: INTRODUCTION, ADDITION, SUBTRACTION

Historically, the idea of how to think about and express number ideas relating to parts of things has caused man a great deal of difficulty. The fact that our system of fractional notation was developed 200 years ago while our set of whole numbers was developed almost 2000 years ago is some indication of this difficulty.

READINESS FOR UNDERSTANDING FRACTIONS[1]

Children's understanding of fractional parts can be invested by asking them to divide a "cake" of circular, rectangular, or square paper between two or three dolls. They are asked to mark on the paper how it should be cut. They are reminded that each doll must have the same amount and that the whole cake must be used. The shape of cake easiest to cut is the rectangle, followed by the circle, followed by the square.

---

[1] For further study see Richard W. Copeland: *How Children Learn Mathematics.* 3d ed. New York: Macmillan Publishing Co., Inc., 1979.

Stages of Development

Two-year-olds refuse to cut the cake, being overwhelmed by its closed shape (or gestalt).

From two to four years of age there is no plan. The child continues to divide, not stopping at two parts, or if he gives each doll the same amount the pieces are small, leaving a large part undivided. There is no relation of the parts to the whole once the cake has been cut.

At four to six years of age halving is possible but dividing in three equal parts is not.

At six to seven years of age division into three equal parts is successfully performed and the procedure is intellectual rather than trial and error or perceptually based.

There is still a **conservation** problem. The children, if asked whether the divided parts of the cake are the same amount as the whole cake, often respond that there is more cake in the pieces (because there are more pieces) or there is less in the pieces (because the cake has been divided).

Not until around ten years of age can the child use an operational or intellectual approach to divide the cake into six equal parts, such as by dividing first into halves and then each half into three equal parts. A year or two earlier the children use a trial and error approach of positioning six dolls around the cake.

INTRODUCING FRACTIONAL NUMBERS

In the simplest sense a fraction may be thought of as a part of some whole. The idea of requiring the parts to be of the same size, or the same measure, is often not recognized by young children, who want "the biggest half." To systematize fractions for measurement purposes, it is necessary to think of fractional parts such as halves as being the same size. Since primary grade youngsters are coping with situations involving fractional ideas, an informal approach to the concept of fractions should begin in the primary grades. A formal or organized treatment of fractions is usually deferred to the middle and upper grades of the elementary school.

Because a fractional notation such as $\frac{1}{2}$ or $\frac{2}{3}$ is used in the physical world to represent several different ideas, it is no wonder that teachers have difficulty in interpreting the meaning of fractions. We will begin with the often used "part of a whole" model.

Fractions as Parts of a Whole

The most basic idea to the child is that of parts of a whole, such as a bar of candy that is to be divided between two children. How much does each receive? If we divide a candy bar into two equal parts, each child receives one part. What shall we name each part? It is one of two equal parts, represented as $\frac{1}{2}$ and called "one-half." This basic idea is extended to include the ideas that there are two halves in a whole, the halves are the same size, and a half taken from a whole leaves a half.

As with other mathematical concepts, notions about fractional numbers should be developed by first manipulating concrete materials. A flannel board is sometimes used.

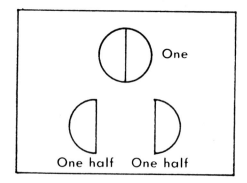

However, this has the disadvantage of often being a show-and-tell approach rather than a first-hand experience for the pupils.

For first-hand experiences, paper strips may be very useful. Each child is given or asked to cut a strip of paper and is then asked to fold the strip so that the two ends meet. Opening up the strip again, what would the part from one end to the fold be called? Now fold the strip into four equal parts. Name each part. Then take another strip and fold it into three equal parts. Name each part. What would the part from one end of the strip to the second fold be named?

The idea of **whole** may also refer to more than a single object, for example "a dozen eggs." In this case the fractional idea $\frac{1}{2}$ results in the number 6. Fractions as a part or parts of a **set of objects** should be introduced after being considered in terms of a single object.

Still later fractions will be used to represent **ratios**—the ratio of boys to girls in class, the ratio of flour to sugar in a cooking recipe, batting averages, and betting odds such as 2 to 1.

FRACTIONAL NUMBER TERMINOLOGY

The symbol $\frac{1}{2}$ represents a number, a **fractional number.** For example, $\frac{1}{2}$ is a numeral, symbol, or fraction which names a point on a line segment halfway between 0 and 1; $\frac{2}{4}$ and $\frac{3}{6}$ are other numerals which name the same point or position. *Fractions are symbols or numerals that name members of a set called the fractional numbers.* In this chapter the term **fraction** is used since it is the term most familiar to both teacher and child.

ADDITION OF FRACTIONAL NUMBERS

Much of this text is devoted to introducing the various mathematical concepts in such a way that youngsters can understand what they are doing rather than having a set of rules to follow blindly. Of course, practice and drill must follow.

Addition of Like Fractions

How much is $\frac{1}{3} + \frac{1}{3}$? Expressed another way, $\frac{1}{3} + \frac{1}{3} = \square$. Geometrically the sum can be shown with vectors on a number line by dividing a unit segment into congruent subunits, each of whose measure is $\frac{1}{3}$.

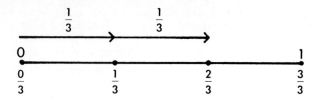

The two abutting vectors $\left(\dfrac{1}{3} + \dfrac{1}{3}\right)$ have a measure of $\dfrac{2}{3}$ of the primary unit.

Similarly, how much is $\dfrac{1}{8} + \dfrac{1}{8}$? Or, $\dfrac{1}{8} + \dfrac{1}{8} = \square$. If a unit segment is divided into eight congruent subunits, then two of these subunits are two-eighths of the original or primary unit. This may be shown as follows:

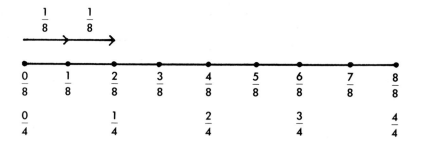

Thus $\dfrac{1}{8} + \dfrac{1}{8} = \dfrac{2}{8}$, and $\dfrac{2}{8}$ may be renamed $\dfrac{1}{4}$.

In these problems what pattern can be observed in the sums as related to the addends?

$$\frac{1}{3} + \frac{1}{3} = \frac{2}{3}$$

$$\frac{1}{8} + \frac{1}{8} = \frac{2}{8}$$

It may be seen that in adding like fractions (fractions with the same denominators), the numerators are added but the denominator of the sum is the same as the denominator of the addends. This is consistent with the conventional interpretation of fractions—the **numerator** is the *number* of parts which we count or add and the **denominator** refers to the *size* of the parts. The **denominator** may be thought of as the *unit of measure* and the **numerator** the *measure*. Thus, for the fraction $\frac{3}{8}$, the unit of measure is eighths and the measure is 3.

A vertical presentation with numerals as the numerators and words as the denominators helps to establish the idea of adding the measures (numerators) and thinking of the denominators as the unit of measure.

1 third	1 eighth
+ 1 third	+ 1 eighth
2 thirds	2 eighths

The addition of like fractions can be visualized with **unit regions** also. To begin at the concrete level use a sheet of paper to represent a **unit region.** If it is divided into congruent parts by folding,

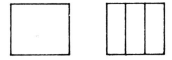

then how is each part named? Two of these parts represent what part of the primary unit? As a mathematical sentence, $\frac{1}{3} + \frac{1}{3} = \frac{2}{3}$ or $2 \times \frac{1}{3} = \frac{2}{3}$.

Similarly, if a unit region is divided into congruent subunits as follows,

how would one subunit be named? two subunits? The sum of two subunits could be expressed as $\frac{1}{8} + \frac{1}{8} = \frac{2}{8}$, renamed $\frac{1}{4}$.

The unit region in such diagrams does not have to be square, but the subunits may be easier to visualize in that form. A fraction board in the classroom is useful in displaying geometrically the addition of fractions. Such boards often define the unit region in the form of a rectangle as shown below:

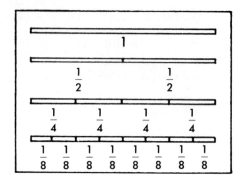

Such displays as the fraction board aid in establishing the idea of how to rename unlike fractions as like fractions before performing addition.

Circle diagrams or pie charts have been used to such an extent in visualizing fraction ideas that youngsters sometimes think of fractions only in terms of circles or pies. Also, with circle diagrams the illustration of ideas which involve a sum greater than 1 necessitates additional circles. For example, $\dfrac{4}{3} + \dfrac{5}{3}$ is difficult to display with circle diagrams. In contrast, the continuity of the number line illustrates such a sum easily. For example, $\dfrac{4}{3} + \dfrac{5}{3} = \square$:

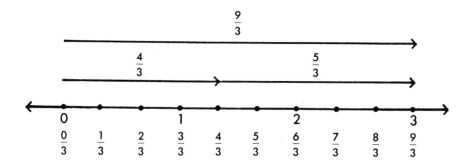

Thus $\dfrac{4}{3} + \dfrac{5}{3} = \dfrac{9}{3}$, $\dfrac{9}{3}$ being renamed 3.

FRACTIONAL NUMBERS: ADDITION, SUBTRACTION

Adding Unlike Fractions

One might begin a treatment of addition of fractions in a college class with a definition, but for children an inductive or discovery approach using concrete materials is better. The number line might be called semi-concrete. A concrete approach might involve folding a strip of paper or using centimeter rods.

In introducing the addition of unlike fractions, first use an example in which the denominator of one fraction is a factor of the other; for example, $\frac{1}{2} + \frac{1}{4} = \square$.

To represent $\frac{1}{2} + \frac{1}{4}$ with a strip of paper, first fold the strip into two equivalent sections. Then open it and fold the original strip into four equivalent sections. One half plus one fourth can then be seen as three fourths of the original strip.

To represent $\frac{1}{2} + \frac{1}{3}$, fold the paper strip into halves and then into thirds. Place the crease of the first third over the one-half fold to represent $\frac{1}{2} + \frac{1}{3}$. Mark this point. The question is how to name it. If we fold the first third into two equivalent sections, how many of these sections are there in the whole strip? Six. And does this help us name the point $\frac{1}{2} + \frac{1}{3}$ as $\frac{5}{6}$?

Considering the problem at a semi-concrete level with a number line:

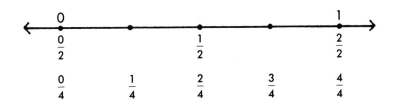

On a fraction board or in the preceding illustration, it can be seen that $\frac{1}{2}$ and $\frac{2}{4}$ name the same segment. If $\frac{1}{2}$ in the expression $\frac{1}{2} + \frac{1}{4}$ is renamed

$\frac{2}{4}$, then addition can be performed on like fractions, $\frac{2}{4} + \frac{1}{4} = \frac{3}{4}$. Similarly, $\frac{1}{3} + \frac{1}{6} = \square$. Renaming $\frac{1}{3}$ as $\frac{2}{6}$, then $\frac{2}{6} + \frac{1}{6} = \frac{3}{6}$ or $\frac{1}{2}$.

For fractions in which neither denominator is a factor of the other, such as in $\frac{1}{2} + \frac{1}{3} = \square$, both fractions will have to be renamed. Again, use the fraction board or a diagram similar to the following:

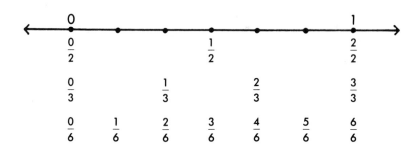

$\frac{1}{2}$ can be renamed as $\frac{3}{6}$ and $\frac{1}{3}$ renamed as $\frac{2}{6}$, then $\frac{1}{2} + \frac{1}{3} = \frac{3}{6} + \frac{2}{6}$ and $\frac{3}{6} + \frac{2}{6} = \frac{5}{6}$.

To explore the same idea with a unit region would involve renaming $\frac{1}{2} + \frac{1}{3}$ as $\frac{3}{6} + \frac{2}{6}$ and dividing the unit region into six congruent subunits. One-half the unit region would be seen as $\frac{3}{6}$, and one-third the unit region as $\frac{2}{6}$.

The Least Common Denominator Method

The idea of least common denominator is usually shown in vertical form.

$$\frac{1}{2} = \frac{\square}{\square}$$

$$+ \frac{1}{3} = \frac{\square}{\square}$$

Children should solve problems involving the adding of unlike fractions geometrically—that is, with the number line—before developing the rote use of the more mechanical least common denominator method.

Youngsters should understand that the least common denominator method is a method of renaming fractions using the multiplicative identity.

How can the fractions $\dfrac{1}{2}$ and $\dfrac{3}{6}$ be renamed arithmetically so that the denominators are the same?

$$\frac{1}{2} \cdot \frac{2}{2} = \frac{2}{4} \qquad \text{Similarly} \qquad \frac{1}{3} \cdot \frac{2}{2} = \frac{2}{6}$$

$$\frac{1}{2} \cdot \frac{3}{3} = \frac{3}{6} \qquad\qquad\qquad \frac{1}{3} \cdot \frac{3}{3} = \frac{3}{9}$$

$$\frac{1}{2} \cdot \frac{4}{4} = \frac{4}{8} \qquad\qquad\qquad \frac{1}{3} \cdot \frac{4}{4} = \frac{4}{12}$$

$$\frac{1}{2} \cdot \frac{5}{5} = \frac{5}{10} \qquad\qquad\qquad \frac{1}{3} \cdot \frac{5}{5} = \frac{5}{15}$$

Thus, $\dfrac{1}{2}$ or $\dfrac{1}{3}$ can be renamed by multiplying by $\dfrac{2}{2}, \dfrac{3}{3}, \dfrac{4}{4}$ and so forth. In so doing an **equivalence class** is produced.

For $\dfrac{1}{2}$, the equivalence class is $\left(\dfrac{1}{2}, \dfrac{2}{4}, \dfrac{3}{6}, \cdots \right)$

For $\dfrac{1}{3}$, the equivalence class is $\left(\dfrac{1}{3}, \dfrac{2}{6}, \dfrac{3}{9}, \cdots \right)$

Inspecting the two classes, it is seen that $\dfrac{1}{2}$ and $\dfrac{1}{3}$ can be renamed in terms of sixths as $\dfrac{3}{6}$ and $\dfrac{2}{6}$.

$$\text{The traditional} \quad \frac{1}{2} = \frac{\square}{6} \quad \text{involves} \quad \frac{1}{2} \cdot \frac{3}{3} = \frac{3}{6}$$

$$+ \frac{1}{3} = \frac{\square}{6} \qquad\qquad\qquad + \frac{1}{3} \cdot \frac{2}{2} = \frac{2}{6}$$

$$\overline{} \qquad\qquad\qquad\qquad \overline{} \;\; \frac{5}{6}$$

The rationale for adding unlike fractions is to rename the fractions so that the denominators will be the same, so that they become like fractions. Then use the rule for like fractions of adding the numerators.

Equivalence classes are generated by multiplying by $\frac{2}{2}, \frac{3}{3}, \frac{4}{4}$, and so forth, which are all names for $\frac{1}{1}$ or 1. A fractional number is not changed when multiplied by 1, only renamed.[2]

The Least Common Multiple. To solve a problem such as $\frac{3}{4} + \frac{1}{6}$ without writing out the equivalence class for fourths and sixths, the notion of least common multiple can be used.

Considering the denominators only, 4 and 6

multiples of 4	4, 8, 12, 16
multiples of 6	6, 12, 18, 24

The **least common multiple** (smallest number for which 4 and 6 are factors) is 12. Therefore, we can rename $\frac{1}{4}$ and $\frac{1}{6}$ in terms of twelfths by multiplying $\frac{1}{4}$ by $\frac{3}{3}$ and $\frac{1}{6}$ by $\frac{2}{2}$.

To find a least common denominator for two unlike fractions, begin by doubling the smaller denominator, then tripling it if it is still smaller than the other denominator. As soon as it is larger than the other denominator, double the other denominator. Continue this process until a number is found for which both the denominators are factors.

Renaming Fractions in Simplest Form

The common expression "reducing fractions" might be better expressed as renaming or finding "the simplest name." To find the simplest name for $\frac{2}{4}$, the arithmetical rationale is to find the common factor and express as follows:

[2] the multiplicative identity.

$$\frac{2}{4} = \frac{2 \cdot 1}{2 \cdot 2} = \frac{2}{2} \cdot \frac{1}{2} = 1 \cdot \frac{1}{2} = \frac{1}{2}$$

A quicker way is to divide both terms by their common factor, in this case 2.

$$\frac{2}{4} = \frac{2 \div 2}{4 \div 2} = \frac{1}{2}$$

Readiness for Understanding Equivalent Fractions

Since the idea of an equivalence class such as $\frac{1}{2}, \frac{2}{4}, \frac{3}{6}, \frac{4}{8} \ldots$ is used as a basis for teaching addition of unlike fractions, are there problems of readiness in understanding that $\frac{1}{2} = \frac{2}{4}$ and $\frac{2}{3} = \frac{4}{6}$?

The expression $\frac{1}{2} = \frac{2}{4}$ seems easy enough to accept, but when represented as a physical problem it can cause a great deal of difficulty. For example, if my car goes 1 cm in 2 seconds and your car goes 2 cm in 4 seconds, do they go at the same speed? Many children think not. They do not see the equality of $\frac{1}{2}$ and $\frac{2}{4}$ in this problem. A problem such as $\frac{2}{3}$ and $\frac{4}{6}$ causes even more difficulty. Even more difficult is which is faster, 1 mile in 3 seconds or 2 miles in 5 seconds.

The expression $\frac{a}{b} = \frac{c}{d}$ is called a proportion (two ratios that are equal). Problems such as $\frac{1}{2} = \frac{2}{4}$ and $\frac{2}{3} = \frac{4}{6}$ are examples. Piaget[3] finds children do not understand the proportion structure until they reach the formal operational level (at around 11 to 12 years of age). This of course means, if true, that many fifth-grade children will have difficulty with the concept.

---

[3] Richard W. Copeland: *How Children Learn Mathematics,* 3d ed. New York: Macmillan Publishing Co., Inc., 1979, pp. 191–193.

The proportion structure is considered in Chapter 14 on Time and also in Chapter 10 on Decimal Fractions and Per Cent since both subjects involve use of proportions.

Adding Mixed Numbers

Mixed numbers can be renamed as improper fractions and then added as follows:

$$3\frac{1}{4} + 2\frac{5}{8} = \square$$

$$\frac{13}{4} + \frac{21}{8} = \square$$

$$\frac{26}{8} + \frac{21}{8} = \frac{47}{8}$$

The rote procedure for renaming $3\frac{1}{4}$ in fourths is to multiply the 3 by the 4 and then add the 1. Youngsters should understand that in multiplying the 3 by the 4 they are renaming the 3 as $\frac{12}{4}$ by multiplying by the identity element, $\frac{4}{4}$.

$$3\frac{1}{4} = 3 + \frac{1}{4}$$

$$= 3\frac{4}{4} + \frac{1}{4}$$

$$= \frac{12}{4} + \frac{1}{4}$$

$$= \frac{13}{4}$$

The problem $3\frac{1}{4} + 2\frac{5}{8}$ developed vertically might be displayed as:

FRACTIONAL NUMBERS: ADDITION, SUBTRACTION

$$3\frac{1}{4} = \frac{13}{4} = \frac{26}{8}$$

$$+\ 2\frac{5}{8} = \frac{21}{8} = \frac{21}{8}$$

$$\frac{47}{8}$$

Both vertical and horizontal forms should be taught. The horizontal form will be used more often as the students progress in high school.

SUBTRACTION OF FRACTIONAL NUMBERS

An idea such as $\frac{3}{4} - \frac{1}{4} = \square$ may be less abstract if first expressed as:

$$\begin{array}{r} 3 \text{ fourths} \\ -\ 1 \text{ fourth} \\ \hline \end{array}$$

In this form the denominator is seen more clearly as a unit of measure, and it is obvious to children that the answer is not 2 but 2 fourths.

In subtracting unlike fractions $\left(\text{e.g.,} \frac{1}{2} - \frac{1}{3} = \square \right)$, the idea of renaming them as like fractions (finding the common denominator) is necessary, as it is in addition. In subtraction, however, the numerators are subtracted.

$$\frac{1}{2} - \frac{1}{3} = \square$$

$$\frac{3}{6} - \frac{2}{6} = \square$$

$$\frac{3}{6} - \frac{2}{6} = \frac{1}{6}$$

After unlike fractions are renamed as like fractions, subtraction is performed on the numerators as whole numbers, and the result named in terms of the unit of measure (the denominator).

The number line, the unit region, the fraction board, or paper folding may be used as necessary to develop an understanding of the renaming of unlike fractions as like fractions.

On the number line, $\frac{1}{2} - \frac{1}{3} = \square$ may be shown as follows: another name for $\frac{1}{3}$ is $\frac{2}{6}$, so count back two sixths from $\frac{1}{2}$ using the sixth scale as the unit measure:

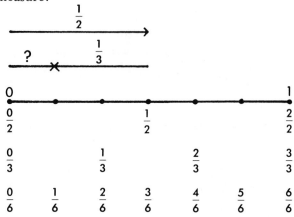

If subtraction is interpreted in its additive form as finding the missing addend when one addend and the sum are known, the problem $\frac{1}{2} - \frac{1}{3} = \square$ may be restated as $\frac{1}{3} + \square = \frac{1}{2}$ and diagrammed as follows:

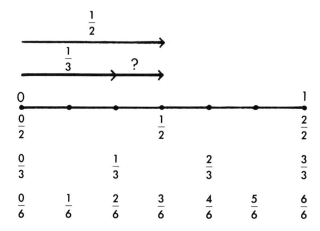

To illustrate the problem $\frac{1}{2} - \frac{1}{3} = \square$ with a unit region, the region is divided into six congruent subunits. Then $\frac{1}{2}$ could be renamed as $\frac{3}{6}$,

FRACTIONAL NUMBERS: ADDITION, SUBTRACTION

and $\frac{1}{3}$ as $\frac{2}{6}$. If two of these subunits are taken away from three, one is left.

During the exploratory stage, addition and subtraction of fractions should be visualized by using such aids as the number line, the unit region, and the fraction board.

The sentence $\frac{1}{2} - \frac{1}{4} = \square$ might be diagrammed as:

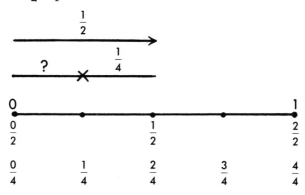

The sentence $\frac{5}{6} - \frac{3}{6} = \square$ may be visualized as:

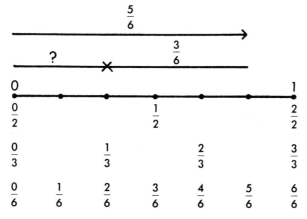

Thus $\frac{5}{6} - \frac{3}{6} = \frac{2}{6}$, renamed $\frac{1}{3}$.

SUBTRACTION OF FRACTIONAL NUMBERS

If subtraction is thought of as the inverse of addition (the additive form) and the problem $\frac{2}{4} - \frac{1}{4} = \square$ is restated as $\frac{1}{4} + \square = \frac{2}{4}$, the number line display would be:

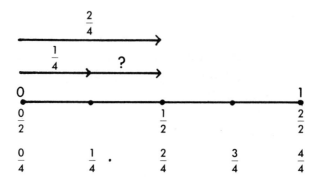

The problem $\frac{5}{6} - \frac{3}{6} = \square$ may be restated as $\frac{3}{6} + \square = \frac{5}{6}$ and shown on the number line as:

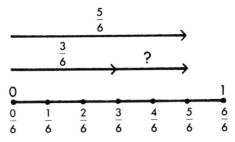

Unit regions may also be used in another manner to illustrate the operation of subtraction. To solve the problem $\frac{5}{6} - \frac{3}{6}$, divide a unit square into six congruent parts. Color five of these to represent $\frac{5}{6}$, then recolor three of the five to represent $\frac{3}{6}$. Those in the original color represent the difference.

The conventional least common denominator method should be learned as a basic way of solving subtraction problems, as it was for addition.

FRACTIONAL NUMBERS: ADDITION, SUBTRACTION

$$\frac{1}{2} = \frac{\square}{6} \qquad \text{then} \qquad \frac{1}{2} \cdot \frac{3}{3} = \frac{3}{6}$$

$$-\frac{1}{3} = \frac{\square}{6} \qquad \qquad -\frac{1}{3} \cdot \frac{2}{2} = \frac{2}{6}$$

$$\frac{1}{6}$$

ERROR PATTERNS IN OPERATIONS WITH FRACTIONS—CAN YOU DIAGNOSE THEM?

Answers

1. (a) $\dfrac{15}{56} = \dfrac{1}{6}$

   (b) $\dfrac{16}{61} = 1$

1. Cancels out common numeral regardless of place value.

2. (a) $\dfrac{3}{9} = \dfrac{1}{3}$

   (b) $\dfrac{4}{9} = \dfrac{2}{3}$

   (c) $\dfrac{5}{12} = \dfrac{1}{4}$

2. Divides by whatever is convenient to simplify fraction.

3. (a) $\dfrac{6}{8} = \dfrac{1}{8}$

   (b) $\dfrac{4}{8} = \dfrac{2}{8}$

   (c) $\dfrac{9}{3} = \dfrac{3}{9}$

3. Divides the larger by the smaller for the new numerator and uses the larger for the new denominator.

4. (a) $\dfrac{3}{4} + \dfrac{1}{2} = 46$

   (b) $\dfrac{1}{2} + \dfrac{2}{3} = 35$

4. Adds both numerators and denominators.

5. (a) $\dfrac{1}{2} + \dfrac{2}{5} = \dfrac{3}{5}$ 5. Adds numerators and uses larger of the denominators as the new denominator.

(b) $\dfrac{3}{4} + \dfrac{2}{6} = \dfrac{5}{6}$

Remediation Procedures

For renaming problems, review ways of renaming fractions using manipulative materials such as the unit region (see p. 173). Relate to the necessary mathematical operation. For example, if $\dfrac{2}{4} = \dfrac{1}{2}$, then what is done to $\dfrac{2}{4}$ to rename it as $\dfrac{1}{2}$? (Divide by the common factor. If there is none, the fraction is in its simplest form.)

EXERCISES

1. Write the next three names for the following equivalence classes:

(a) $\dfrac{1}{3}, \dfrac{2}{6}$ (b) $\dfrac{1}{4}$ (c) $\dfrac{3}{8}$ (d) $\dfrac{2}{16}$ (e) $-\dfrac{1}{5}$

2. What principle did you use in problem 1?
3. What equivalence class is represented in the problem of three boys dividing 12 cookies?
4. Represent with number line or unit regions.

(a) $\dfrac{1}{2}$ (b) $\dfrac{1}{3}$ (c) $\dfrac{2}{3}$ (d) $\dfrac{9}{12}$ (e) $\dfrac{15}{12}$

5. Arrange the following in order from smallest to largest:

(a) $\dfrac{1}{2}, \dfrac{9}{16}, \dfrac{4}{5}, \dfrac{3}{2}$ (b) $\dfrac{200}{300}, \dfrac{1}{5}, \dfrac{9}{20}, \dfrac{50}{300}$

6. Name a number between:

(a) $\dfrac{1}{4}$ and $\dfrac{1}{2}$ (b) $\dfrac{1}{16}$ and $\dfrac{1}{17}$ (c) $\dfrac{1}{200}$ and $\dfrac{1}{201}$

7. How many numbers are there between $\dfrac{1}{200}$ and $\dfrac{1}{201}$?

FRACTIONAL NUMBERS: ADDITION, SUBTRACTION

8. Illustrate with number line diagrams, or by folding paper strips, each of the following: (To represent addends on the number line, it may be more convenient to use loops rather than line segments, as shown in the preceding illustrations.)

(a) $\dfrac{1}{4} + \dfrac{1}{4}$ (b) $\dfrac{1}{2} + \dfrac{1}{4}$ (c) $\dfrac{2}{3} + \dfrac{1}{6}$

(d) $\dfrac{1}{2} + \dfrac{1}{3}$ (e) $\dfrac{3}{4} + \dfrac{1}{3}$ (f) $\dfrac{1}{3} + \dfrac{3}{4}$

9. Demonstrate with an egg carton the solution for:

(a) $\dfrac{1}{12} + \dfrac{4}{12}$ (b) $\dfrac{2}{6} + \dfrac{1}{12}$ (c) $\dfrac{1}{6} + \dfrac{2}{6}$ (d) $\dfrac{1}{2} + \dfrac{1}{3}$ (e) $\dfrac{1}{2} + \dfrac{1}{4}$

(f) $\dfrac{3}{6} + \dfrac{1}{3}$

10. In problem 8, diagram parts (a) to (e) for the operation of substration instead of addition.

11. Using the least common denominator method, solve the following:

(a) $\begin{array}{r} \dfrac{3}{4} \\ -\dfrac{1}{2} \\ \hline \end{array}$ (b) $\begin{array}{r} \dfrac{2}{3} \\ -\dfrac{1}{6} \\ \hline \end{array}$ (c) $\begin{array}{r} \dfrac{5}{8} \\ +\dfrac{1}{3} \\ \hline \end{array}$

FRACTIONAL NUMBERS: MULTIPLICATION, DIVISION

MULTIPLICATION OF FRACTIONAL NUMBERS

What do the expressions $3 \times \frac{1}{2}$, $\frac{1}{2} \times 3$, and $\frac{1}{8} \times \frac{1}{4}$ mean? Could you make up a word or story problem which could be represented by each of these expressions? Youngsters may know "how" to multiply fractions in that they have learned the rule, but still not be able to interpret the idea in the physical world as a basis for solving problems.

Whole Numbers Times a Fractional Number

In our study of the set of whole numbers, the following relationship between the operations of addition and multiplication was observed.

$$
\begin{array}{r}
2 \\
2 \\
+\,2 \\
\hline
6
\end{array}
\qquad \text{or} \qquad
\begin{array}{r}
2 \\
\times\,3 \\
\hline
6
\end{array}
$$

Multiplication was interpreted as the addition of *equal* addends.

Similarly, in the set of fractions:

If $\frac{1}{2} + \frac{1}{2} + \frac{1}{2} = \frac{3}{2}$, then $3 \times \frac{1}{2} = \frac{3}{2}$

The expression $3 \times \dfrac{1}{2} = \dfrac{3}{2}$ may be verbalized as "three one-halves is three halves" or "three times one-half is three halves."

The number line is useful in visualizing this idea. For example, $3 \times \dfrac{1}{2}$ may be visualzed geometrically with a number line as:

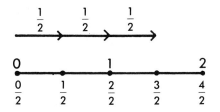

Since 3 can be renamed $\dfrac{3}{1}$, then $3 \times \dfrac{1}{2}$ can be expressed as $\dfrac{3}{1} \times \dfrac{1}{2}$, and $\dfrac{3}{1} \times \dfrac{1}{2}$ is also equal to $\dfrac{3}{2}$.

If $\dfrac{3}{1} \times \dfrac{1}{2} = \dfrac{3}{2}$, what is the relationship of the numerator and denominator in the product to the numerator and denominator of the factors? Youngsters should observe that the product of the two fractions is the product of their numerators divided by the product of their denominators. Several more examples may be considered before the generalization or rule for multiplying fractions is made. This is another example of children's discovering rules from specific examples (the inductive method).

Sample word problems are, "If I give each of three boys one-half of an apple, how many apples will I need?" Or, "If one half yard of material is needed for an apron, how much material will be needed for three aprons?"

A Fractional Number Times a Whole Number

The commutative property holds for multiplication of fractions; therefore if $3 \times \dfrac{1}{2} = \dfrac{3}{2}$, then $\dfrac{1}{2} \times 3 = \dfrac{3}{2}$. Mathematically this is reason enough, but $\dfrac{1}{2} \times 3$ is interpreted differently in the physical world.

Again thinking of multiplication of whole numbers, what is 1×3? If $1 \times 3 = 3$, then what does $\frac{1}{2} \times 3$ equal? One-half times three or one-half of three may be illustrated on the number line as follows:

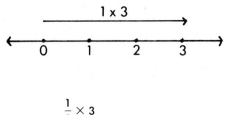

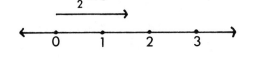

One-half of three is represented differently from three one-halves on the number line.

Although multiplication as an operation can often be interpreted as meaning "of," this is not always the case. When the first factor is a whole number, as in our first problem, $3 \times \frac{1}{2}$, this meaning will not serve. When the first of the two factors is a fraction, however, the "of" interpretation does help visualization. Remember the meaning of the numerator and denominator, that a fraction such as $\frac{1}{2}$ may be interpreted as one of two equal parts. Thus, $\frac{1}{2} \times 3$ can be visualized as "one of the two equal parts in three." "One-half of" produces the same result as "dividing by two." The idea $\frac{1}{2} \times 3$ can also be expressed as $\frac{1}{2} \times \frac{3}{1}$ and solved as $\frac{1}{2} \times \frac{3}{1} = \frac{3}{2}$.

Sample word problems which can be represented by $\frac{1}{2} \times 3$ are, "One-half of three apples is how many?" Or, "If I have three bars of candy and give one-half to Joe, how many does he receive?"

Again, while $\frac{1}{2} \times 6$ and $6 \times \frac{1}{2}$ represent the same number, at the concrete level one-half of six yards of material is not the same as six one-half yard pieces.

A Fractional Number Times a Fractional Number

After introducing the multiplication of fractions by first using the product of a whole number and a fraction, we should consider the product of two fractions.

$$\frac{1}{2} \times \frac{1}{4} = \square$$

At the concrete level, a sheet of paper can be folded into four equal parts. With the paper still folded, fold one more time into two equal parts $\left(\frac{1}{2} \text{ of } \frac{1}{4}\right)$. Open the paper. What is the name of each part?

Similarly, for the problem

$$\frac{1}{3} \times \frac{1}{2}$$

fold the paper first into two equal parts (halves), then fold again into three equal parts $\left(\frac{1}{3} \text{ of } \frac{1}{2}\right)$. What is the name of each part? $\frac{1}{6}$ of the unit.

The number line may be used as a semi-concrete approach for studying multiplication. What multiplication problem would be represented by the following:

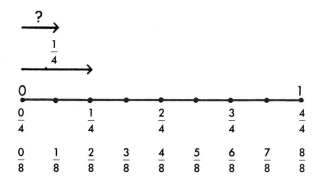

Answer: "One of the two equal parts of one-fourth," or $\frac{1}{2} \times \frac{1}{4} = \frac{1}{8}$.

Some teachers prefer the unit region to the number line. With a unit region, the idea $\frac{1}{2} \times \frac{1}{4}$ may be displayed by first representing $\frac{1}{4}$, and then $\frac{1}{2}$ of $\frac{1}{4}$, which is $\frac{1}{8}$:

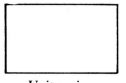
Unit region

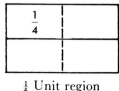
$\frac{1}{4}$ Unit region

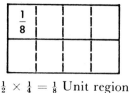
$\frac{1}{2} \times \frac{1}{4} = \frac{1}{8}$ Unit region

The idea $\frac{1}{4} \times \frac{1}{2}$ can be displayed by first representing $\frac{1}{2}$ and then $\frac{1}{4}$ of $\frac{1}{2}$, which again is $\frac{1}{8}$ of the unit region:

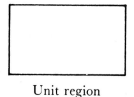
Unit region

$\frac{1}{2}$ Unit region

$\frac{1}{4} \times \frac{1}{2} = \frac{1}{8}$ Unit region

Similarly, $\frac{1}{2} \times \frac{1}{3}$ can be displayed by first representing $\frac{1}{3}$ and then $\frac{1}{2}$ of $\frac{1}{3}$:

Unit region

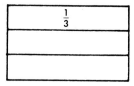
$\frac{1}{3}$ Unit region

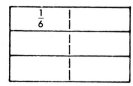
$\frac{1}{2} \times \frac{1}{3} = \frac{1}{6}$ Unit region

One-half of one-third of a unit is one-sixth of the unit.

Similarly, $\dfrac{1}{3} \times \dfrac{1}{2} = \square$ can be displayed as follows:

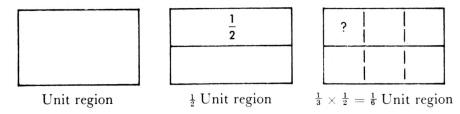

Unit region $\frac{1}{2}$ Unit region $\frac{1}{3} \times \frac{1}{2} = \frac{1}{6}$ Unit region

One-third of one-half of one unit is one-sixth of the unit.

When such a display is verbalized, it should be pointed out that the answer or product, $\dfrac{1}{6}$, is expressed in terms of the unit region; that is, *one-third of one-half of a unit is one-sixth of the unit.*

The multiplication of nonunit fractions is somewhat more difficult to visualize. The expression $\dfrac{2}{3} \times \dfrac{3}{4}$ can be interpreted as two-thirds of three-fourths of a unit. The fraction $\dfrac{2}{3}$ can be interpreted as two of the three parts into which three-fourths has been divided. In the following display the unit region is shown first, then three-fourths of the unit, and finally two-thirds of the three-fourths of the unit:

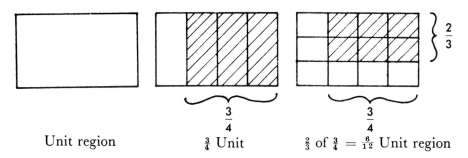

Unit region $\frac{3}{4}$ Unit $\frac{2}{3}$ of $\frac{3}{4} = \frac{6}{12}$ Unit region

Multiplication of Fractions Applied to Word Problems

What types of word problems would then be solved by expressions such as $3 \times \dfrac{1}{2}$, and $\dfrac{1}{2} \times 3$, and $\dfrac{1}{4} \times \dfrac{1}{3}$?

The expression $3 \times \dfrac{1}{2}$ is usually interpreted as "three one-halves," the first factor, 3, indicating the number of units and the second factor, $\dfrac{1}{2}$, the size of the unit. This interpretation is easy to visualize when the first factor is a whole number. A word problem such as, "If each of three girls drinks one-half of a glass of milk, how much milk do all three drink?" could be expressed as $3 \times \dfrac{1}{2} = \square$ or $\dfrac{1}{2} + \dfrac{1}{2} + \dfrac{1}{2} = \square$.

What word problems could be symbolized by expressions in which the first factor is a fraction, such as $\dfrac{1}{2} \times 3$ or $\dfrac{1}{4} \times \dfrac{1}{3}$? The first fraction as a part or parts of the second fraction is usually the idea involved. A word problem which could be expressed as $\dfrac{1}{2} \times 3$ is, "How much is one-half of three apples?"

Similarly, $\dfrac{1}{4} \times \dfrac{1}{3}$ might be the expression for the word problem, "How much is one-fourth of one-third of a pie?" or, "If four boys divide one-third of a pie, how much would each receive?" (The second problem could also be expressed as $\dfrac{1}{3} \div 4$. The division of fractions is discussed in the next section.)

"If one-half of the last quarter of the game is left to play, how many minutes are left?"

"If a recipe serves four people and there are two of you, how would you determine the amounts of the cooking ingredients?"

Multiplication of Numbers Expressed As Mixed Numerals

To solve a problem involving the multiplication of numbers expressed as mixed numerals, rename the mixed numbers as improper fractions and then multiply:

$$3\dfrac{1}{2} \times 2\dfrac{1}{3} = \square$$

$$\dfrac{7}{2} \times \dfrac{7}{3} = \dfrac{49}{6}$$

Why does the rule for renaming $3\frac{1}{2}$ as $\frac{7}{2}$ involve multiplying the 3 and 2 and adding the 1? Because 3×2 renames the whole number, 3, in terms of our unit of measure, $\frac{1}{2}$. Thus, 3 is the same as $3 \times \frac{2}{2}$, or $\frac{6}{2}$. Then, the remaining $\frac{1}{2}$ in the original number $3\frac{1}{2}$ is added to produce $\frac{7}{2}$.

Renaming (Cancellation or Reduction)

In a problem such as $\frac{2}{3} \times \frac{5}{6}$, "cancellation" or "reduction" is sometimes used as follows:

$$\frac{\overset{1}{\cancel{2}}}{3} \times \frac{5}{\underset{3}{\cancel{6}}} = \frac{5}{9}$$

Why does cancellation work? Cancellation or reduction involves finding a common factor, in this example the common factor 2. It would be better to say "divide out the common factor" rather than "cancel" or "reduce." Finding the common factor is a way of renaming a fraction in simplest form. The teacher may be interested in a more complete reason. For example.

$$\frac{4}{6} = \frac{2 \cdot 2}{3 \cdot 2} = \frac{2}{3} \cdot \frac{2}{2} = \frac{2}{3} \cdot 1 = \frac{2}{3}$$

To divide out the common factor, which in this case is $\frac{2}{2}$, is to rename using a form of the identity element, $\frac{1}{1}$, or 1.

EXERCISES

1. Using the number line, rationalize the products of the following:

(a) $2 \times \frac{1}{4}$ (b) $\frac{1}{4} \times 2$ (c) $3 \times \frac{2}{3}$

(d) $\dfrac{2}{3} \times 3$ (e) $\dfrac{1}{3} \times \dfrac{3}{4}$ (f) $\dfrac{1}{3} \times \dfrac{1}{2}$

2. Using the unit region, indicate the products for the following:

(a) $\dfrac{1}{2} \times \dfrac{1}{2}$ (b) $\dfrac{1}{2} \times \dfrac{1}{4}$

(c) $\dfrac{1}{3} \times \dfrac{1}{4}$ (d) $\dfrac{2}{3} \times \dfrac{1}{4}$

3. Make up word problems for each of the following expressions:

(a) $4 \times \dfrac{1}{3}$ (b) $\dfrac{1}{3} \times 4$

(c) $\dfrac{1}{2} \times \dfrac{1}{5}$ (d) $\dfrac{1}{5} \times \dfrac{1}{2}$

4. If a farmer plants only one-fifth of his land, and his son plants one-fourth of this in beans, how much of the farm is planted in beans?
5. What is the rationale of cancelling in multiplying fractions?
6. What name is used for the identity element in each of the following?

(a) $3 = \dfrac{12}{4}$ (b) $5 = \dfrac{10}{2}$

(c) $\dfrac{3}{4} = \dfrac{12}{16}$ (d) $\dfrac{6}{12} = \dfrac{1}{2}$

DIVISION OF FRACTIONAL NUMBERS

The division of fractions as learned by most people is a rote process. To divide fractions the learner is told to "invert and multiply." Such a procedure works, but not one in 50 college students knows why. Few can make up and verbalize a word problem that could be represented by an expression such as $\dfrac{1}{2} \div 3$. Many students will say that one divided by two-thirds is one and one-third.

Because of the difficulties encountered in the teaching of division of fractions, the concepts involved have usually been deferred to the sixth grade, whereas the multiplication of fractions is usually developed in the fifth grade. Now, however, with the advent of many new materials and accelerated programs, these concepts may be introduced earlier.

Two Meanings of Division in the Physical World

If we are going to begin at the concrete level in the physical world, it is necessary to keep in mind that there are two basic interpretations of division, **partitioning** and **measurement**. How then should the expression $6 \div 3$ be interpreted? (Not as "6 divided by 3" at the physical level.)

Which of the following displays could the sentence $6 \div 3 = 2$ represent?

$$XXXXXX = XX \quad XX \quad XX$$

(a set of six elements divided into three equal sets)

$$XXXXXX = XXX \quad XXX$$

(a set of six elements divided into sets of three elements each)

The expression $6 \div 3$ may represent either of these displays. In the first display the six objects are **partitioned** or divided into *three* sets. In partitioning, the divisor represents the number of groups or sets. When the divisor represents the number of sets the quotient represents the number of each set. Verbalizing, "A set of six divided equally into three subsets is how many in each set?"

In the second display, also symbolized as $6 \div 3 = 2$, the interpretation is one of *measurement*. The **divisor**, 3, is the unit of measure or the **number** of groups or sets. "A set of 6 divided into sets of 3 is how many sets?"

It is not difficult to verbalize or to make up word problems involving the division of fractions if the partitioning and measurement interpretations of division (see pp. 117–118) are understood. The representation of division of fractions geometrically is also done on the basis of the partitioning and measurement interpretations. If the divisor is a fraction, use the measurement interpretation. If the divisor is a whole number, use the partitive interpretation. The following are displays of the three basic forms just described:

1. $3 \div \dfrac{1}{2}$ (measurement): How many halves in three?

or with unit regions:

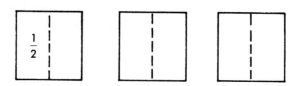

Thus, six one-halves of a unit are in three units.

2. $\dfrac{1}{2} \div 3$ (partitioning): One-half of a unit divided or partitioned into three equal parts leaves how much in each part?

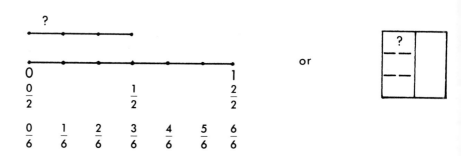

or

One-half of a unit divided in three equal parts leaves one-sixth of a unit are in each part.

3. $\dfrac{1}{2} \div \dfrac{1}{4}$ (measurement): How many one-fourths of a unit are in one-half of a unit?

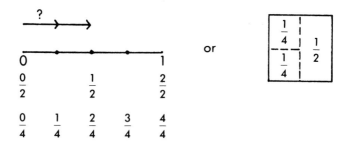

or

There are two one-fourths of a unit in one-half of a unit.

FRACTIONAL NUMBERS: MULTIPLICATION, DIVISION

Observe that in the two cases in which the divisor was a fraction the measurement interpretation was made. In general, then, when dividing by a fraction the measurement interpretation is used. In effect we are establishing a new unit of measure (the divisor) and determining the number of these units that there are in the dividend.

Word Problems. Word problems for the three basic forms, symbolized as $3 \div \frac{1}{2}$ and $\frac{1}{2} \div 3$ and $\frac{1}{2} \div \frac{1}{4}$, might be the following:

1. For $3 \div \frac{1}{2}$

   (a) How many half bushels are in three bushels?

   (b) If it takes one-half yard of material to make an apron, how many aprons can be made with three yards of material? (This problem illustrates the need for understanding the meaning of division of fractions because it may not be clear what operation is needed. This problem also indicates the importance of the interpretation of division as the inverse of multiplication, that is, finding the missing factor when one factor and product are known. Thus $3 \div \frac{1}{2}$ can be written as $\frac{1}{2} \times \square = 3$.)

2. For $\frac{1}{2} \div 3$

   (a) If one-half yard of material is needed to make three handkerchiefs, how much material is required for each handkerchief?

   (b) If one-half of a pie is divided among three boys, how much does each receive?

3. For $\frac{1}{2} \div \frac{1}{4}$

   (a) How many fourths of a cup of milk are there in one-half cup?

   (b) How many one-fourth-inch segments are in one-half-inch segment?

   (c) How many quarters are in a half dollar?

Division by the Least Common Denominator Method

After exploring the operation of division as applied to the physical world, patterns appropriate to a quicker solution should be studied. A pattern for dividing fractions which is relatively easy to visualize is the least common denominator method.

1. $3 \div \dfrac{1}{2} = \square$

   $\dfrac{6}{2} \div \dfrac{1}{2} = \square$ renaming 3 as $\dfrac{6}{2}$ (How many halves in six halves?)

   $\dfrac{6 \div 1}{2 \div 2} = \dfrac{6}{1} = 6$

2. $\dfrac{1}{2} \div 3 = \square$

   $\dfrac{1}{2} \div \dfrac{6}{2} = \square$ renaming 3 as $\dfrac{6}{2}$

   $1 \div 6 = \dfrac{1}{6}$

3. $\dfrac{1}{2} \div \dfrac{1}{4} = \square$

   $\dfrac{2}{4} \div \dfrac{1}{4} = \square$

   $2 \div 1 = 2$

Division by the Reciprocal Method

What does $1 \div \dfrac{2}{3}$ equal? Or, how many two-thirds of a unit are in one unit? A number of students will quickly say $1\dfrac{1}{3}$. If the measurement idea of division is understood, however, it can be seen that the answer is $1\dfrac{1}{2}$ and not $1\dfrac{1}{3}$. We are in effect measuring to find how many line segments two-thirds of a unit in length are in the original unit.

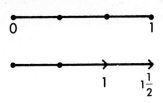

In considering $1 \div \dfrac{2}{3} = 1\dfrac{1}{2}$ or $\dfrac{3}{2}$, it is seen that when the number 1 is

divided by a fraction, $\dfrac{2}{3}$, the quotient is that fraction inverted or the

reciprocal, $\dfrac{3}{2}$.

Similarly, $1 \div \dfrac{1}{4} = 4.$

4 is the **multiplicative inverse** of $\dfrac{1}{4}$

$\dfrac{3}{2}$ is the **multiplicative inverse** of $\dfrac{2}{3}$

The product of a number and its multiplicative inverse is the identity element for multiplication, 1. This is a useful idea in dividing fractions. It provides the reason that the "invert and multiply" rule works.

If the sentence $1 \div \dfrac{2}{3} = \square$ is expressed in its vertical form, the procedure for solving it is somewhat easier to visualize.

$$1 \div \frac{2}{3} = \frac{1}{\dfrac{2}{3}}$$

To rename the denominator, $\dfrac{2}{3}$, as 1, multiply by its inverse, $\dfrac{3}{2}$. If this

is done, the numerator must also by multiplied by $\dfrac{3}{2}$. In multiplying

by $\dfrac{\dfrac{3}{2}}{\dfrac{3}{2}}$, we are multiplying by another name for the identity element, $\dfrac{1}{1}$

DIVISION OF FRACTIONAL NUMBERS

or 1. In this process, the denominator becomes 1 and our answer is the numerator.

$$\frac{1}{\frac{2}{3}} = \frac{1 \cdot \frac{3}{2}}{\frac{2}{3} \cdot \frac{3}{2}} = \frac{1 \cdot \frac{3}{2}}{1} = 1 \cdot \frac{3}{2} = \frac{3}{2} = 1\frac{1}{2}$$

Similarly:

$$2 \div \frac{3}{4} = \frac{2}{\frac{3}{4}} = \frac{2 \cdot \frac{4}{3}}{\frac{3}{4} \cdot \frac{4}{3}} = \frac{2 \cdot \frac{4}{3}}{1} = 2 \cdot \frac{4}{3} = \frac{8}{3}$$

The same procedure developed in a horizontal form is as follows:

$$2 \div \frac{3}{4} = \left(2 \cdot \frac{4}{3}\right) \div \left(\frac{3}{4} \cdot \frac{4}{3}\right) = \left(2 \cdot \frac{4}{3}\right) \div 1 = 2 \cdot \frac{4}{3} = \frac{8}{3}$$

The mathematical basis for "inverting and multiplying" when dividing fractions is that both the numerator (dividend) and the denominator (divisor) are multiplied by the multiplicative inverse of the denominator.

Comparison of the Least Common Denominator and Inversion Methods of Dividing Fractions

The least common denominator method is easier to understand and should be taught first. The youngsters, however, should later be taught the inversion method as a better method because it provides solutions more quickly, since the least common denominator does not have to be found and since multiplication is less difficult than division. The inversion method may, however, become more of a rote procedure than the least common denominator method because the concepts of inversion are somewhat more difficult to grasp and are therefore sometimes ignored.

FRACTIONAL NUMBERS: MULTIPLICATION, DIVISION

EXERCISES

1. Illustrate with a number line, the unit region, or a paper strip the following:

   (a) $2 \div \dfrac{1}{3}$ (b) $\dfrac{1}{3} \div 2$ (c) $\dfrac{1}{3} \div \dfrac{1}{6}$

   (d) $\dfrac{1}{2} \div \dfrac{1}{3}$ (e) $\dfrac{2}{3} \div \dfrac{1}{6}$ (f) $\dfrac{2}{3} \div \dfrac{2}{6}$

2. Which of the parts of problem 1 best express the measurement interpretation of division? the partitive interpretation?

3. Make up word problems for the following:

   (a) $2 \div \dfrac{1}{3}$ (b) $\dfrac{1}{3} \div 2$

   (c) $\dfrac{1}{2} \div \dfrac{1}{3}$ (d) $\dfrac{2}{3} \div \dfrac{1}{6}$

4. Using the least common denominator method, solve the following:

   (a) $2 \div \dfrac{1}{3}$ (b) $\dfrac{2}{3} \div \dfrac{1}{6}$ (c) $\dfrac{1}{2} \div \dfrac{1}{3}$ (d) $\dfrac{1}{3} \div 2$

   (e) $\dfrac{3}{4} \div \dfrac{1}{2}$ (f) $\dfrac{3}{4} \div \dfrac{2}{3}$ (g) $2\dfrac{1}{3} \div \dfrac{1}{2}$

5. Solve the following by the inversion method, giving reasons for each step:

   (a) $3 \div \dfrac{1}{6}$ (b) $\dfrac{2}{3} \div \dfrac{3}{4}$

10

DECIMAL FRACTIONS
AND PER CENT

The meaning of a numeral such as 3333 in base ten notation can be displayed in expanded form as follows:

$$3333 = 3(10^3) + 3(10^2) + 3(10^1) + 3(1)$$

To express fractional ideas in base ten notation, the pattern displayed above is extended to the right by using a decimal to indicate the point of separation of whole numbers and fractions. Thus, to clarify the meaning of a number such as 333.333, the following expanded forms are often used:

3 (hundreds) + 3 (tens) + 3 (ones) + 3 (tenths) + 3 (hundredths)
+ 3 (thousandths)

or

$$3(100) + 3(10) + 3(1) + 3\left(\frac{1}{10}\right) + 3\left(\frac{1}{100}\right) + 3\left(\frac{1}{1000}\right)$$

or

$$3(10^2) + 3(10^1) + 3(10^0) + 3\left(\frac{1}{10^1}\right) + 3\left(\frac{1}{10^2}\right) + 3\left(\frac{1}{10^3}\right)$$

In this decimal or base ten pattern each digit has a place value one-tenth as great as the digit to its left.

INTRODUCING DECIMAL FRACTIONS

If a unit square is divided into 10 congruent regions, how would each be named?

If each of these 10 subunits is divided into 10 congruent regions, how would each of the new units be named?

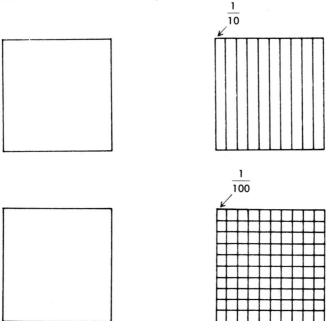

The fraction $\frac{1}{10}$ may also be expressed in decimal fraction form as .1, read as "one-tenth." The fraction $\frac{1}{100}$ may be expressed as .01 and read as "one-hundredth."

To illustrate the same idea with a number line:

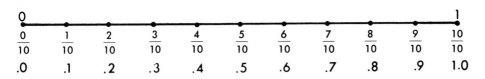

If a segment .1 unit long is divided into 10 congruent segments, how long is each segment?

	0	1	2	3	4	5	6	7	8	9	.1
	$\frac{0}{100}$	$\frac{1}{100}$	$\frac{2}{100}$	$\frac{3}{100}$	$\frac{4}{100}$	$\frac{5}{100}$	$\frac{6}{100}$	$\frac{7}{100}$	$\frac{8}{100}$	$\frac{9}{100}$	$\frac{1}{10}$
	.00	.01	.02	.03	.04	.05	.06	.07	.08	.09	.10

In decimal notation the place value of the number 3333.333 can be illustrated in any of the following forms. The first three forms are found more commonly in the elementary school, and the last form at the secondary and higher levels.

$$3 \text{ (hundreds)} + 3 \text{ (tens)} + 3 \text{ (ones)} + 3 \text{ (tenths)} + 3 \text{ (hundredths)} + 3 \text{ (thousandths)}$$

or

$$3(100) + 3(10) + 3(1) + 3\left(\frac{1}{10}\right) + 3\left(\frac{1}{100}\right) + 3\left(\frac{1}{1000}\right)$$

or

$$3(10^2) + 3(10^1) + 3(1) + 3\left(\frac{1}{10^1}\right) + 3\left(\frac{1}{10^2}\right) + 3\left(\frac{1}{10^3}\right)$$

or

$$3(10^2) + 3(10^1) + 3(10^0) + 3(10^{-1}) + 3(10^{-2}) + 3(10^{-3})$$

That 10^{-1} and $\frac{1}{10}$ are names for the same number can be rationalized by observing the sequence of exponents from left to right in the preceding illustration. The value of the exponent decreases by 1 for each place from left to right, so that 10^1 is followed by 10^0 and then 10^{-1}, and so on. Thus:

$.1, \frac{1}{10}$, and 10^{-1} are names for the same number.

$.01, \frac{1}{10^2}$, and 10^{-2} are names for the same number.

$.001, \frac{1}{10^3}$, and 10^{-3} are names for the same number.

The following diagram compares various forms of fractional notations:

DECIMAL FRACTIONS AND PER CENT

One Tenth	One Hundredth	One Thousandth	One Ten-Thousandth	One Hundred-Thousandth
10^{-1}	10^{-2}	10^{-3}	10^{-4}	10^{-5}
$\dfrac{1}{10^1}$	$\dfrac{1}{10^2}$	$\dfrac{1}{10^3}$	$\dfrac{1}{10^4}$	$\dfrac{1}{10^5}$
$\dfrac{1}{10}$	$\dfrac{1}{100}$	$\dfrac{1}{1000}$	$\dfrac{1}{10,000}$	$\dfrac{1}{100,000}$
.1	.01	.001	.0001	.00001

INTRODUCING THE ADDITION AND SUBTRACTION OF DECIMAL FRACTIONS

In the addition of whole numbers in a base ten or decimal system, units are added to units, tens to tens, and hundreds to hundreds. It follows that tenths should be added to tenths, hundredths to hundredths, and thousandths to thousandths. This idea may be developed with a pocket chart as was the idea of addition of whole numbers; that is, by labeling columns "tenths," "hundredths," "thousandths," and so forth. The results of the addition may then be recorded in a form such as:

$$
\begin{array}{r}
3 \text{ tenths} \\
+\ 3 \text{ tenths} \\
\hline
6 \text{ tenths}
\end{array}
$$

The addition and subtraction of decimal fractions can also be related to the addition and subtraction of common fractions, a procedure already learned. For the problem .3 + .5 = □:

$$
\begin{array}{r}
.3 = \dfrac{3}{10} \\
+\ .5 = +\ \dfrac{5}{10} \\
\hline
\dfrac{8}{10} = .8
\end{array}
$$

Similarly, for the problem $\dfrac{3}{100} + \dfrac{5}{100} = \square$:

$$\begin{array}{l} \dfrac{3}{100} \\[2mm] + \dfrac{5}{100} \\[2mm] \hline \dfrac{8}{100} \end{array} \quad \text{or} \quad \begin{array}{l} .03 \\ + .05 \\ \hline .08 \end{array} \quad \begin{array}{l} (3 \text{ hundredths}) \\ + (5 \text{ hundredths}) \\ \hline (8 \text{ hundredths}) \end{array}$$

On the number line, the problem .3 + .5 = $\square$ may be displayed as:

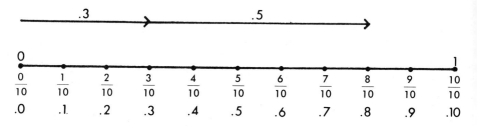

And the problem .03 + .05 = $\square$ as:

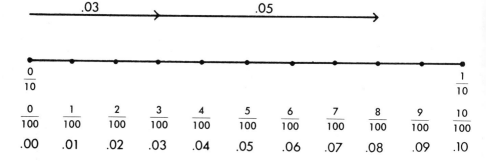

Similarly, in subtraction the problem $\dfrac{8}{10} - \dfrac{3}{10} = \square$ may be presented as:

$$\begin{array}{l} \dfrac{8}{10} \\[2mm] - \dfrac{3}{10} \\[2mm] \hline - \dfrac{5}{10} \end{array} \quad \begin{array}{l} .8 \\ -.3 \\ \hline .5 \end{array} \quad \begin{array}{l} (8 \text{ tenths}) \\ - (3 \text{ tenths}) \\ \hline (5 \text{ tenths}) \end{array}$$

DECIMAL FRACTIONS AND PER CENT

And the problem .8 – .3 may be displayed on the number line as:

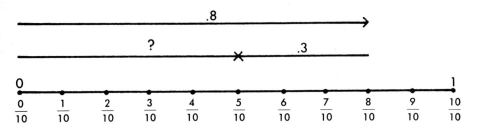

For problems such as $\begin{array}{r}.80\\-.36\\\hline\end{array}$ the idea of renaming is used as in the whole numbers. In this problem, one of the 8 tenths is renamed as 10 hundredths and the 6 hundredths is then subtracted from the 10 hundredths, producing 4 hundredths. Next the 3 tenths is subtracted from the 7 tenths, producing 4 tenths. Thus:

$$\begin{array}{r}.80\\-.36\\\hline.44\end{array}$$

MULTIPLICATION OF DECIMAL FRACTIONS

The method generally employed to teach multiplication of decimal fractions is to use the concepts developed in the multiplication of common fractions. For example:

$$.2 \times .3$$

$$\frac{2}{10} \times \frac{3}{10}$$

$$\frac{2}{10} \times \frac{3}{10} = \frac{6}{100} = .06 \text{ renamed decimally}$$

then $$.2 \times .3 = .06$$

Also,
$$3.2 \times .6 = \square$$

$$3\frac{2}{10} \times \frac{6}{10}$$

$$\frac{32}{10} \times \frac{6}{10} = \frac{192}{100} = 1.92$$

then
$$3.2 \times .6 = 1.92$$

With similar examples the generalization can be developed that the product of two decimal fractions contains the same number of digits to the right of the decimal as does the sum of the number of digits to the right of the decimal in the factors. Zero, of course, must be counted as a digit.

DIVISION OF DECIMAL FRACTIONS

In the previous chapter, fractions were often renamed by multiplying both the numerator and the denominator by the same number. This procedure is also useful in dividing decimal fractions. Multiplying a fraction by a form of the identity element, 1, removes the decimal from the denominator. For a problem such as $\frac{.6}{.3}$, multiply by $\frac{10}{10}$:

$$\frac{.6}{.3} = \frac{.6 \times 10}{.3 \times 10} = \frac{6}{3} = 2$$

This procedure is the basis for expressing the form $.3\overline{).6}$ as $3\overline{)6}$, which is equivalent to multiplying both numbers by 10.

Similarly, for a problem such as $.36\overline{)2.82}$, multiply both divisor and dividend by 100 in order that the divisor be expressed as a whole number. This may be shown with arrows as:

$$.36\overline{)2.82}$$

The same idea could also be represented as:

$$\frac{2.82}{.36} \times \frac{100}{100} = \frac{282}{36}$$

DECIMAL FRACTIONS AND PER CENT

Then, performing the division:

$$
\begin{array}{r}
7.83 \\
36\overline{\smash{)}282.00} \\
\underline{252} \\
300 \\
\underline{288} \\
120 \\
\underline{108} \\
12
\end{array}
$$

Zeros are annexed in the dividend as needed, depending on the number of decimal places desired for the quotient. Since the quotient is rounded off, the answer to the problem above is expressed in terms of "correct to hundredths." Had the remainder been equal to one-half or more of the divisor—that is, 18 or more—the answer would have been 7.84 "correct to hundredths."

EXERCISES

1. Express in expanded notation:
   (a) 111.111   (b) 324.6452
2. Rationalize each of the following:
   (a) $10^0 = 1$ (b) $5^0 = 1$ (c) $\dfrac{1}{100} = 10^{-2}$
3. With number line diagrams, illustrate each of the following:
   (a) .3 + .2 = □   (b) .4 + .3 = □   (c) 1.3 + .5 = □
   (d) .6 - .2 = □   (e) 1.4 - .8 = □
4. What procedure would you use to illustrate that .3 × .5 = .15?
5. What procedure would you use to rationalize moving the decimal in the division problem $3.2\overline{\smash{)}63.84}$?

TYPES OF DECIMAL FRACTIONS

Fractions such as $\dfrac{1}{2}$ may be expressed decimally by dividing the numerator by the denominator:

$$
\begin{array}{r}
.5 \\
2\overline{\smash{)}1.0}
\end{array}
$$

Such fractions are **terminating** decimal fractions; that is, they have a remainder of zero.

A second type of decimal fraction is the **repeating** or **periodic decimal**. The fraction $\frac{1}{3}$, for example, expressed decimally repeats or does not terminate:

$$\frac{1}{3} = .333 \ldots$$

To express a periodic fraction, such as $\frac{1}{7}$, as a decimal fraction, divide the numerator, 1.000. . .by the denominator 7 until a repeating sequence of digits appears:

```
          .1428571 . . .
      7 ⌐ 1.0000000
          7
          ――
          30
          28
          ――
           20
           14
           ――
            60
            56
            ――
             40
             35
             ――
              50
              49
              ――
              10 (here the sequence begins again)
```

The fraction $\frac{1}{7}$, then, expressed decimally is $.142857\overline{142857}\ldots$ (the vinculum or bar is placed over the numerals that repeat to indicate the repeating sequence or period). The fractions $\frac{1}{3}$ and $\frac{1}{7}$ are examples of **repeating** or **periodic decimals**.

In expressing a fraction such as $\frac{1}{17}$ decimally, to how many places must you carry out the division before the sequence of digits begins to repeat? Hint: How many remainders are possible in dividing a number by 17? Since there are only 16 counting numbers less than 17, there can be only 16 different remainders before the sequence begins to re-peat. Thus, for a fraction $\dfrac{1}{n}$, the decimal sequence or period will begin to repeat either before or when $n - 1$ divisions have been performed.

There are decimal fractions which neither terminate nor repeat. These are called **nonterminating, nonrepeating** decimal fractions. If you attempt to express $\sqrt{2}$ as a decimal fraction, you will find that this decimal fraction does not repeat.

EXPRESSING A DECIMAL FRACTION AS A COMMON FRACTION

To express a common fraction such as $\dfrac{1}{7}$ as a decimal fraction, one can divide the numerator, $1.000 \cdots$, by the denominator, 7, until a repeating sequence of digits appears. However, it is more difficult to reverse the process. For example, $.142857\overline{142857} \cdots$ represents what common fraction?

Using a simpler example first, assume that you do not know that the decimal $.3\overline{3} \cdots$ is equal to $\dfrac{1}{3}$. How could you determine the common fraction name for $.3\overline{3} \cdots$? First, let the symbol N represent the un-known common fraction that is equal to $.3\overline{3} \cdots$.

$$N = .3\overline{3} \cdots$$

Multiply both sides of this equation by 10 (because the repeating sequence is only one decimal place):

$$10N = 3.3\overline{3} \cdots$$

Then subtract the first equation from the second (using the property of the equals relation):

$$
\begin{aligned}
10N &= 3.3\overline{3} \cdots \\
-(1)N &= .3\overline{3} \cdots \\
\hline
9N &= 3 \\
N &= \frac{3}{9} = \frac{1}{3}
\end{aligned}
$$

As another example, the decimal fraction $.63\overline{63} \cdots$ is equal to what common fraction? Let $N = .63\overline{63} \cdots$ and multiply by 100 (instead of 10), since there are two digits in the repeating sequence. Now again subtract the first equation from the second:

$$
\begin{array}{l}
100N = 63.63\overline{63} \cdots \\
\underline{-N = .63\overline{63} \cdots} \\
99N = 63 \\
N = \dfrac{63}{99} = \dfrac{7}{11}
\end{array}
$$

For the decimal $.142857\overline{142857} \cdots$, what is the common fraction form? Let $N = .142857\overline{142857} \cdots$ and then multiply each member of this equation by 10^6 (since there are six digits in the repeating sequence):

$$
\begin{array}{l}
1{,}000{,}000N = 142{,}857.142857\overline{142857} \cdots \\
\underline{-N = \phantom{142{,}857.}.142857\overline{142857} \cdots} \\
999{,}999N = 142{,}857 \\
N = \dfrac{142{,}857}{999{,}999} = \dfrac{1}{7}
\end{array}
$$

DECIMAL FRACTIONS AND SCIENTIFIC NOTATION

Numbers are said to be expressed in **scientific notation** if they are in the form of *a product of a number between 1 and 10 and the appropriate power of ten*. In the following examples, the forms on the right are expressed in scientific notation, since each is the product of a number between 1 and 10 and a power of ten:

$$
\begin{aligned}
100 &= 1 \times 10^2 \text{ or simply } 10^2 \\
12 &= 1.2 \times 10 \text{ or } 1.2 \times 10^1 \\
120 &= 1.2 \times 10^2 \\
1200 &= 1.2 \times 10^3 \\
12{,}000 &= 1.2 \times 10^4
\end{aligned}
$$

DECIMAL FRACTIONS AND PER CENT

To express 120 in scientific notation—that is, as the product of a number between 1 and 10 and a power of ten—the decimal must be placed as follows: 1.20. Since this is equivalent to dividing 120 by 100 or 10^2, the second factor, 10^2, must be included as a power of ten. Then, $120 = 1.20 \times 10^2$. Similarly, to express the number 12,000 in scientific notation—that is, as a number between 1 and 10 and the appropriate power of ten—the decimal is placed between the digits 1 and 2. This is equivalent to dividing 12,000 by 10,000 or 10^4. To compensate for this division by 10,000 or 10^4 in expressing 12,000 as 1.2, the second factor as an appropriate power of ten, in this case 10^4, must be included. Thus:

$$12,000 = 1.2 \times 10^4$$

For every place the decimal is moved to the left (a process equivalent to dividing by 10) the power of the second factor, ten, must be increased by 1. Conversely, for every place the decimal is moved to the right, the power of ten must be decreased by 1.

$$1200 = 1.2 \times 10^3$$
$$120 = 1.2 \times 10^2$$
$$12 = 1.2 \times 10^1$$
$$1.2 = 1.2 \times 10^0$$
$$.12 = 1.2 \times 10^{-1}$$

A number such as .001 expressed in scientific notation would involve moving the decimal to the right three places (multiplying by 1000). To compensate, the second factor as a power of ten would be 10^{-3}. The number .001 in scientific notation is then 1×10^{-3}. Similarly, the number .0011 in scientific notation would be 1.1×10^{-3}, and the number .012 would be 1.2×10^{-2}.

Scientific notation is used because it is often a more convenient way of expressing very large or very small numbers. For example, the distance to the sun is 93,000,000 miles. In scientific notation this distance is expressed as 9.3×10^7 miles. Also, in performing operations on large numbers such as $93,000,000 \times 93,000,000$, if the numbers are expressed in scientific notation the problem can be done more quickly by multiplying the first factors and adding the powers of ten in the second factors.

$$9.3 \times 10^7$$
$$9.3 \times 10^7$$

$$\frac{}{279}$$
$$837$$
$$\frac{}{86.49 \times 10^{14}}$$

or 8.649×10^{15}

EXERCISES

1. Express in common fraction form:
   (a) .32 (b) .0202 (c) 2.3
2. Express in decimal fraction form:

   (a) $\dfrac{2}{10}$ (b) $\dfrac{2}{5}$ (c) $\dfrac{20}{5}$ (d) $\dfrac{2000}{5}$

   (e) $\dfrac{10}{2}$ (f) $\dfrac{5}{2}$ (g) $\dfrac{5}{20}$ (d) $\dfrac{5}{2000}$

3. Express the following as terminating or repeating decimal fractions:

   (a) $\dfrac{1}{2}$ (b) $\dfrac{1}{4}$ (c) $\dfrac{1}{6}$ (d) $\dfrac{1}{8}$

   (e) $\dfrac{1}{9}$ (f) $\dfrac{2}{9}$ (g) $\dfrac{1}{11}$

4. Express in common fraction form each of the following:
   (a) $.6\overline{6}\cdots$ (b) $.5\overline{45}4\cdots$ (c) $.3\overline{67}367\cdots$
5. Express in scientific notation:
   (a) 150 (b) 15,000 (c) 15,000,000
   (d) 15 (e) .15 (f) .0015

RATIO AND PROPORTION

A **ratio** is a comparison of two or more numbers. The ratios of boys to girls and hits to times at bat, betting odds of 2 to 1, and changes in cooking recipes all involve such comparisons. The fraction is a way of symbolizing the comparison of two numbers. If there are two boys for every three girls in class, this comparison or ratio of boys to girls can be expressed as "two to three" and symbolized $\dfrac{2}{3}$ or 2:3.

DECIMAL FRACTIONS AND PER CENT

Two ratios that represent the same number are equal. For example, $\frac{2}{3} = \frac{10}{15}$. The form $\frac{2}{3} = \frac{10}{15}$ is called a **proportion**. A proportion in an expression of equality for two ratios.

Many problems in mathematics can be solved by using the proportion. The proportion is now used as a basis for introducing per cent problems in the sixth grade. The science teacher is very much interested in youngsters' understanding proportion, because it can be used so often in solving science problems.

Many problems can be structured or set up as proportions when one comparison or ratio and one of the numbers in the other ratio is known. For example, if three small cans cost 54 cents, how much will seven cans cost? If three cans cost 54 cents, this comparison or ratio can be expressed as $\frac{3}{54}$. The problem can then be verbalized as, "Three is to fifty-four as seven is to what number?" and symbolized as a proportion, $\frac{3}{54} = \frac{7}{x}$. This type of problem is often solved by "cross multiplying"— that is, by solving $\frac{3}{54} = \frac{7}{x}$ as $3 \cdot x = 54 \cdot 7$. Cross multiplying is an application of the **property of proportions:**

$$\text{if} \quad \frac{a}{b} = \frac{c}{d}$$

$$\text{then } a \cdot d = b \cdot c$$

Another way of expressing the problem "If three cans cost fifty-four cents, what do seven cans cost?" is $\frac{3}{7} = \frac{54}{x}$, which is read as, "Three is to seven as fifty-four is to what number?"

The problem as first symbolized is less likely to lead to confusion since if one ratio is "number of cans to price," it follows that the other ratio should also be "number of cans to price." It is more easily seen that the numeral representing the number of cans should be the numerator of the second ratio if the numerator of the first ratio represents number of cans. If one ratio compares soup to nuts, so should the other, and not nuts to soup.

A similar problem in proportion is the following: If candies are three for ten cents, how much would a box of 24 candies cost? Verbalizing, "Three is to ten as twenty-four is to what number?"

$$\frac{3}{10} = \frac{24}{x} \quad \text{then } 3x = 240 \text{ and } x = 80 \text{ cents}$$

Supposed the problem had been, "If candies are three for ten cents, how many should be in a box that is marked 80 cents?" This idea can be expressed as $\dfrac{3}{10} = \dfrac{x}{80}$.

PER CENT

"Per cent" is derived from the Latin *per centum* and means "per hundred." Per cent is then a ratio. Ten per cent, symbolized as 10% is 10 parts per hundred or the ratio $\dfrac{10}{100}$. Thus per cent is the comparison or ratio of a number to 100. It is a convenient idea in the commercial world, a way of making comparisons and figuring rates of gain and loss. The Roman counterpart in the business world was the uncial $\left(\dfrac{1}{12}\right)$.

Expressing Numbers in Fraction, Decimal, and Per Cent Form

The following shows three widely used ways of naming a number:

Common Fraction	Decimal Fraction	Per Cent
$\frac{1}{2}$	0.5	50%
$\frac{1}{5}$	0.20	20%
$\frac{1}{3}$	0.33 $\cdots$	$33\frac{1}{3}\%$
$2\frac{1}{2}$	2.50	250%

DECIMAL FRACTIONS AND PER CENT

To convert a fraction to per cent, proportion is again useful. One half is what per cent? Or, 1 is to 2 as what number is to 100?

$$\frac{1}{2} = \frac{x}{100}$$

$$2x = 100$$

$$x = 50$$

To convert a decimal fraction to per cent, move the decimal two places to the right, a procedure which is equivalent to multiplying by 100.

To convert per cent to a decimal fraction, move the decimal point two places to the left, a procedure which is equivalent to dividing by 100.

Solving Problems in Per Cent

Per cent problems are now introduced in the sixth grade, but the procedure is not based on the memorization of a formula such as $p = b \cdot r$ (principal equals base times rate). In using this formula, pupils had great difficulty in determining which number represented the principal and which numbers represented the base and the rate. It was for the most part a meaningless activity.

Three basic types of per cent problems that are often encountered are:

1. 20% of 30 = □: finding part of a number: 20% of 30 is what?
2. □% of 30 = 6: given two numbers and expressing one as a part of the other (in per cent): what per cent of 30 is 6?
3. 20% of □ = 6: given a number and the part (per cent) that that number is of another number, find the second number: 20% of what number is 6, or 6 is 20% of what number?

The procedure used to rationalize and solve problems in per cent by the proportion method follows. The fact that per cent is a ratio is the starting point.

Type 1: 20% of 30 = □. Here the known ratio is 20% or 20 per 100.

Expressed as a proportion, "Twenty is to one hundred as what number is to thirty?"

$$\frac{20}{100} = \frac{x}{30}$$

$$100x = 600$$

$$x = 6$$

Then, 6 is to 30 as 20 is to 100.

Type 2: $\square$% of 30 = 6. The known ratio is 6 to 30. Rename this ratio in per cent. Verbalizing, "Six is to thirty as what number is to one hundred?" As a proportion:

$$\frac{6}{30} = \frac{x}{100}$$

$$x = 20$$

Then, 20 is to 100 as 6 is to 30, and 20 per 100 is 20%.

Type 3: 20% of $\square$ = 6. The ratio, 20% or $\frac{20}{100}$, is given. The question is then "Twenty is to one hundred as six is to what number?" As a proportion:

$$\frac{20}{100} = \frac{6}{x}$$

$$x = 30$$

Then, 6 is to 30 as 20 is to 100.

Using the same numbers, consider word problems for each of these three types of per cent problems.

1. 20% of 30 = $\square$
   A dress priced at $30 is marked down or "off" 20%. How much will the dress be reduced in price?
2. $\square$% of 30 = 6
   A dress that was priced at $30 is marked down $6. What per cent saving is this?
3. 20% of $\square$ = 6
   In practical affairs this type of problem is used less frequently

than the first two. The problem might be stated as follows: A dress is marked "20% off," which is a saving of $6. What was the original price of the dress? As a proportion, 6 is to what number as 20 is to 100?

A similar problem but with a less obvious solution is the following: A dress, reduced 20%, now sells for $24. What was the original price? The 20% represents the amount reduced, not the new price. If the dress is reduced 20%, the new price, $24, represents what per cent of the original price? The new price, $24, is 80% of the original. Thus, the problem can be restated as 24 is 80% of what number, or 80% of $\square$ = 24. As a proportion, 80 is to 100 as 24 is to what number, $\dfrac{80}{100} = \dfrac{24}{x}$? Then $x = 30$ and $30 was the original price.

Per Cent Problems of "Increase and Decrease"

The college enrollment was 1200 last year and is 1560 this year. What per cent increase is this? The gain or increase of 360 students compared to the original enrollment, 1200, expressed as a ratio is $\dfrac{360}{1200}$. To rename this ratio in per cent or "per hundred," 360 is to 1200 as what number is to 100? $\dfrac{360}{1200} = \dfrac{x}{100}$. Then $x = 30$ and there is a 30 per hundred or 30% increase in enrollment.

Many problems such as $\dfrac{360}{1200} = \dfrac{x}{100}$ can be solved simply by inspection. Note that the denominators are 100 and 1200. Since 100 is $\dfrac{1}{12}$ of 1200, the same relationship should hold for the numerators; then $x = \dfrac{1}{12}$ of 360, or 30.

If in the following year the enrollment drops 30%, what is the enrollment? The 30% drop is from the most recent enrollment, 1560. As a proportion, then, 30 is to 100 as what number is to 1560?

$$\frac{30}{100} = \frac{x}{1560}$$

$$x = 468$$

Since there are 468 fewer students, the new enrollment is 1560 - 468 or 1092. *Note that a 30% increase followed by a 30% decrease does not result in the original number.*

Problems in per cent are sometimes hard to visualize when the increase is more than 100%. For example, if one student flunked last year and two students flunked this year, what per cent of increase is this? The increase, 1, is to 1 as what number is to 100?

$$\frac{1}{1} = \frac{x}{100}$$

$$x = 100$$

This is a 100% increase in students flunked. If next year three students flunk, what is the percent of increase in failures from the first year to the third? The increase is 2, thus 2 is to 1 as what number is to 100? $\frac{2}{1} = \frac{x}{100}$ and therefore $x = 200$. Thus if failures increase from 1 to 3, there is a 200% increase in failures. It is such comparisons as this that furnish dramatic statistics. The newspaper reports, "Boondocks College failures increase 200%."

What was the per cent of increase in failures from the second to third year—that is, from two failures to three failures? The increase of 1 compared to the first 2 can be expressed as the ratio $\frac{1}{2}$. One is to 2 as what number is to 100? $\frac{1}{2} = \frac{x}{100}$, and therefore $x = 50$. Thus, if failures increase from 2 to 3, there is a 50% increase.

EXERCISES

1. Solve the following proportions:

(a) $\frac{3}{4} = \frac{8}{x}$ (b) $\frac{5}{6} = \frac{x}{12}$

(c) $\frac{18}{24} = \frac{3}{x}$ (d) $\frac{x}{5} = \frac{6}{30}$

2. Make up a word problem for each part of exercise 1.
3. What numbers complete the following table?

Common Fraction	Decimal Fraction	Per Cent
$\dfrac{1}{2}$	.5	50%
———	.75	———
———	———	80%
———	.025	———
———	———	$5\dfrac{1}{2}\%$
$\dfrac{1}{50}$	———	———
———	2.3	———

4. Express as a proportion and solve the following:
   (a) 5% of 60 = □   (b) □% of 60 = 3   (c) 5% of □ = 3
5. Make up a word problem for each part of problem 4.
6. If a teacher has a salary of $5000 this year and next year has a salary of $5500, what per cent salary increase did he receive? Solve as a proportion.
7. If a depression necessitated reducing teachers' salaries by 10%, what would the new salary of the teacher in problem 6 be (after the increase)? Solve as a proportion.
8. Complete the following table:

First Number	Second Number	Per Cent of Increase or Decrease
1	2	(a) ———
2	1	(b) ———
2	3	(c) ———
200	300	(d) ———
3	5	(e) ———
12	7	(f) ———

11

PROBLEM SOLVING

The National Council of Teachers of Mathematics lists an eight point Agenda for Action in the 1980s[1] recommending that:

1. problem solving be the focus of school mathematics in the 1980s;
2. basic skills in mathematics be defined to encompass more than computational facility;
3. mathematics programs take full advantage of the power of calculators and computers at all grade levels;
4. stringent standards of both effectiveness and efficiency be applied to the teaching of mathematics;
5. the success of mathematics programs and student learning be evaluated by a wider range of measures than conventional testing;
6. more mathematics study be required for all students and a flexible curriculum with a greater range of options be designed to accommodate the diverse needs of the student population;
7. mathematics teachers demand of themselves and their colleagues a high level of professionalism;
8. public support for mathematics instruction be raised to a level commensurate with the importance of mathematical understanding to individuals and society.

Thus problem solving, the subject of this chapter, is listed as the first agenda item by the National Council of Teachers of Mathematics, and the use of calculators, the subject of the next chapter, is listed as the third agenda item. Both chapters are also concerned with the second agenda item, basic skills.

---

[1] National Council of Teachers of Mathematics, *An Agenda for Action.* April 1980, p. 1.

WHAT IS PROBLEM SOLVING?

Problem solving includes a wide variety of routine and commonplace functions essential in the day-to-day living of every citizen. Problem solving applies mathematics to the world around us.

The current curriculum in mathematics emphasizes computational skills apart from their application. These skills are necessary tools, but tools should not determine the scope and sequence of the curriculum.

A full range of problem solving includes:
1. traditional concepts and techniques of computation applied to real-world problems
2. the use of mathematical symbolism to describe real-world relationships
3. the use of deductive and inductive reasoning to draw conclusions
4. methods of gathering, organizing, and interpreting data; drawing and testing inferences; and communicating results
5. the use of calculators in problem solving
6. the visualization and use of spatial concepts related to problem solving.

Students must learn to formulate key questions, to analyze and define problems, to discover patterns and similarities, and to transfer skills and strategies to new situations. They should be encouraged to have an open mind, to be willing to hypothesize, and to experiment. Problem solving should not be limited to a few pages of "word" or "story" problems scattered among many pages of drill and practice computation as is the practice in many of the current textbooks.

Emphasis in problem solving should be on understanding the processes involved rather than getting the answer. Unfortunately, answers, facts, and "content" rather than process have been the focus of the school mathematics programs most familiar to the student in teacher training.

PROCESS LEARNING

Instruction may be considered in terms of three aspects:

1. Content or knowledge aspects—parts of a flower, when Columbus discovered America

2. Affect aspects—emotional development, positive attitudes, and values
3. Process aspects—information processing capabilities.

It is the third or process aspect that is our prime concern in problem solving. Teachers have not had a guide for organizing process learning.

Recently emphasis has been placed on the thinking process itself. Three major efforts are worth pointing out:

(1) A taxonomy developed by a committee of the American Psychological Association (Bloom's Taxonomy)[2]

6. EVALUATION:	Devise a set of criteria and apply them to arrive at a judgment of quality (e.g., Which otter trap should we build?
5. SYNTHESIS:	Combine various parts of a system to form a unique whole as in solving a problem (e.g., design a humane otter trap to catch otters for redistribution).
4. ANALYSIS:	Identify the parts of a system and the relationships between parts (e.g., identify the contributors to pollution of a stream).
3. APPLICATION:	Employ knowledge in a situation which has not been practiced (e.g., use knowledge of map skills to plan a trip).
2. COMPREHENSION:	Alter knowledge slightly (e.g., by translating tables into graphs).
1. KNOWLEDGE:	Simply recognize or recall something.

Bloom's taxonomy has helped overcome the unfortunate tendency of teachers to organize most of their activities around the lower and simpler levels of thinking. It can help teachers organize activities for the upper levels of thinking. A disadvantage, however, is that the levels listed do not describe the necessary intellectual skills. Also, the developmental sequence in intellectual growth is quite different from Bloom's taxonomy of levels.

(2) A second major approach to process learning is the taxonomy developed by the American Association for the Advancement of Science.[3]

[2] Benjamin S. Bloom. *Taxonomy of Educational Objectives, Handbook I, Cognitive Domain.* New York: David McKay, 1956.
[3] *Science—A Process Approach: Commentary for Teachers.* Washington: American Association for the Advancement of Science, 1965.

SIMPLE:	1. Observing
	2. Classifying
	3. Using Space/Time Relations
	4. Using Numbers
	5. Communicating (graphs, diagrams, etc.)
	6. Measuring
	7. Inferring
	8. Predicting
INTEGRATED:	9. Formulating Hypotheses
	10. Defining Operationally
	11. Controlling Variables
	12. Interpreting Data
	13. Formulating Models
	14. Experimenting

(3) A Growth Plan. The plan of the American Association for the Advancement of Science considered processes of learning related to a single subject—science.

There is now a trend toward more generalized processes applicable to various fields of knowledge. Instead of "science" skills or "reading" skills or "math skills," for example, are there not "thinking" skills or thought processes that underlie necessary processes in each of these fields?

Jean Piaget has studied in great detail the thinking processes of children. These processes change as children grow older. While Piaget has provided a wealth of information relating to how children think, applying it to the classroom is yet to be done.

One approach to a growth plan is that of the Ontario (Canada) Institute for Studies in Education through its Thinking Materials Resource Center.[4] This Center is developing curriculum materials designed to improve the quality of children's thinking. It has developed a booklet titled *Basic Thinking Skills* and an accompanying manual titled "Manual for the Teaching of Basic Thinking Skills."

"Thinking" as an area for development is divided into nine major strands—observation, correlation, seriation, correspondence, proportional thinking, compensatory thinking, probability, classification, and logical multiplication. Curriculum materials for the strands—classification, seriation, and correspondence—have been developed and are in the Manual.

Thinking has been approached as a "task analysis" and divided into

---

[4] Niagra Centre, 187 Geneva St., St. Catherines, Ontario. (Phone: 684-8558.)

components called thinking "skills" for each of the strands listed above. "Skills" may be a misnomer but is here defined as the ability to use various mental or logical processes. For example, what specific thinking skills are necessary for the strand of classification?

This is a beginning toward applying Piaget to classroom activities. All of the nine strands listed are closely related to the thought structures in children which Piaget studied and has described in his writings. However, most of the program is not yet developed.

The following material on problem solving activities provides suggestions for a conventional program. Unfortunately they make no provision for stages of intellectual growth in children.

CLASSROOM ACTIVITIES FOR PROBLEM SOLVING IN THE PRIMARY GRADES

1. Techniques for solving problems in the primary grades include asking:
   (1) What does the problem ask for?
   (2) What facts does the problem give?
   (3) What processes will we need to use to solve the problem?
   Problems may be clarified with the use of:
   (1) concrete materials
   (2) pictures, films, graphs, diagrams
   (3) trips
   (4) informal dramatization of the problem
   (5) resource personnel
2. Developing a sequence for problem solving using phases such as the following:
   Phase 1—primarily oral, partly planned, partly spontaneous activities such as:
   > grouping of toys or objects, putting toys away
   > checking attendance, grouping
   > buying items at a store
   Planning problems such as:
   > "How many more chairs does our group need?"
   > "How many more days until . . .?"
   > "What refreshments do we need?"
   > "What do we need for our trip?" (time, miles, cost, etc.)

Phase 2—written problems using concrete materials (flannel and magnaboards)

Phase 3—using drawings and diagrams to solve written problems

Phase 4—abstractions (number sentences) such as $3 \times 3 = \square$ and $5 - 2 = \square$ for diagrams in phase 3.

3. Development of written solutions might proceed as follows:

Level 1—Jan has 4 apples.

She ate 2 of them.

How many apples has she now?

_____ - _____ = _____

Jan has _____ apples now.

Level 2—Mike has 14 blue cars and 3 red ones.

How many cars does he have altogether?

$14 + 3 = \square$

$14 + 3 = 17$

Level 3—Dave has some hockey cards. John gave him 17 more. He now has 38 cards. How many cards did he have in the beginning?

Let $\square$ represent the number of cards Dave had in the beginning.

$\square + 17 = 38$

$21 + 17 = 38$

$\square = 21$

Dave had 21 hockey cards in the beginning.

Level 4—Janet bought some bread for 27¢ and some milk for 34¢.

She gave the checkout girl $1.00. How much change will she get?

Let x represent Janet's change.

$100 - (27 + 34) = x$

$100 - 61 = x$

$100 - 61 = 39$

$x = 39$

Janet will receive 39¢ change.

At this point a definite solution format has been established, one which most textbooks and teachers expect children to follow, i.e.,

(a) Let x or □ represent the answer to be found
(b) then build an open number sentence to include the unknown, the known, and appropriate operation or operations
(c) find the solution to the sentence
(d) make a final statement which provides the answer to the problem.

CLASSROOM ACTIVITIES FOR PROBLEM SOLVING IN UPPER ELEMENTARY GRADES

1. Let children make up their own problems as a project (complete with solutions). These could be based on a hobby or interest, a walk to the boiler room or cafeteria, etc. The teacher may wish to give guidelines, e.g., include many addition and subtraction problems with numbers in the thousands.
2. Teacher and/or class can make up problems on class trips or projects, e.g., mileage, miles per gallon, cost per pupil, etc.
3. Write problems about a story—similar to creative writing.
4. Make a series of problems based on a neighborhood industry or construction site. Do research so these problems are based on as much fact as possible.
5. After making or reading graphs, make up problems about the facts.
6. Use problems with no numbers for two purposes.
   (a) Dave has some apples. His mother gave him some more. (Identify the operation.)
   (b) Advanced "fun problems" to develop logical thinking and organization, e.g.,
      cannibal, missionary problem
      finding counterfeit coins in limited weighings on balances
      toothpick problems
      finding all the triangles or other shapes in drawings
7. Different money problems, e.g., How many ways can you make 17¢?
8. *Estimations* are important. To encourage this, give many problems where children estimate the answers before solving the problems.

9. Solve some problems by *only* drawing pictures, no written words.
10. Use problems with missing or irrelevant data.
11. Use problems with the question missing.
12. Use problems where you can insist on two different solutions.
13. Use a "Problem a Day" in the back corner for children who really want a challenge. Good examples are often found in math paperbacks, party game books, and the children themselves will often bring them in if you initiate it.
14. Encourage critical thinking about problems in textbooks, e.g., "Susan walked 3 blocks in 5 minutes. How long would it take her to walk 60 blocks?" *Who would want to walk 60 blocks?*
15. Restate a problem with different numbers.
16. Use problems with different solutions to the same question.

EXERCISES

1. Compare Bloom's taxonomy and the taxonomy of the American Association for the Advancement of Science from the standpoint of their use in problem solving in a math class at both the primary and upper elementary grade levels.
2. Make up a problem for each of the six levels shown in Bloom's taxonomy chart.
3. Make up some problems and describe accompanying charts, graphs, or concrete materials that might aid children in solving the problems.
4. Analyze one or more of the nine strand topics listed in "A Growth Plan" and as described in the writings of Piaget. Describe how that topic could be applied to an elementary school math program. (The topics of correspondence (one-to-one) and seriation are dealt with in Piaget's *The Child's Conception of Number*. The topic of classification and logical multiplication are dealt with in Piaget's *The Early Growth of Logic in the Child*.)
5. Make up a problem for each of the basic operations—addition, subtraction, multiplication, and division. Indicate grade or grades for which appropriate.

12

THE CALCULATOR IN THE CLASSROOM

INTRODUCTION TO THE CALCULATOR

In 1972 electronic companies introduced the four function hand-held calculator at retail prices of around $200. Within four years more durable calculators were available for less than $10. In 1978 the National Assessment of Educational Progress[1] reported that three out of four nine year olds have access to at least one calculator. Yet in 1980 there were still few calculators in the schools. Basal textbook series have not integrated calculators into their programs.

Will the schools ignore the development of the calculator as an instructional tool or capitalize on it? Those favoring total prohibition of the use of the hand or pocket calculator in the elementary school include many parents and teachers. Their position is based on the idea that the calculator is a "crutch" and that its use will discourage children from learning the basic number facts. Reys[2] reports that 80 per cent of elementary school teachers said calculators should be available to children but cite standardized tests which stress paper and pencil computation as the principal reason for not using calculators.

Children should learn and commit to memory the basic number facts. Calculators do not solve a basic fact problem such as 3 + 8 = 11 as quickly as it can be done if memorized. To solve this problem on a

[1] Robert E. Reys: "Calculators in the Elementary Classrooms," *The Arithmetic Teacher,* Nov. 1980, pp. 38–39.
[2] *Ibid.*

hand calculator involves 4 motions: 3, +, 8, =. But for a problem such as 354 + 78 or 32 × 76, the calculator comes into its own in terms of speed and accuracy of solution.

A primary concern has been that children would not learn their basic facts or computational procedures if calculators are used too soon. Statewide math assessment tests are revealing that it is not the basic facts or computations that are the biggest problem but rather understanding and being able to solve real world or "word" problems.

In our emphasis on basic drill and computation in math instruction, that is, learning and relearning the complicated step by step procedures (algorisms) for solving addition, subtraction, multiplication, and division problems, the goal has been quick and accurate solution. Some 75 per cent of the math instruction time in the elementary school is spent on computational procedures.

Even our behavioral objectives are designed to "get answers," being couched in such phrases as "Given any two single-digit addends the learner will write the sum." A pedagogical problem in the preceding statement is the word "given." If the child is "given" the input for the problem, what has he learned? Certainly not how to set up the problem in terms of what numbers are needed and what operation or operations are necessary.

To solve a math problem from the real world involves much more than computation. Computation is only the last step or next-to-last step, the last step being an evaluation of whether the answer is reasonable or not, based on an estimate or approximation of what the answer should be. It is worth examining our math textbooks to see what percentage is devoted to word problems and what percentage to drill and practice on computation.

If children do not have to spend so much time "computing," they can spend more time on how the problem should be set up, what operation or operations are called for and whether the answer appears to be reasonable. This is closer to the nature of learning mathematics and also closer to the nature of the kind of problem the child faces in real life. Calculators can do much to replace the routine and boring part of mathematics—lengthy computation.

Relative to the criticism of "dependence" on the calculator, can you do the problem 73 × 872 without a paper and pencil? Are you not "dependent" on paper and pencil? Is it any easier to keep paper and pencil at hand than a calculator? Then, too, some children will never be successful at solving problems such as 1869 ÷ 72 on paper using the conventional algorism. Should they be denied the use of a calculator?

Is it not more significant that they know when to divide and what to divide by than that they be able to execute a long step-by-step procedure for computing the answer?

Food for thought is a statement by Shumway[3] that

> Arabic numerals, zero, paper and pencil algorisms, and so on were not introduced to teach mathematics but to make calculations easier. The hand-held calculator was invented for the same reason.

It has been said that taking a calculator to math class is like taking field glasses along on a hike. Calculators can be used to **understand** math concepts rather than just to **apply** concepts. That calculators can be used to teach understanding will be seen in exercises to follow.

Instructional Materials on How to Use the Calculator

Children learn how to use the calculator very quickly—usually within the first hour—with at most a worksheet that confronts them with various possibilities appropriate to their grade level. They tend to learn mostly about operations they are already familiar with. If they are not familiar with division, for example, they simply ignore that key. They learn from the machine and from each other with new ideas and shortcuts quickly shared. Time probably should not be spent on film strips, cassettes, and so on, which simply "show" how to use the calculator.

Interest in Using the Calculator

There is usually high initial interest in using the calculator, which persists over a long time if students are given interesting things to do. They even demand to be given things to do. The problem exercises and games that follow give some examples that can be used. The problem with conventional math textbook series is that they have few interesting things to do that exploit the power the calculator provides.

Should students work independently or with each other in solving a set of problems? Two college methods classes were introduced to the use of the calculator by the writer. One class did not respond nearly as well to a page handout of problems to be explored individually

---

[3] Richard Shumway: "Hand Calculators: Where Do You Stand?" *The Arithmetic Teacher*, Nov. 1976, p. 570.

as did the other class, in which the problems were tackled one by one by the entire class, information shared, and questions asked. Self-directed work did not seem to be as much fun or as interesting as shared problems.

Grade Level and the Calculator

The meaning of counting should be introduced by placing the counting numbers in one-to-one correspondence with sets of objects as is usually done. But it is interesting to discover later how to count with the calculator by pressing 1, +, =, =, =, $\cdots$

The calculator to the child is a toy that says, "Come, play with me." It really means "Learn with me."

The basic single-digit addition and subtraction facts can often be obtained more quickly with our fingers as a computer than with the hand calculator. Committing the answers to memory provides an even faster way and is the best way. Suggested teaching procedures to introduce and finally arrive at memorized answers for the basic facts have been described in the chapters on the basic operations.

Children should be introduced to the basic operations of addition, subtraction, multiplication, and division as described in preceding chapters, that is, with concrete objects being joined, separated, divided, and so on. Number operations should be related to sets of objects if word problems are to be understood. The calculator can, however, serve as a recorder of what has been done or is to be done with the objects or pictures of objects. For example, a set of 3 objects and a set of 4 objects, if joined, will make how many? Or, two football teams will require how many helmets?

By manipulating sets of objects, the basic arithmetical operations are related to things of the physical world, creating what are in effect word problems or problems dealing with things in our environment. The hand calculator can then furnish the teacher with a quick answer as to whether the meanings and purpose of the basic operations and place value have been learned.

Just when to begin and how much calculators should be used will depend on the philosophy and ability of the teacher. But they should be used more and more as children move through the middle and upper elementary grades, so that the emphasis can be on problem solving rather than computation. Having children practice computation may improve computational speed but not speed in solving word problems.

And if computational speed is our objective rather than solving word problems, the calculator is faster.

Some of the advantages often listed for using the calculator in the classroom are:

1. Calculator use encourages discovery and exploration of number problems.
2. It checks or verifies answers.
3. It provides instant feedback.
4. It provides a video approach for practice in the basic facts.

Low achievers enjoy working with Dataman[4] and the Lil Professor.[5]

Estimation or Approximation of Answers

Considerable attention should be paid to approximating or estimating what the answer should be before solving a problem rather than just writing down what the calculator says is the answer. Errors made when using the calculator, such as pressing the wrong key, are often large. If an approximation of what the answer should be has been made, the error is then obvious and provides immediate confirmation (or non-confirmation) of the answer.

"Checking" with a Calculator Problems Done by Hand

Some educators hold that the calculator should be used only to check problems done conventionally. But using the calculator only to check hard computations teaches the child little if anything about mathematics. It may overemphasize the importance of the one right answer. Similarly, using the calculator to perform component steps of a paper-and-pencil algorism such as long division is like using a good watch to check a sun dial.[6]

Teachers may think that in having children do many computation problems they are teaching an understanding of a process such as addi-

[4] Manufactured by Texas Instruments.
[5] Ibid.
[6] A. Kesner and T. Slesnick: "Myths About Calculators in the Schools." *Calculators Computers Magazine,* Sept.–Oct. 1978, p. 78.

tion when in fact all that is being learned is a procedure, process, or algorism for getting the correct answer, and a slow one at that.[7]

Why do we put great emphasis on practice of basic computational algorisms such as long division? To get the right answer quickly. Would not the calculator do a better job?

Order of Operations

In solving problems involving two or more "steps" or operations such as 5 + 2 × 8, one person may solve as 7 × 8 = 56 and another as 5 + 16 = 21. Who is right?

Mathematicians have agreed on certain rules concerning the order of operations—that is, first multiply and divide, then add and subtract. Some call this the "My Dear Aunt Sally rule"—MDAS or "multiply, divide, add, subtract" for ease in remembering the order.

In solving an equation:

1. Work from left to right performing each multiplication and division operation as you come to it.
2. Go back and work from left to right again performing each addition and subtraction operation as you come to it.

$$5 \ + 2 \times 8$$
$$= 5 \ + (2 \times 8)$$
$$= 5 + 16$$
$$= 21$$

Similarly,

$$46 - 3 \times 2 + 8 \div 4 \times 5$$
$$= 46 - 6 + 8 \div 4 \times 5$$
$$= 46 - 6 + 2 \times 5$$
$$= 46 - 6 + 10$$
$$= 40 + 10$$
$$= 50$$

Parentheses are sometimes used to indicate which operations should be done first.

[7] *Ibid.*

For example,

$$46 - 3 \times 2 + 8 \div 4 \times 5$$
$$= 46 - (3 \times 2) + ((8 \div 4) \times 5)$$

PLACE VALUE ACTIVITIES

Many of the problems children have in mathematics are due to their lack of understanding of place value. Following are some practice and exploratory activities.

1. Press 1, +, =, =, =   What will appear after 9? after 19, after 99?
2. Can you predict the next number? 0 + 10 =, =, =, · · · How many times to display 250?
3. "Beat the calc" game—one child solves the problem on the calculator, the other solves the problem mentally or on paper. A third person draws cards with numbers expressed in standard notation.
   - a. 20 + 3   Calculator solves as 2, 0, +, 3, =
   - b. 30 + 5
   - c. 80 + 4
   - d. 100 + 20 + 4
   - e. 4000 + 300 + 20 + 1
   - f. 10 × 2
   - g. 3 × 100
   - h. 35 × 10
   - i. 400 ÷ 100
   - j. 740 ÷ 10
   - k. 4600 ÷ 100
4. Using only the keys with numerals on them and
   - a. using one key once, what is the largest number you can get? the smallest?
   - b. using two keys once or the same key twice, what is the largest number? the smallest?
   - c. using any key or keys as many times as you want, what is the largest number? the smallest?
   - d. if children have studied decimal fractions, include the decimal key for *b* and *c*.
   - e. find a number smaller than .004 other than zero.

5. "Wipe-out" game—children take turns making a number vanish from their calculator displays. Clear key may not be used.
   a. Press 307   Replace 7 with 0 (by subtracting seven).
   b. Press 384   Replace 8 with 0.
   c. Press 4281   Wipe out the 4.
6. Enter each of the following:
   a. three hundred forty-five
   b. three thousand forty
   c. four hundred nine
   d. thirty-two hundred seven
   e. for students who have studied decimal fractions,
      (1) fifty and forty thousandths
      (2) four and twenty-seven hundredths
7. Round off to nearest thousand
   a. 12415
   b. 12642
   c. 14875
   d. 24862

COMPUTATION AND NUMBER THEORY ACTIVITIES

1. Generate the counting numbers 1, 2, 3, $\cdots$
   Try 1 + 1 = , + 1 =, + 1, =
   Also try 1 + =, =, =, $\cdots$
   And + 1 =, =, =, $\cdots$
   Now generate the even numbers 2, 4, 6, $\cdots$
   Then 10, 20, 30, $\cdots$
2. Generate the fifth multiplication table.
   Try 5 × 1 =, 2 =, 3 =, $\cdots$
   Then generate the seventh multiplication table.
3. Nim (game for two people, one calculator)
   a. Take turns pressing either 1 +, 2 +, or 3 +. Winner presses the number to get 21.
   b. Take turns pressing any counting number 1–9 and +. Target number: 67.
4. Game—"Before"
   Press 1 - = . Then key in a number such as 10 and ask a stu-

dent what will appear when you press =. (9). How about if we press = again? (8)

Try variations such as 5 − .

5. Basic computation practice
   a. $3 + 5 =$ d. $324 + 37 =$
   b. $3 \times 5 =$ e. $45 \div 9 =$
   c. $32 \times 56 =$ f. $423 \div 7 =$

6. Find the missing numeral.
   a. $3 + 8 + 7 - \square = 5$
   b. $35 + 72 - \square = 27$
   c. $36 \times \square = 785$
   d. $253 \times 76 = \square$
   e. $910 \div \square = 26$

7. Find the missing numerals.

   a.   45   b. $\square$26   c.   6 9 4 2
        8$\square$ 5$\square$8   1$\square\square\square$
        $\square$6   12$\square$ 1 2 9 0
       ─────   ─────   ─────
        161   1093   10 2 0 0

8. "Broken key" game
   a. 6 key is broken. Display 361.
   b. 8 and + keys are broken. Display 588.
   c. +, −, 6 keys are broken. Display 36.

9. How many cards in this set? 1, 8, 15, 22, · · · 113

10. Generate each of the counting numbers 1 to 6 using the keys 4, $\times$, $\div$, +, −, = . For example, to generate 1, divide 4 by 4.

11. Fewest key strokes.
    a. Target number, 24. Legal keys 2, +, −, $\times$, $\div$, = .
       Primary grades might do as $2 + 2 =$. Shorter $22 + 2 =$
    b. Target number, 24. Legal keys 4, +, −, $\times$, $\div$, = .
    c. Target number, 17. Legal keys 5, +, $\times$, −, $\div$, = .

12. $5 + 3 \times 7 - 2 = \square$ Answer 24 (See p. 227)

13. a. Which is smaller, $\dfrac{8}{11}$ or $\dfrac{9}{12}$?

    b. Enter a common fraction that, converted to decimal notation, produces a single repeating numeral, then one that repeats in pairs.

    c. Enter a fraction that does not repeat (in the calculator display).

13

THE EXCEPTIONAL CHILD AND MATHEMATICS[1]

This chapter is designed to provide the regular classroom teacher with basic information concerning mathematics instruction for the exceptional student. Specific objectives are:

1. To develop a rationale for serving the exceptional student in the regular classroom.
2. To provide basic information concerning the nature and needs of exceptional youngsters likely to be involved in the mainstream.
3. To provide an overview of current practices and procedures for mainstream programming of such students.
4. To develop a basic understanding of assessment procedures.
5. To provide specific programming recommendations for curriculum design, strategies, materials.

INTRODUCTION

The trend in providing special education services to handicapped students, stimulated by current federal requirements, is to educate youngsters in what is termed "the least restrictive environment." Very simply explained, this practice involves structuring the child's environment in such a way as to permit his/her successful functioning in as close to a

[1] This chapter was written by Barbara Grasso Ehren. Exceptional Child Education Department, Florida Atlantic University.

normal setting as possible. Federal law, in fact, requires that "to the maximum extent appropriate handicapped children . . . are educated with children who are not handicapped."[2] For many handicapped students this means spending time in the mainstream of education, the regular classroom. To the regular elementary school teacher this practice will likely involve mathematics instruction of children with various exceptionalities.

While many teachers at first react hesitantly to serving handicapped students in the regular classroom, they are often surprised at how well many of these children do in the mainstream. One of the keys to the child's success is the supportive classroom teacher who, with assistance, learns to understand the child's strengths and weaknesses and to make modifications in the learning environment. Many teachers come to the realization that many handicapped learners function at the same instructional level as the non-handicapped youngsters.

EXCEPTIONALITIES

To this point, the discussion has dealt with the handicapped. It should be noted that the broader term "exceptional" refers to those individuals whose needs cannot be adequately served without some form of special education. Included in this population are the gifted and talented as well as individuals with various handicapping conditions. Although the special needs of the gifted and the talented cannot be overlooked and will be dealt with to some degree, the emphasis in this chapter is on serving handicapped learners.

This latter group includes the mentally retarded, hard of hearing, deaf, speech and language impaired, visually handicapped, emotionally disturbed, orthopedically impaired, other health impaired, deaf-blind, multi-handicapped, and those with specific learning disabilities. Within all of these exceptionalities, there exists a range of severity from mild to severe, defined by the degree to which these youngsters are handicapped by specific impairments. Classroom teachers are likely to encounter children in the mild to moderate range, with most mainstreamed youngsters being mildly handicapped. Most commonly, they will serve the learning disabled, the educable mentally retarded, the emotionally handicapped, the speech and language impaired, and those

[2]PL 94–142

THE EXCEPTIONAL CHILD AND MATHEMATICS

physically handicapped children (such as hearing impaired, visually impaired, orthopedically impaired and other health impaired) whose needs can be met in the regular classroom.

The Learning Disabled

Learning-disabled children are children of average or above average intelligence who have specific problems in learning related to a disorder in one or more of the basic psychological processes. These problems are typically manifested in failure to achieve academically according to ability. In light of the current emphasis on identifying and serving this population, these children will be seen frequently by the regular classroom teacher.

It is important for the teacher to understand that these youngsters are not mentally retarded. Most important is the notion that the learning-disabled youngster presents his/her own individual pattern of abilities and disabilities; it is very difficult to describe general characteristics. Some youngsters may be performing two grade levels behind expectancy in reading and yet be at grade level in math. Some have equally severe difficulties in math and reading, while others may exhibit strengths in mathematics performance. Learning styles will vary. Some children will learn math facts better by listening to drill tapes; others need to use flash cards.

Of the many specific areas of difficulty encountered by learning-disabled youngsters some problems have a direct impact on mathematics learning. A **visual perceptual problem,** for example, may interfere with a child's ability to keep his/her place while doing math work, especially if he/she has to copy from the board. This problem is often manifested by the following types of errors:

(a) Incorrect copying of the problem:

$$\begin{array}{r} 15 \\ +12 \\ \hline \end{array} \quad \text{becomes} \quad \begin{array}{r} 15 \\ +\ 12 \\ \hline \end{array}$$

(b) Putting the answer in the wrong place:

$$\begin{array}{r} 3 \\ +1 \\ \hline \end{array} \qquad \begin{array}{r} 4 \\ +2 \\ \hline 4 \end{array}$$

(c) Misplacing the decimal in money problems:

$3.00 becomes $30.

Other types of visual perceptual difficulties may involve difficulties in discriminating likenesses and differences as well as spatial relationships and directionality. Failure to learn concepts of big/small, long/short, left/right may be related to inability to discriminate the differences perceptually. Many youngsters make errors related to reversal or inversion of numbers:

5 is perceived as 3 (type of reversal).
6 is perceived as 9 (type of inversion).

Another common problem is **lack of time orientation**. Learning various mathematical concepts involving time may be difficult for some. Such a problem will also be manifested in behavior that teachers often interpret as poor work habits, i.e., failure to complete tasks, not completing tasks on time. These behaviors may actually be related to lack of time concept rather than contrariness.

Children may also be **distracted** by irrelevant stimuli in the environment and may not be able to concentrate on the task at hand. This difficulty is most often seen when the child is doing independent seat work.

Many children have **memory problems**. They may understand math concepts and processes, but may not be able to recall basic facts or processes quickly. If given a calculator, some of these children may even become quite good at problem solving.

A child with **motor control difficulties** may have a difficult time performing written work. It may take such a child a long time to complete written responses. Such behaviors as shakiness of handwriting, too little or too much pencil pressure, or tight pencil grip may be observed.

Other common problems of learning-disabled youngsters may be more related to **abstract reasoning difficulties**. At a lower level of performance, a child may have difficulty relating to a numeral as representing a number concept. For example, the child may see the numeral "4," be able to say it and write it, but may be unable to count out four objects to demonstrate understanding of the meaning. At a higher level, especially with regard to complex operations and problem solving, the child may find it difficult to manipulate symbols in his/her head and may just not be able to "put it all together". A child having such difficulties may be able to solve a verbal problem if the solution is demonstrated step by step, but may not be successful at coordinating all phases without assistance.

For those children with **language-based learning disabilities,** math vocabulary (e.g., What does "plus" mean? What does "subtraction" mean?) may be difficult. Typically these youngsters will learn simple computation processes and facts more easily than problem-solving strategies since the latter set of skills requires manipulation of language structures and concepts.

The teacher must also keep constantly aware of the impact of **reading disabilities** on performance in mathematics. If a child cannot read the directions or read a problem to be solved, his/her success in math tasks requiring reading will be thwarted. Such performance may not adequately reflect the child's abilities in mathematics.

The Mentally Retarded

These children have reduced intellectual functioning, i.e., their mental ability is below what would be expected of a youngster of their age. Additionally, they lack what is termed "adaptive behavior," the ability to adjust to various changes in the environment and to function both independently and in social situations. The degree of retardation will determine the extent to which the mentally retarded child is below chronological age expectations.

Regarding the **mildly mentally retarded** or **educable mentally retarded,** although criteria may vary from state to state, a ballpark range is an IQ of 50 to 70. In considering the academic achievement of mentally retarded youngsters, one must use the child's **mental age** (derived from the IQ test), using $IQ = \dfrac{MA}{CA} \times 100$, not his chronological age, as a reference point. Caution must always be taken, however, in attaching a mental age equivalent to a child as absolute truth. The mental age is derived from intelligence tests which are at best fallible. Perhaps the most significant problem experienced is that teachers often lower expectation levels of performance to align with the IQ number, often despite the progress of the student.

Although it cannot be overemphasized that the term "mild mental retardation" is not synonymous with "learning disabilities," many problems in mathematics learning are shared by both the mildly mentally retarded and the learning disabled. The mentally retarded child typically presents a more even profile of strengths and weaknesses, not evidencing the degrees of discrepancy of the learning disabled.

The Emotionally Handicapped

These youngsters have persistent and consistent **personality** or **psychological adjustment problems** over time. Their presenting behaviors may be of an aggressive, acting-out variety or they may show more withdrawal. In any case, these behaviors are likely to be counterproductive to school functioning, with lack of academic progress typically resulting. In practice, it is often difficult to ascertain whether underlying learning disability may be at the root of emotional disorders. The most glaring area of difficulty that the classroom teacher will likely encounter with this group is managing counterproductive behaviors. The emotionally handicapped youngster may not stay in his seat, may talk out and be generally disruptive, may not complete tasks. He often has a poor self-concept, may have negative attitudes toward school and may have difficulties in interacting with peers.

Other Handicapping Conditions

The problems of the speech-impaired will not likely impact mathematical functioning per se. However, those students with a **primary language disorder**, who would, in most instances, be considered learning disabled, will present those language-based difficulties described previously.

Physically handicapped youngsters such as the **hard of hearing** and **deaf, visually handicapped, orthopedically impaired,** and **other health impaired** present a wide variety of characteristics. It is beyond the scope and intent of this chapter to delve into the specific nature of these impairments. It is hoped that the strategies described later may prove helpful for these youngsters. Although many physically handicapped children will be served in the regular classroom, it is expected that the teacher will receive specific information regarding the nature of the handicap from special education personnel. Perhaps the single most important concept for classroom teachers to realize regarding the physically handicapped is that a physical handicap in no way implies mental deficiency. A normally intelligent hard-of-hearing child with adequate use of language will have no problem understanding math as long as he receives the necessary information through the senses. An orthopedically handicapped child (perhaps with cerebral palsy) who has normal intelligence may be terrific in learning math processes even though his fine motor difficulties make it very difficult to use manipulative aids or to write answers.

Assessment Considerations

A key issue in the mainstreaming of handicapped students relates to assessing their level of functioning as well as diagnosing specific areas of strength and weakness in mathematics. It is important, therefore, to consider both achievement tests and diagnostic procedures.

An overall consideration regarding assessment deals with performance on group versus individually administered tests. Many handicapped children do more poorly on group math tests than classroom performance would predict. Several factors may be related:

1. The child may not be used to working in large groups and may become distracted or feel too insecure to perform optimally.
2. The child may not be used to working with a speed component, e.g., on a timed test.
3. The visual format of the test may be confusing, e.g., too much on a page, items too small, confusing layout design.
4. The child may not be able to understand directions or he may not be able to read the directions.
5. The use of an answer key to bubble in responses may be a new experience or may be too confusing.
6. The math problems on the test may be mixed frequently and the child may not be able to switch rapidly from one type of problem to another.

With these potential problems in mind, teachers should be cautious about interpreting achievement results. A word of caution in the opposite direction: Some group tests in computing total scores may yield an overall grade level of achievement higher than the child's actual instructional level.

Individually administered tests are likely to produce more accurate achievement results as long as content validity is intact. This type of test is often administered as part of the evaluation procedures prior to placement in special education. Two commonly used tests in this category for math achievement are the Peabody Individual Achievement Test—PIAT (Dunn & Workwardt, 1970) and the Wide Range Achievement Tests—WRAT (Jastak and Jastak, 1965). Each of these instruments has a subtest to assess mathematics.

However, in the area of diagnostic work in mathematics, the most widely used instrument is the Key Math Diagnostic Arithmetic Test (Connolly, Nachtmann and Pritchett, 1971). This test has 14 subtests divided into three areas: content, operations, and application. It is designed for kindergarten to eighth grade and yields a profile of strengths and weaknesses that is helpful in planning math instruction.

Growing in popularity is the use of criterion-referenced assessment procedures to pinpoint specific skills which may need attention. Teachers typically find that this kind of assessment provides a practical base for program planning. The Brigance Diagnostic Inventory of Basic Skills (Brigume, 1976) is a criterion-referenced instrument used widely. It assesses math skills from kindergarten through sixth grade in the areas of numbers, operations, measurement, and geometry.

Classroom teachers are urged to use informal assessment procedures to assist in pinpointing areas of skill strength and weakness for purposes of instruction. The use of error analysis in uncovering patterns of error is extremely helpful in planning teaching strategies.

Donna Lynn, age nine, studies an item from the Key Math Diagnostic Arithmetic Test.

PROGRAMMING CONSIDERATIONS

Planning Mathematics Instruction

Current practices in providing special education for handicapped students require the writing and implementation of an Individualized Educational Program (IEP) for each student. The elementary classroom teacher should be a part of the planning of the educational goals for the child. If the child is to spend time in the regular classroom, the classroom teacher will participate in implementing a program.

Decisions need to be made with regard to math instruction. Who will do what and for what length of time? What curriculum changes should be made? What specific skills *must* a child have at a given grade level? Which ones can he live without? What should the order of skill presentation be? Does the child need more functional skill development? What strategies and materials are appropriate?

These decisions must in all cases depend on the individual needs of the child. They will not be made on the basis of any given exceptionality label, but on the given child's profile of behavior and skills. For example, it makes no sense to talk about a math curriculum for the mentally regarded; rather, one decides what skills *this* mentally retarded child needs.

Strategies for Teaching

1. Be certain that directions are stated in clear, simple language. Directions should not be at a level of difficulty higher than the content to be tapped. For children with reading difficulties this factor is especially important.
2. Specify where any given breakdown is occurring. It is not sufficient, for example, to note that a child cannot do long division accurately. The question is: At what point in the process is the error being made?
3. Analyze a skill into its component parts. Divide into small steps. Divise an order of progression for the child to use in computation or problem solving, e.g., first do this, next do this, etc.
4. If the child gets confused with visual format,
   (a) make dittos with fewer items, fold or tear existing worksheets and give a child one section at a time.

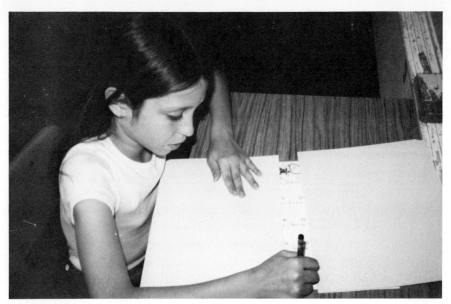

Two sheets of oak tag are used to mask out problems thus helping the child to attend to fewer items at a time.

      (b) let the child use a masking device, such as a piece of cardboard, or paper to cover items to be completed later.

      (c) mark boundaries of problems with heavy marker lines.

      (d) make sure prepared materials are clear and well done.

5. For children who have reading difficulties, record problems to be solved on cassette tapes.

6. Use color coding, to highlight operations or processes, such as +, -, X, ÷ in red; or code steps in long division in different colors.

7. For children who are easily distracted, alter the physical environment slightly to assist them. Turn furniture around, use a study carrel.

8. Give tasks in shorter segments. E.g., if the activity would ordinarily take twenty minutes to complete but the child only has a ten-minute attention span, give half the work, let the child turn it in, and only after that give the second half.

9. Avoid tackling two problems at once. Do not give a worksheet reinforcing a new concept while requiring completion within a short time limit if the child either has trouble with that concept or has difficulty operating in that time frame.

10. Do add a realistic time limit to practice of a skill the child has

          THE EXCEPTIONAL CHILD AND MATHEMATICS

Working in a study carrel helps Beth, age nine, to concentrate without distraction. Her work with money problems is aided by the use of real coins.

Positioning a desk facing a wall or board helps many children to attend to tasks.

already mastered, being careful to avoid boring or frustrating the child.

11. Allow child to use aids: counting on fingers, math tables, calculators.

12. Regarding point 11: If you target quick recall of facts as an objective, handle it apart from computation or problem-solving objectives. That is, do fact drills at one time, but let the child use aids in computing or problem-solving activities. Maybe later, as the child progresses, you will be able to combine both sets of skills.

13. Use the Language Master to write math facts and record verbally. The child plays back the card, sees and hears the fact, and repeats it.

14. For children who learn well through auditory means, reinforce math facts with auditory tapes.

15. Teach concepts and computation in context of functional use, e.g., trading baseball cards to teach missing addend.

16. Vary the kinds of activities. Not all math has to be done with paper and pencil. Try having the child work at the board; use portable lap boards, an overhead projector.

17. Plan varied movement patterns. Do ten math problems; get up;

The Language Master may be used for aiding recall of math facts.

THE EXCEPTIONAL CHILD AND MATHEMATICS

Board work provides an opportunity for changing activity type, as well as physical movement possibilities.

This math game station may be used for two to five youngsters at a time, as a math skill reinforcement activity.

sharpen pencil; do ten more problems; turn in paper; go to chalkboard, etc.

18. Set up math stations with math reinforcement games.
19. Assign the child to a math buddy who can assist him/her without doing the work for him; or, if the handicapped child is the one good in math, let him/her be the buddy.
20. Praise liberally for effort and achievement demonstrated, but be specific in stating reasons, e.g., rather than using too general praise such as "Good girl," state the specific behavior that is being noted, such as "I like the way you finished all ten problems in fifteen minutes."

The Gifted Child

Definitions of the gifted vary widely. Various combinations of intelligence (usually above 120 IQ) and creativity are utilized as criteria. In any case, this group includes children of above average intellectual potential.

Math programming for the gifted is usually one of two types: **vertical,** which entails progression to a higher or more advanced content level; or **horizontal,** which means expansion at a particular level in order to provide wider, more in-depth knowledge of a particular concept or process.

While many teachers enjoy teaching gifted children because they learn readily, these children can often create problems if not treated appropriately. Gifted children often become bored when work is repetitive and unchallenging. Boredom then creates the need for stimulation, which often takes the form of disruptive behavior in the classroom. Therefore, a worthwhile method for teaching gifted children is individualized math programming, which can be geared to horizontal and/or vertical learning in conjunction with the regular program. There are many creative programs that may challenge the gifted child if tailored to his individual abilities. The only category of activity to be avoided is "busy work." Gifted children not only recognize the nature of "extra" practice sheets, but may be insulted by them.

Many teachers involve gifted children as "buddies" for other children having difficulty with mathematics. While this approach can be rewarding for both children, the teacher should remember that the gifted child is not a substitute for the teacher and, though gifted, may not make a good teacher. Being "smart" may involve being impatient with and then disliked by other members of the class.

Activities for the gifted may include setting up a mathematical learn-

THE EXCEPTIONAL CHILD AND MATHEMATICS

ing station or stations which can be changed frequently for variety. Stations serve as independent study sources and can be utilized to stimulate gifted children, especially if other members of the class are doing repetitive or drill work.

Sample activities to include at the stations are:

1. Activity sheets with metric measurement tools and items to be measured.
2. "Problem for the Day": a specific mathematical problem to be worked out and placed in a "Solution Box."
3. Manipulative inquiry: printed problems to be solved using an abacus, Cuisenaire rods, number blocks, tangrams, geoboards, etc. (See Chapter 17 for other ideas).
4. Various commercially produced or teacher-made games with objectives, directions, and rules specified. (Ideas may be gotten from various books on math games. Also see pp. 247-251.)
5. Computer investigation: functions, uses, principles of operation to be either implemented or discovered by the student.

EXERCISES

1. Visit an exceptional child class.
   (a) Note materials used for arithmetic.
   (b) Observe a mathematics lesson.
   (c) Record specific behaviors of different children.
   (d) Ask the special education teacher questions regarding the lesson and behavior of the children.
2. Visit a school and tutor an exceptional child. Report on the experience.
3. Plan a lesson for a gifted child.
4. Send for and evaluate catalogues from vendors who carry special math materials. (Following is a partial list).

American Guidance Service (AGS)
Publishers Building
Circle Pines, MN 55014

BFA Educational Media
2211 Michigan Ave.
P.O. Box 1795
Santa Monica, CA 90406

C.C. Publications Inc.
P.O. Box 23699
Tigard, OR 97223

Centurion Industries, Inc.
167 Constitution Drive
Menlo Park, CA 94025

The Continental Press, Inc.
Elizabethtown, PA 17022

Curriculum Associates, Inc.
5 Esquire Road
North Billerica, MA 01862

Developmental Learning Materials (DLM)
7440 Natchez Avenue
Niles, IL 60648

Educational Performance Associates, Inc.
(Milton Bradley)
600 Board Avenue
Ridgefield, NJ 07657

Educational Teaching Aids (ETA)
159 West Kenzie Street
Chicago, IL 60610

Ideal School Supply Company
11000 South Lavergne Avenue
Oak Laron, IL 60453

Mafex Associates, Inc.
90 Cherry Street
Johnstown, PA 15907

Modern Education Corporation
P.O. Box 721
Tulsa, OK 74101

Opportunities for Learning, Inc.
8950 Lurline Avenue, Dept. W9440
Chatsworth, CA 91311

Science Research Associates, Inc. (SRA)
155 N. Wacker Drive
Chicago, IL 60606

Teachers Market Place
16220 Orange Avenue
Paramount, CA 90723

Teaching Resources Corp.
50 Pond Park Road
Hingham, MA 02043

THE EXCEPTIONAL CHILD AND MATHEMATICS

SUGGESTED MATERIALS

Assessment Materials

See page 246 for addresses of companies.
Basic Arithmetic Skill Evaluation
(diagnostic and prescriptive system, grades 1-6—Opportunities for Learning, Inc.)
Brigance Diagnostic Inventory of Basic Skills
(a criterion-referenced instrument that includes math skills, K-6—Curriculum Associates, Inc.)
Classroom Mathematics Diagnosis System
(assessment tests, teaching strategies, practice sheets, learning center ideas—Opportunities for Learning, Inc.)
Key Math Diagnostic Arithmetic Tests and Key Math Metric Supplement
(individual assessment of arithmetic skills, K-6—American Guidance Service)
Kraner Preschool Math Inventory
(criterion-referenced assessment of basic math skills and concepts, ages 3-6½—Teaching Resources)

Math Programs

See page 246 for addresses of companies.
Arithmetic Fact Kit
(practice cards in basics, SRA)
Change Maker
(program for change-making skills—Opportunities for Learning, Inc.)
Chip Trading Activities
(program using a natural approach to learning basic math concepts—Opportunities for Learning, Inc.)
Computational Skills Laboratory I (grades 1-3) and II (grades 4-6)
(pre/post tests, activity cards; skill book presents basic computational skills—SRA)
Distar Arithmetic
(structured basal program, grades K-3—SRA)
Early Math
(self-discovery approach to primary math using cassettes, workbooks—Opportunities for Learning, Inc.)
Experiences in Number Readiness
(manipulative readiness materials—Milton Bradley)
Goal: Mathematical Concepts
(readiness activity kit—Milton Bradley)
Grocery Shopping Kit
(hands-on practice of basic skills using real life shopping activities—ETA)
How to Solve Story Problems and Moving Up in Story Problem
(activity cards—DLM)

How to Tell Time
  (complete time telling program—Opportunities for Learning, Inc.)
IDM—Independent Drill for Mastery
  (math computation drill program with audio tapes and duplicating masters—DLM)
Mathematics Involvement Program
  (manipulative experiences in math concepts—SRA)
Math House Proficiency Review Tapes
  (self-teaching audio cassettes with duplicating masters—Mafex)
Oregon Math Computation
  (basic computation program—C.C. Publications, Inc.)
Oregon Math Story Problems for Non-Readers
  (beginning level story problem solving—C.C. Publications, Inc.)
Remedial Arithmetic
  (aural-oral cassette program in basic math facts and skills—Opportunities for Learning, Inc.)
Starting Off With Numbers
  (systematic, individualized program for developing fundamental math concepts and skills—DLM)
Take Time
  (program in time-telling—C.C. Publications, Inc.)
Time Sequence
  (time-telling program with flash cards and worksheets—Opportunities for Learning, Inc.)

Workbooks—Duplicating Masters

All About Fractions
  (drill for fractions, percent—Mafex)
Arithmetic Step by Step
  (kit of duplicating Masters, K–3 with guide—Continental Press, Inc.)
Aztec Math
  (duplicating masters or workbooks of self-directed high-interest activities—Teachers Market Place)
Basic Math for Children with Learning Disabilities
  (worksheets—Opportunities for Learning, Inc.)
Disney's Mathematics Fun
  (series of books using Disney characters—Teachers Market Place)
Galactimath 1 and 2
  (drill books—Mafex)
Joy Series
  (30 duplicating books, high interest drill—Mafex)
Marvelous Math Spirit Masters
  (duplicating masters at high interest level—Opportunities for Learning, Inc.)
Math for Special Learners
  (high-interest, low reading level duplicating masters—Opportunities for Learning, Inc.)

Pacemaker Practical Arithmetic
(workbooks on fundamental money knowledge at second grade reading level—
Opportunities for Learning, Inc.)
Pizazz
(workbooks, grades 1–6 in basic math—ETA)
Remedimath
(primary and intermediate workbooks using cartoon characters—Mafex)
Your Daily Math 1 and 2
(workbooks for individualized instruction—Mafex)

Games

Bingo Games: Money, Shape, Time
(Mafex)
Dart Math
(a dart board game using Velcro, for addition, subtraction and multiplication—
Modern Education Corp.)
Happy Metrics
(resource books of games and activities—Opportunities for Learning, Inc.)
Let's Go Shopping
(reinforces basic math skills in the context of a shopping game, intermediate—
Teachers Market Place)
Math Soup Games
(30 games, all materials, in basic skills—Opportunities in Learning, Inc.)
Math Wheels
(games cards—Teaching Resources)
Motivating Math Gamebooks
(books containing gameboards and pieces, grades K–5—Teachers Market Place)
Playground Math Games
(essential math skills reinforced through physical activities—Mafex)
Ready-in-a-Minute Math Games
(reproducible game boards—Opportunities for Learning Inc.)
Shopping Lists Game I and II
(making change games—DLM)
Special Basegames
(78 games, complete materials in basic arithmetic skills—Opportunities for Learn-
ing, Inc.)
Squibit Games
(8 math/word building games—Mafex)
Stac Pacs
(sets of games with manipulatives, grades 1–6—Teachers Market Place)
Sum Fun (bingo); Metric Fun (bingo); Metric Playing Cards; Dec-a Ten (card game)
(Ideal School Supply Co.)
Unique Math Games
(4″ X 6″ cards of games and activities—Opportunities for Learning, Inc.)

Aids

Basic 6-Digit Calculator
  (large easy to read display—Opportunities for Learning, Inc.)
Data Man (Texas Instruments)
  (calculator math strategy games—Mafex, among other vendors)
Digitor
  (mini-computer—Centurion Industries, Inc.)
Electronic Cash Register with Calculator
  (ETA)
ETA Pre-Number Kit
  (manipulative for number concepts—ETA)
Fraction Circles; Fraction Squares; Lacking Numbers; Portable Study Carrels; Number Rods; Jumbo Counting Frame; Touch to Learn (Beaded Clock, number cards); Place Value Building Set
  (Ideal School Supply Co.)
Large abacus; Number Equalizer Balance; Math Big Box
  (Manipulative materials); Calculation Cubes; Number Dice
  (DLM)
Let's Learn Math Facts Course
  (records or tapes of problems—Teachers Market Place)
Little Professor (Texas Instruments)
  (calculator for practice of facts—Mafex, among other vendors)
Math Cards
  (set of concept vocabulary, facts flashcard—Mafex)
Quiz Kid Racer
  (displays arithmetic problems for number fact drill—calculator type—Opportunities for Learning, Inc.)
TLD Tactile Learning Cards (multiplication); Touch Time Clock
  (Modern Education Corp)

Learning Centers Material[3]

The Big Book for Collection: Math Games and Activities
  (manipulative aids for learning center—Teachers Market Place)
Daigger's Math Tutors
  (non-consumable learning module requiring no writing, utilizing placement of tiles—ETA)
How to Create Math Centers
  (100 centers suggestions—Opportunities for Learning, Inc.)
Math Resources Learning Center
  (Frank Schaffer—activity cards, worksheets, game-board—Teachers Market Place)
Miliken Math—Independent Math Activities
  (activities for grades 1-6 for use at Learning centers—Mafex)

[3] Note that many other materials listed are suitable for use in learning centers.

Projects for the Math Lab
  (100 activity cards, self-directed—Opportunities for Learning, Inc.)
Sports 'n Things Math Cards
  (series of 86 9 X 6 cards using sports and high interest areas as context for math
  skill practice—Opportunities for Learning, Inc.)

REFERENCES AND SUGGESTED READING

Cawley, J. F., and S. J. Vitello. "Model for Arithmetical Programming for the Handicapped Children." *Exceptional Children*, 39 (No. 2): 101–110, 1972.

Cratty, B. *Active Learning Games to Enhance Academic Abilities*. Englewood Cliffs, N.J.: Prentice-Hall, Inc., 1971.

Forer, R. K., and B. Koegh. "Time Understanding of Learning Disabled Boys." *Exceptional Children* 37 (No. 10): 741–744, 1971.

Gallagher, J. *Teaching the Gifted Child*, 2d ed. Boston, MA: Allyn & Bacon, 1975.

Gearheart, B. R., and Weishahn, M. W. *The Handicapped Child in the Regular Classroom*. St. Louis, MO: C.V. Mosby Co., 1976.

Hammill, D. D., and N. R. Bartel. *Teaching Children with Learning and Behavior Problems*. Boston, MA: Allyn & Bacon, 1975.

Homan, D. R. "The Child with a Learning Disability in Arithmetic." *The Arithmetic Teacher*, pp. 199–203, March, 1970.

Johnson, S. W. *Arithmetic and Learning Disabilities*. Boston, MA: Allyn and Bacon, Inc., 1979.

Lowenbraun, S., and J. Q. Affleck. *Teaching Mildly Handicapped Children in Regular Classes*. Columbus, OH: Charles E. Merrill Publishing Company, 1976.

Mercer, C. D. *Children and Adolescents with Learning Disabilities*. Columbus, OH: Charles E. Merrill Publishing Company, 1979.

Otto, W., R. A. McMenemy, and R. J. Smith: *Corrective and Remedial Teaching*, 2d ed. Boston, MA: Houghton Mifflin Company, 1973.

Smith, R. M. *Clinical Teaching: Methods of Instruction for the Retarded*. 2d ed. New York: McGraw-Hill Book Co., 1974.

Taylor, G., and S. Watkins. "Active Games: An Approach to Teaching Mathematical Skills to the Educable Mentally Retarded." *The Arithmetic Teacher*, December, 1974, pp. 674–678.

Turnbull, A. P., and J. B. Schulz. *Mainstreaming Handicapped Students: A Guide for the Classroom Teacher*. Boston, MA: Allyn & Bacon, Inc., 1979.

Wallace, G., and S. C. Larsen. *Educational Assessment of Learning Problems: Testing for Teaching*. Boston, MA: Allyn & Bacon, Inc., 1978.

14

TIME

A six-year-old neighbor came home early from school because she was sick.

"How long have you been sick, Jennifer?"

"Yesterday, the day after yesterday, and today."

Understanding time requires more than having it explained. St. Augustine despaired in his *Confessions* when discussing the notion of time that "if no one asks me, I know; if I want to explain it to a questioner, I do not know. . . ."[1]

Teaching children how to tell time has been approached in a very naive way—a "show and tell" procedure based on the assumption that all you have to do is use a good visual aid and "explain" how the clock works.

Understanding time requires logical thought processes and not just perceptual or sensory processes. Yet "time" is often taught in the same way as "colors" are taught—that is, by pointing at a color and naming it, for example, saying "That is red." "Now what color is it?" "Red." The right verbal response has been obtained.

Concentrated work on teaching time has usually been deferred to the third grade, which is one evidence of the difficulties involved. And this fits fairly well with the developmental level for understanding time, around nine years of age. On the basis of his research on children's understanding of time Piaget concluded that children were at a complete loss in attempting to understand instruments for telling time, such as watches and hourglasses, until around nine years old.[2]

---

[1] Francis J. Sheed (translator): *The Confessions of St. Augustine.* New York: Sheed & Ward, Inc., 1954.

[2] Jean Piaget: *The Child's Conception of Time.* New York: Basic Books, Inc., Publishers, 1969, p. 176.

It is true that children are attempting to use clocks before this time because our culture is very time conscious. They read clocks perceptually, learning that when the little hand points to 2 it is time to go home or when the big hand gets to 12 it is time to watch "Captain Kangaroo."

But real understanding of time involves certain basic intellectual or logical constructions. It is amazing that these necessary operations were identified and published in French by Jean Piaget in 1946 and yet not published in English until 1969, almost 25 years later. It may be another 25 years before the results of his research are implemented in our program of instruction involving teaching children how to tell time. Where else to get a better study of children's concepts of time than from a psychologist who is also Swiss?

ORDERING OR SUCCESSION

Telling time involves coordinating some motion such as walking to the store with the motion of the hands on the clock or the sand in the hourglass. This coordination of two motions can be called a **coseriation**. The coordination of two motions or two successions of events is more difficult than one might think.

As one experiment, Piaget placed one bottle upside down on top of another with a control valve between. At fixed intervals water is allowed to flow from the top to the bottom container. After all the water has moved from the top to the bottom container the child is given six pieces of paper with pictures of the two empty flasks on each. The child is asked to draw on each picture what the water looked like in both flasks after each flow. Not until around nine years of age does the child understand the coordination of these two successions of events— the water getting less each time in the top container and more each time in the bottom container.

DURATION

The second operation necessary to understand time is that of **duration**. Using the experiment just described the question now is: Did it take "as long" for the water to rise from here to here (pointing at the bottom flask) as it did to fall from here to here (pointing at the comparable positions on the top flask)? Again, not until around nine years of age can the question be answered successfully.

Since the two flasks have a different shape the water moves faster in the narrower flask. The preoperational child answers on the basis of this perceptual factor, that since the water moves faster in one flask it must take more (or less) time. But at around nine years of age he realizes that the "time" or "duration" of flow must be the same, since no more water can flow out of one flask than flows into the other.

A second experiment involves having two dolls hop along a table (the interviewer can move them by hand). The dolls are "started" and "stopped" at the same time, and the child is asked if the dolls started and stopped at the same time.

The experiment is then repeated, with the dolls being started and stopped at the same time but with one doll taking longer hops so that it goes further. The child is again asked if the dolls started and stopped at the same time.

This **succession** of events usually is not understood until seven years of age, the child thinking the dolls did not stop at the same time because one went further. Similarly, **duration** is not understood, the child thinking it took more time for the doll that went further.

ISOCHRONISM

Children often think that the speed of the moving clock hand changes as it measures some other motion. Thus the clock hand goes fast if you do something fast and slowly if you do something slowly. They do not understand conservation of velocity or speed. They fail to grasp the **isochronism** of watches. Yet the fundamental hypothesis on which all time measurement is based is the existence of motions that take the same time to recur under the same conditions [isochronism].[3]

SYNCHRONISM

Different clocks must also "tell" the same time for a given event or motion. While the second hand on the wall clock moves faster and goes further than the second hand on a wristwatch, they both measure the same time. Children less than nine years of age usually lack the transitivity necessary to realize this.

The child is asked to make marks on a paper at regular intervals as he watches the second hand on the wall clock make one rotation. He is

[3] *Ibid.,* p. 176.

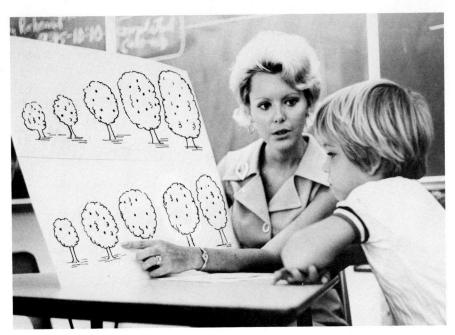

Six and seven-year-olds study succession of events in terms of ages of two trees. The tree in the top row was planted one year after the tree in bottom row but it grows faster, as shown by drawings for each year of growth. As it gets bigger than the other tree, the six year old thinks it is older. He equates age with size.

Bobby, six, thinks the car that reaches the finish line first goes faster even if the other car that was further away almost overtakes it.

then asked again to make marks on a piece of paper at the same speed while watching the second hand on a wristwatch make one rotation. The child is then asked if it took more, less, or the same time for the two events, and why.

The logic is that of transitivity; if making marks took a certain time on the big clock, and if making marks (at the same speed) took a certain time on the little clock, it must be concluded that the two clocks measured the same time. Instead, the prelogical reasoning is that the big clock took more time because it went further or faster.

THE CONSTRUCTION OF TIME UNITS

Necessary conditions for understanding time have just been described. A last necessary condition, according to Piaget, is to divide a period of time into number units which can be repeated and applied to other actions or motions one may wish to measure.

As one experiment, ask a child to count to 15 in unison with a metronome (set to beat each second) while looking at the hand on a stopwatch that, of course, also records 15 seconds during the same time interval. The stopwatch is then covered and the metronome set to beat more quickly as again the child counts in unison with the metronome to 15.

The child is then asked to predict how far the hand on the stopwatch went during the time he counted to 15. Preoperational children are unable to synchronize the two motions and reason that the clock hand went farther because they counted more quickly. Or, they may say the clock hand took more time because it went more slowly.

PROPORTIONS

Piaget finds children unable to use the proportion construct, $\frac{a}{b} = \frac{c}{d}$, until the formal operations level—that is, around 11 or 12 years of age. It is interesting that many children do not even realize the equivalency of two fractions such as $\frac{1}{2}$ and $\frac{2}{4}$ as applied to speed as a ratio of distance to time.

If one car travels 1 kilometer in 2 minutes and another car travels 2 kilometers in 4 minutes, then they travel at the same speed.

$$\text{Expressed as a proportion,} \frac{1}{2} = \frac{2}{4}.$$

Similarly, one car goes 4 centimeters in 4 seconds and another goes 5 centimeters in 4 seconds. Did it take the same time and did the cars travel at the same speed? *More quickly* is equivalent to *more time* for many children.

Since this intellectual construct, that of a proportion, is not present in many children until they leave the elementary school, it is given only brief attention here. Those students interested in an enrichment activity for intermediate grade students and who would like to pursue the matter further, please see footnote for exercise 3 on page 260.

It is worth mentioning at this point that **probability** is also being in-

Marge, nine, can successfully compare the speed of two cars based on ratios of distance to time traveled.

troduced into the elementary school math curriculum. Since this also involves the proportional schema, it may be only appropriate for more able students.[4]

CONCLUSION

Once children can master the diagnostic activities described they are ready, cognitively speaking, to understand time measurement by clocks. It is then that time should be studied in terms of number units on the clock face and what they mean.

Before this time, however, it is probably worthwhile to "socialize" the child to time and clocks, as children are socialized to the number symbols before they really understand them (see p. 37). Children may derive some pleasure from being able to "read" the time and relate it to something they wish to do even though they do not yet have the intellectual operations for understanding the basic principles involved in measuring time. An example would be the making of paper plate clocks

[4] For full discussion see Richard W. Copeland: *How Children Learn Mathematics*, 3d ed. New York: Macmillan Publishing Co., Inc., 1979, Chapter 13.

TIME

and being able to read times such as *9 o'clock* and *half past 4*. These might be termed language arts experiences.

Research

Experimental data on children's notion of time have usually been limited to children's ability to use time words,[5] to form and interpret historical and chronological sequences,[6] or to tell clock time.[7] In fact, in light of the relatively slow development of the concept of time, Gothberg, Pistor, Oakden, Sturt, and Bradley all recommend that instruction in history be deferred to as late as age 11 or 12.

Conservation

The equality of time intervals is unaffected by the events that take place in those intervals. **Conservation of time** is this notion—namely, the recognition that the length of a time interval is independent of any event that occurs in that time interval. For certain kinds of events children below the age of eight—and for some events children below the age of eleven—fail to conserve time. These children[8] appear to ignore relevant time information and instead base their judgments of the duration of an event upon physical stimuli, such as distance or speed.

On the subject of conservation of time Murray concludes that:

> . . . young children do not appreciate the uniformity and homogeneity of clock time even though 70% to 80% of six year olds can correctly tell hour time from

[5] Louise Bates Ames: "The Development of the Sense of Time in the Young Child." *Journal of Genetic Psychology,* **68**:97-125, 1946.

M. Lucile Harrison: "The Nature and Development of Concepts of Time Among Young Children." *Elementary School Journal,* 34:507-514, 1934.

Kopple C. Friedman: Time Concepts. *Elementary School Journal,* 44:337-342, 1944.

[6] E. C. Oakden and Mary Sturt: "The Development of the Knowledge of Time in Children." *British Journal of Psychology,* 12:309-336, 1922.

N. C. Bradley: "The Growth of the Knowledge of Time in Children of School Age." *British Journal of Psychology,* 38:67-78, 1947.

Frederick Pistor: "How Time Concepts Are Acquired by Children." *Educational Method,* 20:107-112, 1940.

J. D. McAulay: "What Understandings do Second Grade Children have of Time Relationship?" *Journal of Educational Research,* 54:312-314, 1961.

[7] Laura Gothberg: "The Mentally Defective Child's Understanding of Time." *American Journal of Mental Deficiency,* 53:441-455, 1949.

Doris Springer: "Development in Young Children of an Understanding of Time and the Clock." *Journal of Genetic Psychology,* 80:83-96, 1952.

[8] K. Lovell and A. Slater. "The Growth of the Concept of Time: A Comparative Study." *Journal of Child Psychology and Psychiatry.* 1:179-190, 1960.

a clock. It would seem that skill in "knowing" clock time is not closely related to the conservation aspect of the concept of time just as counting skills are not closely related to number conservation.[9]

EXERCISES

1. Test some five to nine-year-olds on their ability to understand such concepts as conservation of time, transitivity, and synchronism.[10]
2. Survey some primary-grade math books and evaluate in terms of whether the experiences are of a socialization (language arts) sort or cognitive in character.
3. Students who plan to teach fifth or sixth-grade children may want to study children's concepts of speed as a ratio of distance to time. This involves the mathematical idea of a proportion, which children do not understand until the formal operational level.[11]
4. Discuss the significance of Murray's conclusion that the "knowing" or "reading" of clock time by children does not seem closely related to the conservation aspect of time.
5. Report on a research article related to children's understanding of time. Some references follow (for ability to use time words see a, b, c; for telling clock time, see d, e):
   a. Louise Bates Ames: The Development of the Sense of Time in the Young Child. *Journal of Genetic Psychology*, **68**:97–125, 1946.
   b. M. Lucile Harrison: The Nature and Development of Concepts of Time Among Young Children. *Elementary School Journal*, 34:507–514, 1934.
   c. Kopple C. Friedman: Time Concepts. *Elementary School Journal*, **44**:337–342, 1944.
   d. Laura Gothberg: The Mentally Defective Child's Understanding of Time. *American Journal of Mental Deficiency*, **53**:441–445, 1949.
   e. Doris Springer: Development in Young Children of an Understanding of Time and the Clock. *Journal of Genetic Psychology*, 80:83–96, 1952.
6. Discuss the conclusions of Gothberg, Pistor, Oakden, Sturt, and Bradley that because of the slow development of the time concept history instruction should be deferred until ages 11 or 12 (see p. 259).

[9] Frank B. Murray: "Conservation Aspects of the Concept of Time in Primary School Children." University of Delaware. *Journal of Research in Science Teaching*, 6 (no. 3): 264, 1969.

[10] For tests in a form designed for ease in administering, see section on time in Copeland's *Math Activities For Children*. Columbus, Ohio: Charles E. Merrill Publishing Company, 1979, pp. 150–161.

[11] See Jean Piaget: *The Child's Conception of Movement and Speed*. New York: Ballantine Books, Inc., 1971, p. 227.

Or, Richard W. Copeland: *How Children Learn Mathematics*, 3d ed. New York: Macmillan Publishing Co., Inc. 1979, pp. 192–194.

15

GEOMETRY

WHY STUDY GEOMETRY?

The first mathematical experiences of children as they explore objects in space are geometrical rather than arithmetical. But as far as formal instruction is concerned, youngsters have had little experience in school with geometry except for a few activities in measuring and naming shapes.

Why do many teachers skip the pages on geometry in their mathematics textbooks? From a psychological standpoint, geometry has been at best a dreary experience for many students who have become teachers. Apparently, they have not seen geometry as Euclid, Aristotle, or Pythagoras did. Geometry, as remembered by many teachers, was that of Euclid as taught in high school, with many "proofs" which could only be "learned" by memorization.

Euclid, in 300 B.C., systemized the achievements in geometry of such mathematicians as Pythagoras, Eudoxus, and their predecessors in a set of 13 books called the *Elements*. The *Elements* are not the practical geometry of measurements but a strictly logical and formal development of plane and solid geometry. Struick describes the tremendous importance and influence of Euclid's work thus:

> The *Elements* form, next to the Bible, probably the book most reproduced and studied in the history of the Western World. More than a thousand editions have appeared since the invention of printing and before that time manuscript copies dominated much of the teaching of geometry. Most of our school geometry is taken, often literally, from [the first] six of the thirteen books; and the Euclidean tradition still weighs heavily on our elementary instruction. . . .[1]

[1] D. J. Struick: *A Concise History of Mathematics.* New York: Dover Publications, Inc., 1948, Vol. II, pp. 58-59.

Unfortunately, as Struick points out, geometry does still "weigh heavily" on our elementary instruction as far as teacher attitudes are concerned. Geometry instruction has been approached from a logical rather than a psychological standpoint. While many changes are still needed if children's stages of development are to be the important factor that they should be, the trend at the elementary school level today is away from the formal toward what might be called the informal, the intuitive, or the experimental. The goal is one of learning through experience—an inductive approach.

Rigorous proofs are not the goal for children but rather the joy of discovery as they explore the space around them. With a geoboard and rubber bands, children experience the joy of creating geometric patterns. In so doing they often discover many interesting geometric ideas. G. H. Hardy characterizes the mathematician as "a maker of patterns".[2]

GEOMETRY FOR CHILDREN FIVE TO NINE

Basic awareness of space develops without direct guidance, and is frequently thought to be fairly complete by the time the child enters school. But research shows that correct awareness of spatial relationships is far from complete for the five to nine-year-old. How many six-year-olds know that a stick does not change length when it is moved, that changing shape does not change amount, that an object looks different from different points of view?

Sensorimotor organization of space begins at birth when the permanence of objects is not even realized. A ball shown and then hidden from the view of a baby will not be looked for because the baby no longer thinks the ball exists. The infant with his lack of hand-eye coordination sees visual and tactile kinesthetic space as separate entities, not as related parts of the whole. Space seems to have no organization. He cannot even correctly place the feeding bottle.

As the infant begins to accumulate a background of sensorimotor experiences, the first spatial (topological) relation he seems capable of grasping is that of **proximity**. Dry clothing, a bottle which gives nourishment, Mother's nearness, and other tactile experiences that involve his body and sensations of nearness help him to establish a perceptual notion of this first basic concept.

Proximity is soon followed by a perceptual awareness of **separation**—

[2]G. H. Hardy: *A Mathematician's Apology*. New York: Cambridge University Press, 1961.

mother leaving—a lack of nearness. With coordination of vision and grasping, and consequent object manipulation, the child is better able to differentiate between objects and to note separation of one object from another, such as beads on a bead frame, which he enjoys separating from each other.

A third essential topological relation, that of **order** or spatial succession, is established when two neighboring though separate elements are arranged one before another. There is a certain order of beads on the bead frame—yellow, red, green, for example.

A fourth topological relationship determined perceptually is that of **enclosure**, or **surrounding**. Some of the first geometrical activities involve noting "inside" and "outside" relations. The dog is "in" the yard. The horse is "outside" the barn. Very young children may not make such distinctions correctly—drawing an eye outside the head, for example. Neither are "order" relations observed correctly, as in attaching arms to legs. The neck as an ordered element "between" or enclosed by head and body appears relatively late in children's drawings. (See photo.)

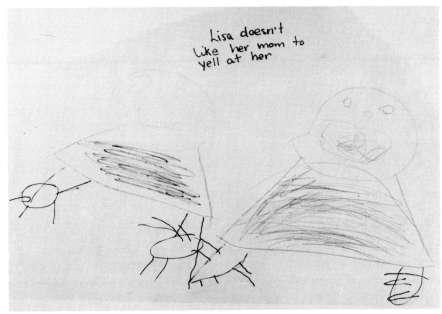

Which Is Mother? Children's drawings, as in photograph above, reveal their spatial concepts as well as feelings. The order relations of head, neck, and body are not yet represented. There is no neck. It is not clear whether the small lines on the legs are arms, toes, or both.

The Order Relation

The idea of ordering things in some way is an important mathematical activity. When objects are arranged in a line or linear series, the relation of proximity provides a basis for another important topological relation, that of **order**, or sequence. The "order" from left to right of beads on a bead frame may, for example, be A, then B, then C.

To study children's ability to order, the children can be asked to make a bead chain "like" one you have already set up. They are given beads and asked to place them "in the same order" or "like mine."

If the model set of beads is then placed in a circle, can the child follow the same order in placing his beads in a row or line? Also, can he reverse order, or put his beads in an opposite order, for example, E, D, C, B, A when shown an order A, B, C, D, E?

At first there is complete inability to make a copy of a row of different-colored beads using another set. At three to four years of age children correspond items intuitively, irrespective of order. Following

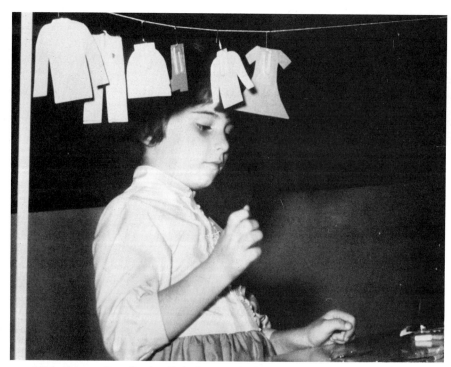

Michelle, age five, "orders" clothes on clothesline. She is unable to reverse order.

this, they learn to coordinate pairs, then successive pairs, and finally series of increasing length. This accomplishment involves the breakdown and reconstruction of the topological relationships among the beads of proximity, separation, order, and a constant direction of travel.

These experiments can be varied using paper cutouts of clothes to be hung on a clothesline in a certain "order."

At ages four to five, a child can "copy" a straight order if he is allowed to place his copy near the model and to check his work by trial and error. He is unable to produce a circular or reverse order.

Around six or seven years the child has arrived at a stable and rational conception of order. He understands the order in a series as a unified whole and can solve reverse order and circular order problems. The ability to solve such problems at this time is due to the attainment of the important reversibility of thought, the necessary component for solving conservation problems.

The Euclidean Concept of Shape

It is commonly assumed by many teachers that one "sees" an object in space and that the mind makes a copy of it much like a photographic plate. Hence, we point at a shape such as a square, tell the child what it is, and then expect the child to be able to draw what a square is since he has "photographed" it. Piaget considers this to oversimplify and completely misrepresent the facts.

What the child is able to construct in his mind depends on sensory data, but the **reconstruction** or **representation** of space in his mind must also involve an intellectual operation of coordinating sensory data into a meaningful whole.

To reconstruct or represent an idea such as a square, the child should handle the model of a square with his hands, tracing its outline with his fingers, beginning and stopping at the same point on the square so that he coordinates the particular relations involved in a square. Motor activity (operations) by the child is most important; looking at the object is not enough. A week later, sensory impressions are gone and recall depends on what was constructed in the mind.

Piaget remarks that there is a remarkably close correlation between the way the child explores the models and his ability to draw them. Reconstruction of shapes is not just a matter of isolating various perceptual qualities, such as noting number of corners or straightness of sides. The mental construction of shape rests upon the child's active process of hand movement as he traces the outline of the object. The abstraction is based on the child's own actions.[3]

Between the ages of four and six and a half there is a progressive ability to differentiate between Euclidean shapes. At six and a half to seven the child is able to coordinate the sensory impression of an object he had handled, such as a rhombus, and is able to recognize the shape if it is shown in a collection of different objects, or is able to draw the object he has handled. This ability to convert sensory impression into a mental reconstruction of an idea requires "operational" thought.

A second and more important question is whether the child can construct or represent an object without having a model to copy. Can he represent a geometric idea such as a square? It is one thing to recognize a square, but another to reconstruct or draw one. The ability to recognize a shape slightly precedes the ability to draw it.

The ability to represent or draw a square constitutes a test for a mental age of four, but the rhombus is not mastered until six and a half to seven years. If the child lacks the necessary motor coordination, he can be given matchsticks and asked to make a shape such as a rhombus,

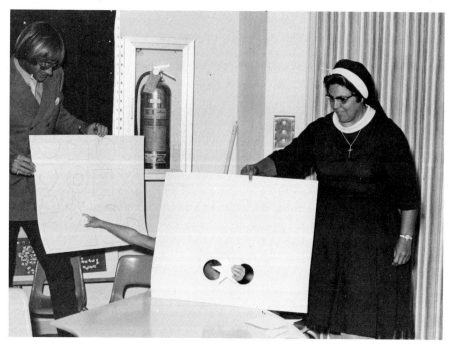

Relating a tactile to visual impression.

[3] Jean Piaget and Barbel Inhelder: *The Child's Conception of Space.* New York: W. W. Norton & Company, Inc., 1967, p. 79.

GEOMETRY

but Piaget found that the ability to make a shape such as a triangle with three matchsticks occurs no earlier than the ability to draw a triangle.[4] The fact that such a problem can be solved no earlier with its component shapes (matchsticks) than by drawing confirms that the problem is a lack of the necessary operational thought rather than of motor ability. A drawing is an imitation of reality constructed by the mind and not a perceptual photograph or copy.

As children explore such shapes as triangles, trapezoids, and squares, they begin to see that our physical world contains many models of these ideas—the pattern in the linoleum on the kitchen floor, the pattern in the stained glass windows in the churches, or the pattern or shape of their desks. On the day that this paragraph was written, two youngsters were looking at an umbrella tent (in which, of course, they were much interested). The top of the tent had the following design.

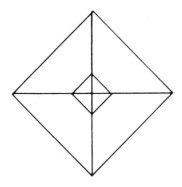

The youngsters wanted to know the names used to describe these patterns. How many basic geometric figures such as triangles, squares, and trapezoids do you see? There are two squares, 16 triangles, and four trapezoids. As one analyzes such patterns, one begins to see his environment in a new way and also comes to appreciate the mathematics of geometry. Geometry does become a study of space. Incidentally, what shape is a stop sign? a railroad crossing sign? a yield sign? a caution sign?

Curves

Basic Euclidean shapes may be described in terms of curves. The set of points represented by a drawing made without lifting pencil from

4 Ibid., p. 78.

paper is referred to as a **curve.** Thus, a line segment may be thought of as one specialization of a curve. The accompanying figures are examples of curves.

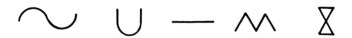

Curves (all open except for last figure)

If, in representing a curve, the drawing starts and stops at the same point, no point is touched more than once, and the pencil is not lifted from the paper during the drawing, then the curve is referred to as a **simple closed curve.** A triangle and a circle are examples of simple closed curves. The following figures are illustrations of simple closed curves:

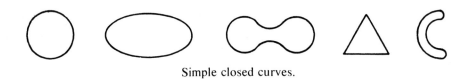

Simple closed curves.

Polygons

A simple closed curve that is the union of line segments is called a **polygon.** Triangles, squares, and rectangles are examples of polygons. If all the line segments are congruent and all angles are congruent, the figure is a **regular polygon.** Equilateral triangles and squares are examples of regular polygons. The following are illustrations of regular polygons:

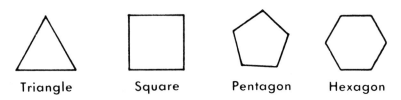

| Triangle | Square | Pentagon | Hexagon |

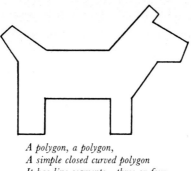

A polygon, a polygon,
A simple closed curved polygon
It has line segments—three or four
Or five or six, or even more!

Triangles and Quadrilaterals

Triangles may be classified according to their sides as **equilateral**—all three sides are congruent: **isosceles**—two sides are congruent; and **scalene**—no two sides are congruent.

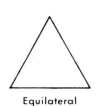

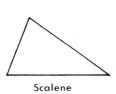

Equilateral   Isosceles   Scalene

They may also be classified according to their angles as **acute**—all angles are less than a right angle; **right**—there is exactly one right angle; and **obtuse**—there is exactly one angle greater than a right angle.

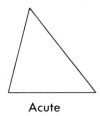
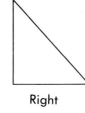
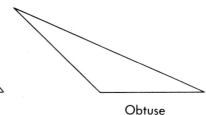

Acute   Right   Obtuse

In the right triangle the side opposite the right angle is called the **hypotenuse,** and the other two sides are called **legs.**

A figure bounded by four distinct line segments is a **quadrilateral.** There are many specializations of the quadrilateral—the rhombus, square, rectangle, and trapezoid, for example. The **rhombus** is a quadrilateral with all four sides congruent. If the angles are also congruent, the rhombus is a square. The **trapezoid** is a quadrilateral with one pair of opposite sides parallel. A **parallelogram** is a quadrilateral with opposite sides congruent and parallel. If the angles are also congruent, the parallelogram is a rectangle.

| Square | Rectangle | Parallelogram | Rhombus | Trapezoid |

The Concepts of Vertical and Horizontal

In introducing the Euclidean concepts of parallel, vertical, and horizontal, it should be realized that such concepts are more difficult for children than commonly supposed. Young children's spatial organization is different from that of the adult. To the child △ may be a triangle and yet ▽ is not. To explore the concept of horizontal, show a child a drawing of a tilted glass,

and ask him to draw how the water would look if we put water in the glass. Not until around nine years of age can children perform this task successfully. Before that they draw the water parallel to the base of the glass or parallel to the base and side.

Even if the child is shown a tilted glass with water in it, he cannot draw what he saw correctly a few days later because he does not yet have the necessary intellectual structures. His difficulties with directions such as north or east in mapmaking and in understanding geography are a reflection of this condition.[5]

EXERCISES

1. Test some five to seven-year-olds' understanding of the order relation by the following:
   (a) Show a row of seven to nine different colored beads on a rod and ask the child to make a row "like" yours from a collection of beads including the same colors.
   (b) Show the beads in a circle to see if the child can copy a circular order. Give him a soft wire hoop on which to string his beads. Can he also order his beads on a straight rod using the circle as a model (transposition of circular to linear order)?
   (c) With beads on a string in the form of a figure 8, ask the child to make a copy of the order on a straight piece of string.
   (d) Shown a row of beads, can the child make another row in reverse order? These experiments can be varied by using paper cutouts of doll clothes arranged in a certain order—for instance, as hung on a wash line. Such testing is not only diagnostic but provides appropriate readiness activities for the concrete operational thought level.
2. Make cardboard cutouts of various Euclidean "shapes" and a screen with two holes in it for the child to put his arms through, as shown in the photograph on page 266. Make a poster display of drawings of the same shapes for the child to look at as he handles each cardboard shape. Ask him to pick from the poster the shape he has handled (through the screen) but could not see. Also, remove the poster to see if he can "represent," or draw the shape he has handled. Try these tests on some five to nine-year-olds. Use only the simpler shapes such as circles, ellipses, and squares for the younger children. (For more information see pp. 18–43 of Piaget and Inhelder: *The Child's Conception of Space.* New York: W. W. Norton & Co., 1967.)
3. Test some five to nine-year-olds on their concepts of horizontal as described on p. 270. Can they make a map of their neighborhood? This of course requires the concept of a reference system such as north-south (vertical) and east-west (horizontal).

[5] For further study see Richard W. Copeland: *How Children Learn Mathematics,* 3d ed. New York: Macmillan Publishing Co., Inc., 1979, Chaps. 18 and 19.

EXPLORING SHAPES WITH A GEOBOARD

A geoboard is most useful in exploring geometric ideas. Shapes are quickly and easily represented with rubber bands.

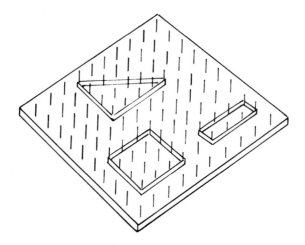

Geoboards can be made with a square piece of wood and nails spaced one inch apart vertically and horizontally, or they may be obtained commercially. Rubber bands of different colors help explore geometric relations. In the geometry of measurement, area and perimeter can easily be determined.

Geoboard Activities—Non-metric

1. Make some different shapes by stretching rubber bands around some of the nails. These are polygons whose sides are line segments.
2. Can you make the following shapes?
    (a) Triangle.
    (b) Parallelogram.
    (c) Pentagon.
    (d) Rhombus.
    (e) Square.
    (f) Rectangle.
3. Which of the shapes in problem 2 did you make as regular polygons?
4. Which of the shapes in problem 2 had to be regular polygons?

5. Triangles with the same shape are called **similar triangles**. Make two similar triangles on your geoboard.
6. Triangles that are the same size and shape are called **congruent triangles**. Make two congruent triangles adjacent to each other so that they form:
   (a) A square.
   (b) A rectangle.
   (c) A larger triangle.
   (d) A parallelogram.
7. Polygons
   The polygon that Bill made on the geoboard has four (4) sides.

   Can you form a figure which has three sides? Five sides? More than five sides?
   How many different shapes can you make with four sides? Do any of these have special names? Can you find any of these figures in the classroom, at home, or outside?
8. Name the following specializations of the quadrilateral and represent each on a geoboard.
   (a) One pair of opposite sides parallel.
   (b) Both pairs of opposite sides parallel.
   (c) Opposite sides parallel and all angles congruent.
   (d) Opposite sides congruent and all angles congruent.
   (e) One pair of opposite sides congruent.
9. Polyominoes
   There are a group of islands called the 4-Square Islands. These islands are made up of four squares, each of which has one side in common with its neighbor square.

         This is one of them: This is not. Why?

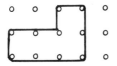 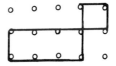

   Can you make all the islands in the 4-Square Islands group?
   How many are there?

10. If Allen lives at A and Betty lives at B, how many ways can Allen go to Betty's house? He cannot travel down, to the left, or diagonally.

```
o   o   oB

o   o   o

A°  o   o
```

Geoboard Activities—Measurement

1. How many line segments the same length as the one shown here can you find on the geoboard?

2. On the geoboard let this represent 1 square unit.

   (a) How many square units are within this figure?

   (b) How many square units are within this figure?

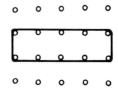

GEOMETRY

(c) How many square units are within this triangle?

(d) How many square units are within this triangle?

3. (a) Construct all the different rectangles you can which have an area of 4 square units. Did you find at least three?
   (b) Determine the perimeter of each of your rectangles.
   (c) Which has the greatest area with the least perimeter?
4. How many different-sized squares can you find on the board?
5. Make a figure and ask your neighbor to find the area.
6. Make a figure whose perimeter is:
   (a)   8 units
   (b) 10 units
7. Make a 6-sided figure with perimeter of 16 units.
8. (a) Construct the largest square possible on your geoboard. What is the area?
   (b) Join successive midpoints of adjacent sides. What is the area of the new square?
9. Construct a parallelogram with an area of 3 square units.
10. Construct a rectangle with an area of 4 square units which is exactly twice as long as it is wide.
11. Construct a triangle having an area of 1 square unit.
12. Construct a trapezoid having an area of 5 square units.
13. Construct a hexagon having an area of 5 square units.

LINES, RAYS, PLANES, AND ANGLES

Children are unable to conceive of a line as a set of points until approximately 11 years of age, but some current math textbooks introduce these ideas two or three years earlier.

Lines, Line Segments, and Rays

Once children have reached the developmental stage necessary to consider such ideas as lines, rays, and angles as sets of points, we can proceed with a more formal instructional program. It may still be worthwhile to begin with a "line" in terms of its meaning to children, asking, "What represents a line on the highway or on the board?" and, "Why do you call it a line?" "It is straight." Similarly, what does "a ray" mean to children? "What is a ray of light from a flashlight or from the sun?" and, "What characteristics does it have?" "It is straight, it has an end point [or rather a beginning point], and it appears to proceed infinitely far in one direction."

A line may be symbolized $\overleftrightarrow{AB}$ and is represented as:

Through any two points A and B there is exactly one line. It extends infinitely far in two directions.

The part of the line to the right of and including point A may be described as *ray AB*, symbolized as $\overrightarrow{AB}$. Similarly, ray BA, the set of points on the line to the left of and including B, is symbolized as $\overrightarrow{BA}$. Rays extend infinitely far in one direction.

Line segment AB, symbolized as $\overline{AB}$, has two end points, A and B. Strictly speaking, we draw a "line segment" not a "line" on the blackboard, unless we indicate in some way, such as with an arrowhead, that there is no endpoint for the line.

Also, strictly speaking, we do not *draw* "lines," "rays," or "line segments," but rather *representations* of these ideas since a line, for example, has length but no thickness. It is probably not worthwhile to make an issue of these distinctions with children.

Planes

The idea of a plane in geometry is suggested by a flat surface extending infinitely. A ceiling, table top, wall, or floor suggest a section of a plane. A plane is also a set of points, and although it has no thickness, it does extend infinitely. In considering a table top, for example, care must be taken to point out that it represents only a section of a plane. Thus, if the plane that includes the table top were impenetrable, there would be no way of getting from the floor to a point above the table top.

Since any two points determine the position of a line, how many points are needed to indicate the position of a plane? Three non-colinear points. Some time should be spent in discussing this idea because youngsters have trouble visualizing that only three points, not on a line, are necessary to name a plane. The expression "not on a line" is important because three points on a line determine only the line and not a plane. That three points not on a line determine a plane can be visualized by considering the question: Can a three-legged stool be wobbly? No, because the ends of the three legs can only be in one plane. The four-legged stool or table, however, often needs a piece of wadding under one leg to place it in the same plane as the ends of the other three legs.

Intersection and Union of Sets of Points

In considering the relationship of lines and planes in space, the idea of intersection is again important. The intersection of a line and a plane in space may be a point, a line, or empty (that is, line and plane do not intersect).

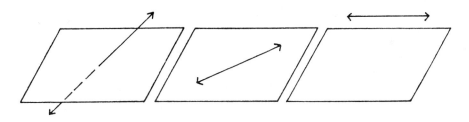

The **intersection** of two sets of points is the set which contains those points found in both sets. In the illustration

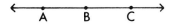

$\overline{AB} \cap \overline{BC} = B$ is read, "The intersection of line segment AB and line segment BC is point B." The statement $\overline{AB} \cap \overrightarrow{BA} = \overline{AB}$ is read, "The intersection of line segment AB and ray BA is line segment AB." Since ray BA has as its end point B and extends infinitely to the left through A, the ray has as one of its subsets the line segment AB. Since the intersection of two sets by definition includes only those points common to both sets, the intersection of ray BA and line segment AB is the line segment AB.

The **union** of two sets of points is the set which contains those points found in either or both of the two given sets. Again, in the preceding diagram, the union of line segment AB and line segment BC is line segment AC, symbolized $\overline{AB} \cup \overline{BC} = \overline{AC}$. The union of ray BA and line segment AB is ray BA, symbolized $\overrightarrow{BA} \cup \overline{AB} = \overrightarrow{BA}$. Remember that ray BA has end point B and extends through A.

These ideas of line segments and rays and of intersection and union of sets of points are challenging to college students and yet can be grasped and enjoyed by fifth and sixth graders as well.

Angles

If youngsters are questioned as to what constitutes an angle, many answers will result, but the one most often heard will involve a description of the interior of an angle.

We will define an angle in terms of our previous discussion of points and rays. **An angle is the set of points formed by two distinct rays with a common end point.** The point of intersection is called the **vertex**, and the rays are called **sides** of the angle.

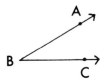

In this diagram of angle ABC, symbolized $\angle ABC$, point B is the vertex. The letter naming the vertex should be the middle letter in naming the angle; that is, either $\angle ABC$ or $\angle CBA$. The two rays with a common end point which name the angle are ray BA and ray BC.

The sets of points shaded in these diagrams indicate the interior and exterior of an angle:

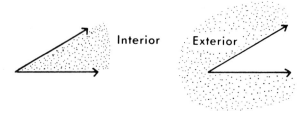

Interior   Exterior

In reference to a plane which includes a given angle, one can think of three sets of points whose union represents the plane—the angle, its interior, and its exterior. The angle is a set of points separate and distinct from both interior and exterior.

A line may be thought of as an angle by designating a point on the line and considering the line as two rays which have this point as a common end point.

EXERCISES

1. Name three models that suggest a point, a line, and a plane.
2. How many lines pass through a particular point? two particular points?
3. A line contains how many points?
4. A plane contains how many points? how many lines?
5. A point may be in how many planes?
6. A line may be in how many planes?
7. Three particular points may be in how many planes?
8. The faces of a pyramid with a triangle base suggest how many planes? The edges suggest how many lines?
9. The intersection of any two lines in space is _____ or _____ .
10. The intersection of a line and a plane in space is _____, _____, or _____ .
11. The intersection of two planes in space is _____ or _____ .
12. Represent three lines on a sheet of paper. How many points are common to two of the lines? Sketch the possibilities for four different answers.
13. Sketch and name the possible solution sets for the intersection of an angle and a plane.
14. The intersection of two angles in a plane may be:
    (a)   (b)
    (c)   (d)
    (e)   (f)
    (g)   (h)

THE GOLDEN RECTANGLE

The golden rectangle has often been used by artists as an esthetically pleasing ratio of length to width in constructing buildings and even human figures. The ratio of length to width was called **phi** and is 1.618 to 1. The ratio is unique in that it can mathematically reproduce itself in an infinite series of smaller rectangles by swinging an arc the length of the shorter side to the longer side. In so doing, a new rectangle is formed at right angles to the preceding one, yet with the same ratio of length to width.

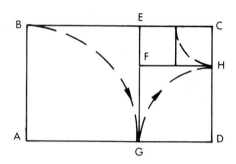

SYMMETRY

The idea of an **axis of symmetry** can be explored by folding a sheet of paper so that the edges coincide. The folding of cutouts of triangles, squares, parallelograms, and so forth should also be investigated to determine whether there is an axis or axes of symmetry for each of the figures. The folds suggest axes of symmetry when the edges coincide. An equilateral triangle, for example, has three axes of symmetry. It can be folded in three ways so that its edges coincide.

Presented in exercise 13 following is a copy of a lesson on the axis of symmetry used as an experiment in the fourth, fifth, and sixth grades of an elementary school. The children grasped the idea with little difficulty and seemed to enjoy the lesson.

A more formal statement of definition for an axis of symmetry may be developed later, as follows: A figure is symmetrical with respect to a line (axis of symmetry) if for each point A on the figure there is a point B such that the line is the perpendicular bisector of the line segment AB. To amplify this definition, consider the following drawing. Does it have an axis of symmetry?

GEOMETRY

If the figure is symmetrical with respect to a line (has an axis of symmetry) the line is probably vertical. If such a line is sketched on the figure as follows

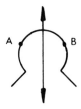

and if for any point A there is a point B such that the line is the perpendicular bisector of the line segment joining points A and B,

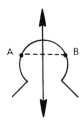

then the figure is symmetrical with respect to the line. Note that the definition states for *each* point A. For each and every point A, there must be a point B that satisfies the definition; otherwise there is no axis of symmetry.

A figure in plane geometry may be symmetrical with respect to a line or a point or both. A circle has a **point of symmetry** as well as an infinite number of **axes of symmetry**. (See exercise 6 following.)

A three-dimensional figure may be symmetrical with respect to a plane. A sphere is symmetrical with respect to any plane which passes through its center.

EXERCISES

1. By folding a sheet of notepaper, determine the number of its axes of symmetry, if any.
2. Cut out an equilateral triangle, an isosceles triangle, and a scalene triangle. Determine the number of axes of symmetry for each model.

3. Cut out a square, a rectangle, a rhombus, and a trapezoid. Determine the number of axes of symmetry for each model.
4. What number of axes of symmetry do the following have:
   (a) An ellipse   (b) A regular pentagon   (c) A regular hexagon
5. Do the following have an axis of symmetry? If not, why not?

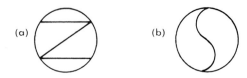

(a)   (b)

6. A circle, an ellipse, and a line segment each have a point of symmetry—the center. The figure

also has a point of symmetry. Can you state a definition for a point of symmetry?
7. Which of the figures named in problems 2, 3, 4, and 5 have a point of symmetry?
8. Which of the figures in exercise 13 have a point of symmetry? axis of axes of symmetry?
9. Thinking of a sphere as being symmetrical with respect to a plane passing through its center, can you state a definition for symmetry with respect to a plane?
10. Would a round layer cake with smooth outside surfaces be symmetrical with respect to one or more planes? A cake, cubic in shape, would have how many planes of symmetry?
11. A pyramid, each face of which is an equilateral triangle, would have how many planes of symmetry? If the base were a square, how many planes of symmetry would there be?
12. Identify models of geometric objects in your classroom that have
    (a) an axis or axes of symmetry
    (b) a point of symmetry
    (c) a plane or planes of symmetry.
13. Determine the axis (axes) of symmetry for the following:

1

2

3

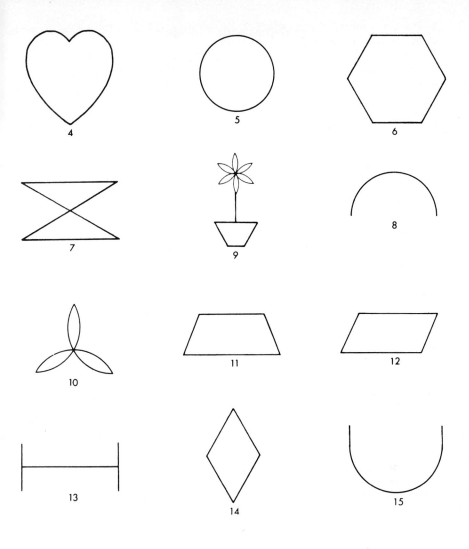

THE TANGRAM

The **tangram** is a type of jigsaw puzzle involving basic Euclidean shapes. The one shown on the next page has seven pieces—4 triangles, 2 squares, and 1 parallelogram. The pieces are manipulated to form various shapes, such as making a rectangle with two triangles.

The tangram provides an interesting way of exploring space. It can be a fun way of studying geometric relationships involving the basic Euclidean shapes. It can also be used to study area measurement.

Activities with Tangrams

Trace the following figure on a piece of paper or cardboard and then cut along each line:

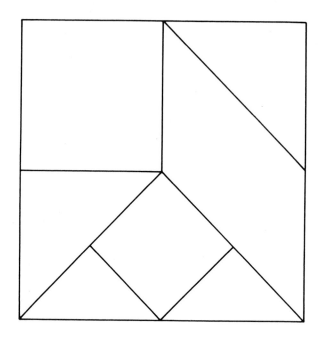

1. Making triangles
   (a) Make a triangle using 2 pieces. Make another with 2 other pieces. What kind of a triangle is it?
   (b) Make a triangle with 3 pieces. What kind is it? Can you find another way to make one with 3 pieces?
   (c) Make a triangle with 4 pieces.
   (d) Make a triangle with all 7 pieces.
2. Making rectangles
   (a) Make the smallest rectangle you can.
   (b) Make a rectangle with 3 pieces. With 4 pieces.
   (c) Make a rectangle with all 7 pieces
3. Making parallelograms
   (a) Make a parallelogram with 3 pieces.
   (b) Make a parallelogram with 4 pieces.
   (c) Make a parallelogram with all 7 pieces.
4. Area
   (a) If the length of each side of the large square is 2 inches, what is its area?

(b) Then what is the area of the large triangles?
(c) What is the area of the parallelograms?
(d) What is the area of the small triangle?
(e) What is the area of the small square?
(f) What is the area of each of the following?

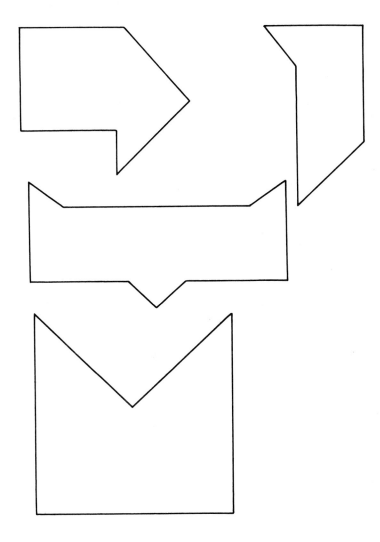

16

MEASUREMENT

READINESS FOR LEARNING MEASUREMENT

When should children begin measurement activities in school? One might assume that if a child can read the numerals on a ruler he is ready for linear measurement, since all he has to do is lay the ruler beside the object being measured and count the appropriate number of ruler lengths.

That there is more to measurement at the operational thought level than indicated in the preceding paragraph is shown by a simple experiment.

Conservation of Length

If a child is shown two sticks placed side by side so that he can see they are the same length,

and then one is moved either up or down,

the child of seven or less usually thinks the stick in the higher position is longer. He focuses his attention on the end of the stick that was above the other stick and concludes that this stick must be longer. It is not a matter of lack of communication. The question can be varied by asking, "Would an ant walk further on one stick than the other?"

This concept of conservation or invariance of length is an intellectual or logical concept and one that conflicts with what the child thinks he sees. Our senses may give us an incorrect answer.

The child must reach an intellectual or logical level at which he can reason that they are the same length. How do we know they are the same length? Because we can put the sticks side by side again. The reversibility of thought necessary to solve this question is not present in most children of seven years or less, but you will probably have to try the experiment yourself before you believe it. It shakes a lot of mothers when their children are unable to respond correctly.

An important question in readiness to measure is: How can the child use a measuring unit such as a ruler if its length changes (to him) as it is moved in measurement?

Conservation of Distance

In measuring the distance between two objects, does this distance remain invariant if another object is placed between the two objects? This poses another psychological problem for the child. Children often think placing an object between two other objects changes the distance between the objects. These children are not ready to measure.

Children also have a reversibility problem in that they often think that the distance AB is not the same as the distance BA if point B is higher than A. They think it is farther "up" than "down."

Transitivity of Length

If children are asked to compare the height of two towers (see photo, p. 288) using a common measuring term such as a stick, they at first

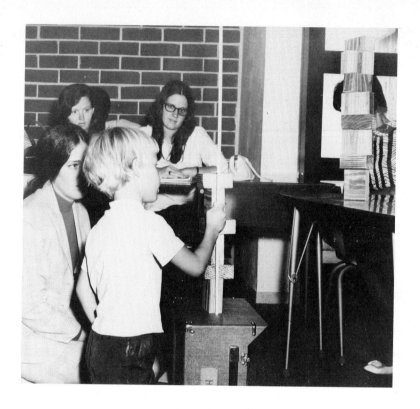

do not see how the stick can help. The logic of using the stick *C* to measure towers *A* and *B* involves the logic of transitivity. If *C* is as long as tower *A* and also as long as tower *B*, then towers *A* and *B* must be the same length. Not until seven to eight years of age can children use such reasoning.

Number and Measurement

Present practice involves introducing children to measurement in the first grade, apparently on the assumption that if a child understands numbers (that is, if he can count) and can move a ruler, then he can measure.

But the simple tests just described, such as conservation of length and transitivity, reveal that there are problems of spatial understanding and logic that make measurement more difficult than understanding number per se. Conservation of number (see p. 35) is usually mastered before conservation of length.

A six-year-old attempts to build his tower the same height as model tower on a higher table.

As described by Piaget, "Unlike the unit of number, that of length is not the beginning stage but the final stage in the achievement of operational thinking . . . the elaboration of the operations of measurement is far slower . . ."[1]

The conclusion would be that measurement ought to be introduced no sooner than in the second grade.

[1] Jean Piaget, Barbel Inhelder, and Alina Szeminska: *The Child's Conception of Geometry.* New York: Basic Books, Inc., Publishers, 1960, p. 149.

Conservation of area occurs at about the same time as conservation of length. The Piaget test of conservation of area involves showing a child two identical, square pieces of cardboard painted green, with a cow on each. The child is asked if each cow has the same amount of grass to eat. Small wooden barns are then placed on each field, but the barns are spread out over the entire field on one model. The child who answers on the basis of how it looks thinks that there is less grass to eat on the field that has more space between the barns.

The logic or mathematics necessary to solve the area problem correctly involves the idea that if equals (barn areas) are subtracted from equals (the fields), the results, or grass areas, must be equal. The child who understands number and this idea can solve the problem.

Conservation of area task. Patti, six, thinks there is more grass in the field with the barns spread out, even though there are four barns in each field.

MEASUREMENT

Conservation of area task. This six-year-old thinks the rectangle is larger, even though it was formed from two triangles which, together, were the same size as the triangle shown.

Reduction to Scale, or Ratio

The ability to read a map, or to construct one, involves the use of scale drawing, or a reduction to scale. The ability to use a ratio such as 1 inch to 50 miles in making a map involves a thought level and mathematical competence not usually found until around 11 years of age.[2] Also necessary for social studies activities such as geography or map making is a vertical and horizontal axes framework to be used as a basis for positioning objects (see p. 270).

[2] Jean Piaget and Barbel Inhelder: *The Child's Conception of Space.* New York: W. W. Norton & Company, Inc., 1967, Chap. 14.

When children are ready for such concepts they should have the opportunity to make maps of things in which they are interested, whether it is playground, city, or neighborhood.

EXERCISES

1. Try the conservation of length and distance tests on children in the five-to-eight-year range to convince yourself of the existence of the stages of development. For further information, see Piaget, Inhelder, and Szeminska's *The Child's Conception of Geometry* (New York: Basic Books, Inc., Publishers, 1960), Chapters 3 and 4.
2. Examine math textbooks used in the elementary schools in your area and make a scope and sequence chart of measurement activities.
3. Obtain some blocks, each of a different size, and build a tower on a table. On another table of a different height, ask a six, seven, or eight-year-old to build a tower that is as tall as yours. Put a screen between the two towers but allow the child to go and look at the model tower as often as he wishes. After the child has made some preliminary trials, give him a stick and ask if it will help. For a detailed study of stages in ability to make a linear measurement, see Piaget, Inhelder, and Szeminska's *The Child's Conception of Geometry*, pages 69 to 128; or Copeland's *How Children Learn Mathematics* (New York: The Macmillan Publishing Co., Inc., 1979), Chapter 14.
4. Make a report on stages of development in ability to make a map as described in Piaget, Inhelder, and Szeminska's *The Child's Conceptions of Geometry*, Chapters 13 and 14.

BEGINNING ACTIVITIES IN MEASUREMENT

As young children play, there are many available readiness activities for measuring. In a sandpile, a bucket may be filled with sand by using a smaller container. Blocks are often arranged in rows or made into a tower. Sticks are compared to see which is longer. Sample beginning measurement activities are listed at the end of this chapter.

The laboratory approach to teaching mathematics probably involves more measurement activities than any other kind of activity. (See Chapter 17.)

In teaching linear measurement, unmarked rulers, strips of paper, or sticks may be used first, followed by rulers marked off in standard units. Children should have many activities requiring measurements—heights, weights, lengths of rooms, and so forth.

Youngsters enjoy measurement at each grade level. For example, they are learning to tell time, and the time that they have to go to bed or that a certain television program comes on may be very important to them. They measure their height and weight. In science they measure rainfall, wind speed, barometric pressure, the growth of plants and animals, the amount pets should be fed, and the proper sizes of their animals' cages.

A measurement involves a *measure* and a *unit of measure.* In a measurement of 3 meters, the unit of measure is the **meter,** the measure is *3.*

THE METRIC SYSTEM

The United States is now the only major country which has not converted to the metric system of measurement. Congress once again in 1974 voted as it has repeatedly since 1869 to keep the American system of measurement in the 17th century, where three lengths of a king's foot is a yard.

The basic advantage of the metric system is that it is a base ten system, as is the Hindu-Arabic system of numeration. For example, in the metric system there are 10 millimeters in 1 centimeter, 10 centimeters in 1 decimeter, and 10 decimeters in 1 meter.

In computations with measurements, such as adding 12 centimeters (cm), 2 meters (m) and 3 millimeters (mm), there are no fraction problems other than assigning to these measures the correct place value.

$$
\begin{array}{rl}
12 \text{ cm} = & 0.12 \text{ m} \\
3 \text{ mm} = & 0.003 \text{ m} \\
2 \text{ m} = + & 2.00 \text{ m} \\
\hline
& 2.123 \text{ m}
\end{array}
$$

In contrast, in the English system there are 12 inches in a foot, 3 feet in a yard, $16\frac{1}{4}$ yards in a rod, and 320 rods in a mile. The English system would be simpler if there were 10 inches in a foot, 10 feet in a yard, and 10 yards in a rod. To appreciate the difficulty in using the English system, find the sum of the following: 3 rods, 21 yards, $7\frac{1}{2}$ feet, 142 inches. Each pair of addends involves different conversion units. Such addends cannot be added directly, as can numbers in the metric system, in which even the fractions are expressed in base ten.

Metric Units of Measurement

The standard metric length unit is the **meter**, which is a little longer than a yard (39.37 in.). The prefixes **milli, centi-, deci-** represent respectively thousandths, hundredths, and tenths of a meter. The prefixes **deca-, hecto-, kilo-** represent 10 times, 100 times, and 1000 times the length of a meter. The same prefixes are used relative to the standard weight unit, the **gram,** and the standard volume unit, the **liter.**

The measuring units with prefixes **deci, deca-** (**deka-**) and **hecto-** are not often used, but they help display the base ten characteristic of the metric system.

It may be worthwhile to have a display such as the following to show the complete base ten character of the metric system.

Length

10 millimeters	=	1 centimeter
10 centimeters	=	1 decimeter
10 decimeters	=	1 **meter**
10 meters	=	1 decameter
10 decameters	=	1 hectometer
10 hectometers	=	1 kilometer

The basic unit of weight in the metric system, the **gram,** is about the weight of a paper clip—much lighter than many people would guess. The basic volume unit, the **liter,** is a little more than a quart (1 quart = 0.946 liter).

Weight			Volume		
10 milligrams	=	1 centigram	10 milliliters	=	1 centiliter
10 centigrams	=	1 decigram	10 centiliters	=	1 deciliter
10 decigrams	=	1 **gram**	10 deciliters	=	1 **liter**
10 grams	=	1 decagram	10 liters	=	1 decaliter
10 decagrams	=	1 hectogram	10 decaliters	=	1 hectoliter
10 hectograms	=	1 kilogram	10 hectoliters	=	1 kiloliter

MEASUREMENT

Conversions in the Metric System

While it is much easier than making conversions in the English system, making conversions in the metric system causes difficulty for the new student. For example, 1 mm = □ cm? The question is one of moving the decimal point, but in which direction and how many places?

The following diagram is useful until the learner becomes more familiar with the units.

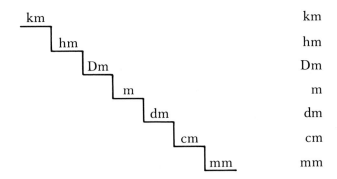

To convert *3.2 cm* to meters, count the number of steps from *cm* to *m*, which is 2, and since the direction is to the left, move the decimal to the left two places.

Hence, 3.2 cm = .032 m

Similarly, 4 km = □ m

3 steps to the right from *k m* to *m*

Hence, 4.0 km = 4000 m

For practice in metric conversions, see the following diagram. The numerals represent centimeters (cm). Place the letters on the ruler in the place or places indicated to see if you get the message. The letter H has already been positioned.

METRIC INCHES ALONG

What will happen to the inchworm when we use the metric system?

H

Find the correct mark for each letter. Write the letter above the ruler.

I always try to get to the core of the problem

H → 6.8 cm

R → 208 mm

G → 23.2 cm, 92 mm

O → 14 cm

U → 224 mm

N → 8.4 cm, 12.4 cm

C → 6 cm

A → 76 mm, 156 mm

E → 1 dm, 2 dm

B → 216 mm

L → 4 cm, 17.6 cm, 32 mm

T → 192 mm, 13.2 cm, 16 mm

I → 11.6 cm, 18.4 cm, 8 mm

, → 24 mm

(From *The Math Group*, 5625 Girard Ave., South, Minneapolis, Minnesota 55419.)

296

EXERCISES

1. A decimeter or 10 centimeter ruler is shown below.

Ten centimeters is called a **decimeter**. Ten decimeters is called a **meter**. Then:

(a)   1   m = ☐ centimeters (cm)
(b)   1   m = ☐ decimeters (dm)
(c)   60 cm = ☐ dm
(d) 0.8 dm = ☐ cm

2. (a) A centimeter is about the same length as what familiar object or objects?
   (b) A meter is about the same length as what familiar object or objects?

3. A ruler 10 times the length of a meter is called a decameter.
   A ruler 100 times the length of a meter is called a hectometer.
   A ruler 1000 times the length of a meter is called a kilometer.
   Then:

(a) a kilometer   = ☐ hectometers
(b) a kilometer   = ☐ decameters
(c) a kilometer   = ☐ meters
(d) a meter   = ☐ kilometer
(e) 3.6 kilometers = ☐ meters
(f) 40 meters   = ☐ kilometers

4. Formulate a rule for changing the unit of measure such as from meters to centimeters and from kilometers to meters.

5. A small can of orange juice contains 0.177 liter. How many ml does it contain?

6. Which is longest? Which is shortest? Estimate, then measure in centimeters and millimeters.

a	d	g
b	e	h
c	f	i

7.

(a) Length _____
(b) Width _____
(c) Height _____
(d) Volume _____

(e) If each ml of volume of the box weighs 1 gram, what is the weight of the box?

(f) If the box is full of water, approximate its weight.

8. Bring an object to class which is marked in the metric system. Explain the marking.

9. Have the class divide in three groups with each group developing a laboratory station and 10 problems for practice in metric measurement. Each group chooses one of the following: length, weight, volume. Groups rotate and solve problems developed by other groups.

10. Can you now think metric?

In each of the following questions, underline the correct answer.

(a) A gram is about the weight of: an apple, a dime, a pound.

(b) A meter is about the height of: a door, a table, a chair seat.

(c) Water freezes and boils at: $32°C$ and $212°C$, $100°C$ and $200°C$, $0°C$ and $100°C$.

(d) A measuring cup would hold about: 2 ml, 20 ml, 200 ml.

(e) The weight of a newborn baby in kilograms is about: 3, 30, 300.

(f) The height of a tall man in centimeters is about: 20, 200, 2000.

(g) Normal body temperature is about: $37°C$, $56°C$, $98.6°C$.

(h) A soft drink measures in liters about: 1.5, 1, 0.3.

(i) A liter of water weighs in grams about: 100, 10, 1000.

(j) The length of a new lead pencil is about: 50 mm, 100 mm, 200 mm.

(k) The thickness of a dime would be about: 0.1 mm, 1 mm, 5 mm.

(l) The standard of length in the metric system is the: millimeter, centimeter, meter.

(m) A desk top is 65 centimeters across. This is equivalent to: 650 mm, 0.65 m, 6.5 m, 0.065 km.

INTRODUCING CHILDREN TO THE METRIC SYSTEM

Children begin to work with ones, tens, and hundreds, or a base ten place value number system, in first and second grades. The metric system is also a base ten system, but there are new names to learn, such as kilometers. There are also decimal or base ten fractions to consider, such as centimeters.

While children will not work formally with fractions in base ten as tenths, hundredths, thousandths until fifth or sixth grade, these fractions are an important part of the metric system. Since the basic unit for measuring length, the **meter**, is a little longer than a yard, to measure something less than a yard in length involves fractional measurement (using decimeters, centimeters, or millimeters). One way to avoid this fraction problem is to begin with the centimeter or decimeter as the measuring unit.

It may be appropriate for the third or fourth grade to begin a study of the metric system. Not until this time are the necessary operational factors of conservation and transitivity present for most children (see p. 286).

By eight years of age children understand conservation of length, realizing that when an object is moved it does not change length. They also understand transitivity of length, that if a measuring stick is the same length as two objects then those objects must be the same length. Metric measurement should thus begin with a linear measurement unit.

Readiness for understanding conservation of weight should be present at eight to nine years of age. Volume conservation does not occur until a year or so later.[3] Therefore, a study of the metric unit of weight (grams) should probably precede the study of the volume unit (liters).

Teaching temperature in the metric system is relatively easy. Heat is measured in degrees Celsius. On the Celsius (centigrade) thermometer water freezes at $0°$ and boils at $100°$, which fits with our base ten number system. This is in contrast to the Fahrenheit scale of $32°$ and $212°$ for the freezing and boiling points of water.

Teaching a Lesson on Length

First the children are asked to measure some objects with a body unit, such as the width of their hands. They soon realize the need for a standard unit. They are then provided with a measurement unit consisting of a paper strip 1 decimeter in length.

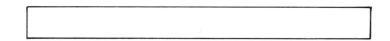

This basic measurement unit of 1 **decimeter** (the length of an orange Cuisenaire rod) is $\frac{1}{10}$ of a meter or 10 cm, but the children are not told this. The children are asked to measure the length and width of various objects such as their books, desk, and so forth to the nearest ruler length.

It is soon discovered that a smaller unit of measure will provide a more precise measurement and lessen the fraction problem. If centi-

[3] Richard W. Copeland: *How Children Learn Mathematics*, 3d ed. New York: Macmillan Publishing Co., Inc., 1979, pp. 345–349.

cubes (see following section) are available, give one to each child so that they can mark their ruler in ten equal parts. They are then, of course, measuring with a commonly used measuring unit, the centimeter. They will later measure their height with this unit.

Each of these is called a **centimeter** because there are 100 in a meter. The children can then measure objects using all three of these basic units—centimeters, decimeters, and meters. Paste ten of the decimeter units end to end to make a meter unit.

Skill develops with adequate practice. Children begin to learn how to annex or drop zeros. Some want to use a still smaller unit on their ruler, the millimeter, noting that there are 10 in the centimeter, and 1000 in the meter. For long distances some are curious about the kilometer (1000 meters).

It is important that before measuring each object, a guess or approximation of its length should be made to help visualize the length of the measuring units. This estimation also serves as motivation, since children want to check and see how accurate they are in estimating. Estimating activities can involve both guessing how long a particular object is and finding a particular object which has a specified length, such as 3 decimeters.

The Centicube

This is a drawing of what is usually called the centicube.

Each edge is 1 centimeter in length. It is the size of the white Cuisenaire rod. This volume of water weighs 1 gram.

Centicubes are made of plastic and are available from most of the math lab supply companies.[4] They are very useful because they tie

---

[4]See footnotes p. 316 for catalog addresses.

together the length, weight, and volume units of measurement in the metric system. They can be hooked together in a row so that 10 centicubes are the same length as a decimeter or an orange Cuisenaire rod.

In terms of weight the centicube is designed so as to weigh 1 gram; thus 1000 of them weigh 1 kilogram.

In terms of volume, since each edge of the centicube is 1 centimeter in length, its volume is 1 cubic centimeter, or 1 cm^3. The weight of this much water (1 cm^3) is 1 gram.

The volume of the centicube, 1 cubic centimeter, can also be expressed as 1 **milliliter**, or 1 ml. Thus the volume of 1000 centicubes is 1000 cm^3 or 1000 ml or 1 **liter**.

CONSIDERATIONS IN TEACHING ELEMENTARY SCHOOL CHILDREN THE METRIC SYSTEM

1. Have children measure things in which they are interested rather than using worksheets or pages from textbooks.
2. Emphasize approximating measurement before actual measurement.
3. Emphasize measuring *in* the metric system, rather than making conversions to the English system. Children who are in elementary school today will work only with the metric system as adults.
4. In making conversions use only approximations such as the following:

> meter . . . a little longer than a yard
> centimeter . . . not quite half an inch
> kilometer . . . somewhat longer than half a mile
> liter . . . slightly larger than a quart or same
>   size as a one-pound coffee can
> milliliter . . . 5 milliliters equal 1 teaspoon
> gram . . . about the weight of a paper clip
> kilogram . . . a little more than 2 pounds

5. It may be advisable to teach only the commonly used prefixes—centi-, milli-, and kilo-. The prefixes deca-, and hecto- are rarely used, with deci- being used somewhat more often. Commonly

used prefixes for length, weight, and volume are shown in the following table:

Length	Mass (Weight)	Capacity
kilometer (km)	kilogram (kg)	
meter (m)	gram (g)	liter (l)
centimeter (cm)		
millimeter (mm)		milliliter (ml)

NOTE: Abbreviations, such as km are not followed by a period.

6. Measurement may be used as motivation for fractions, decimals, and arithmetic. There are no sources of application of arithmetic quite comparable to those that arise from measurement.
7. It should be emphasized that it is the correlation between the metric units and the base ten system which makes the metric system better than the English, not the arbitrarily chosen length or weight standard. The metric system is not more "accurate," as often claimed by students. We can measure to billionths of an inch.

OTHER MEASUREMENT ACTIVITIES FOR CHILDREN

Length

1. Using your foot as a measuring unit, how long is the classroom?
2. Using the width of your thumb, what is the width of your tablet? Compare your measurement with that of a friend.
3. With fingers spread out, the distance from the end of your little finger to the end of your thumb is a span. How many spans wide is your desk?
4. The distance from your elbow to the end of the middle finger is a cubit. How many cubits are you in height? First estimate your answer. Write the results in your notebook.
5. Can you measure the circumference of a paper plate? How?
6. Measure in centimeters the lengths of the following line segments, but first estimate your answers.

MEASUREMENT

	My estimate	Measurement
_____		
_____		
_____		

7. Using a trundle wheel or a tape measure, how long is the playground? How wide?
8. Discuss with your teacher different ways of measuring length.

Weight

1. Using a two-pan balance, which is heavier:
   (a) A pencil or a crayon?
   (b) An eraser or a pen?
   (c) A nickel or a pencil?
2. Does it matter what shape a weight is? Begin with two balls of plasticene the same size. Then flatten one.
3. Name some objects which you think weigh less than a kilogram; more than a pound. Weigh them to see if you are right.
4. Do you think your pencil weighs more or less than a gram? Check to see if you are right.
5. What two weights in grams can be used instead of a kilogram weight?
6. How much does a one-page letter with envelope weigh?
7. Make a chart to show how much it costs to send letters of different weights by parcel post.
8. What is the average weight for girls (or boys) your height?

Time

1. What time do you do these things:
   (a) Get up?
   (b) Eat breakfast?
   (c) Get home from school?
   (d) Watch TV?
2. What time do you like best? Why?
3. What time does the sun rise? set?

4. Make a chart to show how many hours each member of your class is in bed each night.
5. Can you make a sand clock with two bottles and a piece of plastic? How long does it take for the sand to pour from one bottle to the other?
6. What things travel faster than you? slower than you?
7. Make a clock face with a paper plate. Show what time you get up and what time you go to bed.
8. How fast do cars go? What is the speed limit in your neighborhood?
9. How long does it take a car to stop going 20 miles an hour? 40 miles per hour? 60 miles per hour? Can you make a chart to show this?

Graphs

1. Make a chart to show how many children missed school each day last week.
2. Make a graph to show the temperature on the school playground for each hour during the school day.
3. Make a graph to show how the volume changes for cubes 1 cm, 2 cm, 3 cm, and 4 cm on each side.
4. Make a graph to show how the area changes for squares 1 cm, 2 cm, 3 cm, and 4 cm on a side.

MEASUREMENT

17

THE MATHEMATICS LABORATORY – AN INDIVIDUALIZED APPROACH TO LEARNING[1]

Children are very much a part of the physical world. They like to explore the many objects they see, sometimes to the dismay of parents. Physical objects such as plants, rocks, a bird's eggs, cows are all subjects worthy of attention. Boys much prefer wading through a puddle of water to walking around it. Firsthand experience with objects is very necessary for learning. It is a basis for Piaget's concrete operational level of thought.

Children should be encouraged to compare objects—to determine the *relations* that exist between their characteristics or properties and the properties of other objects. Mathematics is a study of relationships. Is one object heavier, thinner, lighter, darker, smoother, rougher, bigger, smaller, taller, shorter, thicker, the same shape? Younger children will study such relations; later they will measure to make more precise determinations. It is necessary that the children themselves make these determinations, as in a laboratory setting, for a real idea of number and geometry to develop.

The mathematics laboratory approach is a recognition of this need for first-hand experience by each child with objects in his physical world. If real learning is to take place, mathematical ideas should be abstracted

[1] From Richard Copeland: *How Children Learn Mathematics. Teaching Implications of Piaget's Research,* 3d ed. New York: Macmillan Publishing Co., Inc., 1979, Chap. 21. © Copyright Richard W. Copeland, 1979.

from the physical world. The relation of geometry to the physical world is often less difficult to see than that of number. The child cannot pick up and handle a number.

Number is an idea or abstraction and not an object in the physical world, but it does need a physical framework in which to develop for children. Dogs, cars, houses are objects in our physical world, but a "two" is not. The world of number is completely separate from the physical world. And yet, we can use ideas from the world of number to describe *relationships* between objects in our physical world. For example, which is heavier, longer, wider, or taller, and by how much? Measurement is an important activity in the math laboratory. It is also important to find ways to record or express these relationships in order to systematize our work and for others to see or use. Charts and graphs will be useful.

Number, in its cardinal sense, may be thought of as a *property of a set*. For example, in considering the three sets below one finds that each has the same number property, which we call "two." Each set contains two objects, although we see no 2 in the picture. The number 2 is a property of each set. We find that there are two in each by matching the objects in each set with the corresponding set of counting numbers.

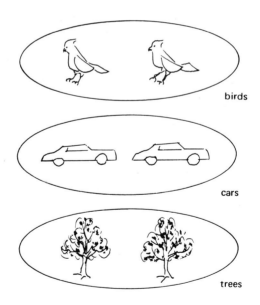

birds

cars

trees

Matching of objects in one set with objects in another set is a prelude to counting. In comparing two sets, are they the same (in number) or is one larger? Which one? How much larger?

This is in sharp contrast to the way children have often learned to count: by simply memorizing a sequence of sounds "one, two, three," and so forth. The futility of such a process is seen by asking such a child to tell you how many objects you hold in your hand. If he has just learned to memorize a sequence of sounds, he is unable to match the number names with the objects in your hand. He has not established the idea of one-to-one correspondence that is basic to counting.

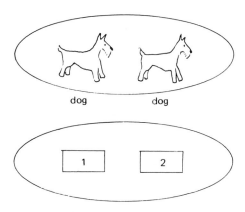

Similarly, the child may learn the addition facts by memorizing, with no real understanding, sums from a table. He may memorize $3 + 4 = 7$ and still tell you there are more coins in the box on the right than on the left.

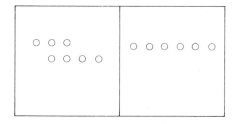

Children must develop mathematical concepts from operations they perform on physical objects. The many experiments described have shown that this involves an individual developmental process. Each child has his own span of development of necessary concepts.

To help meet such needs, schools may include classrooms designed as **mathematics laboratories.** The math lab is a classroom designed to allow children individually to perform the physical manipulations or concrete operations that are necessary for real learning of mathematical concepts.

Such real learning, based on first-hand experiences in the physical world, places mathematics in the realm of something that is fun, that can be enjoyed, and that can be understood. The child sees some purpose in what he is doing; number is not just tables and sums to be memorized. From a psychological standpoint, this consciousness of purpose is most important. The method of inquiry is an experimental one: Can you find out? Did you discover anything? Important from a psychological standpoint is the inductive or discovery approach to learning. The child is provided a situation from which he should discover for himself or "disengage" the mathematical structure involved.

For example, does each of the two sets shown below contain the same number of objects?

How about these two sets?

Would the number always be the same when the order of the subsets is reversed? Could you give us a general rule (the commutative property)?

HOW TO BEGIN A MATH LABORATORY

Many teachers have used a laboratory situation, such as playing store, for part of their mathematics program. Children are allowed to go to the store and buy something and then are asked to make the proper exchange in terms of money for goods purchased. Children may also take a train trip or figure the cost of their morning milk. Such practical activites give some meaning to the mathematics learned.

These procedures are, however, still not a laboratory learning situation in terms of an individualized approach to learning; they are usually a total class endeavor with the whole class doing or attempting to do the same problems at the same time. For some, it has meaning; for others, it does not.

A laboratory situation should allow for individual work as a basis for learning. It may, however, be advantageous in many situations for children to work in pairs or even in small groups. This will allow each

THE MATHEMATICS LABORATORY

child a measure of freedom to develop concepts on his own. Working in pairs or small groups may contribute to social needs and build vocabulary development. Vocabulary development is important in mathematics as elsewhere.

In starting a math laboratory a teacher often begins in a small way, such as with an arithmetic corner in the classroom containing such useful apparatus as counting frames, abaci, blocks, measuring tools, and so forth (see photo below).

Children in Hazelmere Infants' School, Colchester, Essex, England, performing experiments of weight relations. Note other weighing scales in background. (Courtesy Miss Lena Davidson, Head of School.)

A spare room, if one is available, may be a place for children to go when they want to work with the available materials when they have finished their regular lessons. There are enough interesting things such as mathematical games in the laboratory to draw children to it.

Class Organization

In a conventional classroom situation, children may be working problems in a textbook. If grouped for instruction, they may be working in different books. The emphasis may be an individualized one, but it is still a vicarious type of experience with possibly little meaning for the children.

In a laboratory situation, children may be given "assignment" cards that are usually problems that require using some of the materials in the math laboratory. There is much measuring, comparing, sorting, and questioning.

Assignments may be on an individual basis or in the form of some type of grouping. Allowing children to work in pairs provides for much first-hand experience and also allows opportunity for discussion of the problem. In experiments, one child may perform and the other record.

Mathematics Laboratory in Hazelmere Infants' School, Colchester, Essex, England. (Courtesy Miss Lena Davidson, Head of School.)

After evaluating their findings, they decide on the best way to make a record of their findings; for example, a graph, model or table. While pairing or grouping is important for vocabulary development and sharing ideas, it may mean that only one person is learning and the other simply following. The teacher can observe easily enough and make grouping changes as necessary. It may be advisable to make grouping changes as new assignments are undertaken.

Children may be grouped by friendship, mixed ability, or common ability. Each has its advantages and disadvantages. The Paiget experiments can serve as a basis for determining common-ability groups.

A beginning teacher may allow only one group a day to do the practical "discovery" work while the others continue their regular routine. This will allow a pilot approach to the new procedure to see how it works, and later the program can be broadened as the teacher feels more secure with it. This will also allow time for obtaining additional materials. Friday afternoon, as an informal time, may serve as a basis for beginning a laboratory program.

Children who have been in a formal classroom atmosphere will need some time to develop self-sufficiency and confidence. Some have not been allowed to pick up a pencil until told to do so. They have been used to doing only what they were told. There will be some noise and confusion in the changeover and the teacher will have many questions to answer, but gradually the children will proceed more and more on their own. This will finally allow the teacher to perform her true role of advisor and questioner as she moves from group to group.

Classroom Arrangement

In the traditional school, desks are placed in rows so that all children face the blackboard and the teacher. For a teacher-centered learning situation, this is a logical arrangement. Class discussion is largely recitation. The entire class considers the same question and reads the same page at the same time. Pupils do not leave their desk without permission.

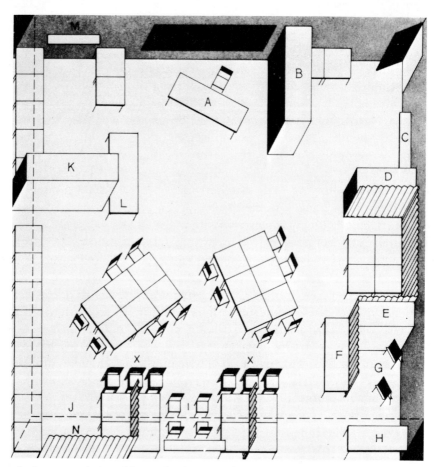

A classroom designed for active learning. (From *I Do and I Understand.* Nuffield Junior Mathematics Project. Courtesy John Wiley and Sons, New York, N.Y.)

THE MATHEMATICS LABORATORY

If learning is to be on an individual basis with actual rather than vicarious experience, a different physical arrangement of the classroom is necessary. Also, a more permissive classroom atmosphere must exist. Children should be allowed to move about as they seek answers to questions.

In many elementary classrooms, there are now tables and chairs in place of desks. The chairs and tables may be moved about as necessary for varied work and grouping. Since children will be working as individuals or in small groups, and often in different activities, cupboards and partitions should be placed at right angles to the wall to allow for some separation of the learning groups. The back of the cupboards and the partitions can serve as display areas for the results of the group work. Children often prefer to work at the tables in a standing position, in which case chairs should be stacked as shown in the preceding illustration.

In some experimental "open" schools, children are not grouped by grade or age. Instead there may be 90 to 120 children in a large room with several teachers. The children move from one activity to another as they are able. The range of activities will be greater than in the conventional classroom, as will the variety of learning materials.

MORAL BEHAVIOR

Discipline and Justice

The conservation of moral values depends upon the ability to think logically just as does the conservation of such mathematical concepts as number. Children's thoughts on such moral questions as cheating, lying, or tattling are, of course, extremely important in their development into wholesome adults.

As Brearley and Hitchfield[2] point out, a study of children's ideas on punishment leads one to rethink the whole question of rules and regulations in the school. The ability to resolve a conflict by not giving way to an immediate urge involves a process of "decentration." This includes not only considering the act itself but also remembering what preceded and being able to anticipate what will follow.

Justice does not grow out of rules imposed by an adult, which are

[2]Molly Brearley and Elizabeth Hitchfield: *A Guide to Reading Piaget.* New York: Schocken Books, Inc., 1966, p. 130.

often not understood by children. In asking children why they should not "copy" from a neighbor, Piaget found that only 5 per cent of eight and nine-year-olds and 10 per cent of 10 to 12-year-olds define it as deceitful.[3] The great majority reply in terms of "we will get punished" or, in today's vernacular, "it's a no-no."

Justice requires nothing more than the mutual respect and solidarity that holds among children themselves and often develops at the adult's expense rather than because of him. As the solidarity among children grows, the notion of justice emerges in almost complete autonomy.

Children come to see that retribution or the infliction of suffering to right a wrong is only justified to make the offender realize he has broken the bond of solidarity, and retribution is largely ineffective. The law of reciprocity, the ability to put oneself in another's place, tends toward a morality of forgiveness and understanding. Young children, of course, are only groping toward reciprocity and have many regressions.

Piaget concludes:

> Equilitarianism would therefore seem to come from the habits of reciprocity peculiar to mutual respect rather than from the mechanism of duties that is founded upon unilateral respect.[4]

In a laboratory where children are pursuing their work at their own rate and level with purposes that they have made their own, cheating does not appear. It would be pointless. It is the externally imposed standard exercise and stress on correctness that encourages cheating to avoid humiliation.[5]

MATERIALS AND THEIR USE

We have emphasized the use of various concrete materials which children can see, handle, measure, and so forth, to develop mathematical ideas. Such materials should include objects that are of an appropriate size for children to handle, that do not roll easily, and that are harmless. Ease of storing when not in use is also a factor.

For the lower grades, such materials might include wooden blocks, dried peas or beans, matchboxes, plasticene, bricks, milk straws, sand,

---

[3] Jean Piaget: *Moral Judgment of the Child.* New York: Free Press, 1932, p. 285.
[4] *Ibid.,* p. 285.
[5] Brearley and Hitchfield, *op. cit.,* p. 138.

pipe cleaners, tongue-depressor sticks, counting frames such as a coat hanger with wooden beads on it, and for place-value concepts an abacus and pocket chart. Containers are needed for most of these materials. Large sheets of polyethylene are needed as a floor or table cover when working with sand, as are tools for transferring sand. Containers should be provided that hold the same amount but are different in shape, to determine whether the children have reached the stage of conservation or invariance of quantity.

Vocabulary development is a valuable part of such activities. The containers may be described as wide, narrow, tall, thin. The mathematical relations of *the same as, more than,* and *less than* can be studied:

$$\square \text{ holds more than } \square$$

$$\square \text{ holds less than } \square$$

In studying length children may compare ribbons of different colors and lengths. They may be first asked which is "longer," the "red" or the "black." Which is "shorter?" And finally, to "order" the ribbons by finding the "shortest," "the next longer," and so forth. They should order from shortest to longest and also from longest to shortest.

Children can compare the many lengths around them such as pencils and table edges. They will also need to be tested on conservation of length:

| | Which is longer? Or are they the same?

| ' Which is longer? Or are they the same?

|_ Which is longer? Or are they the same?

Children should not begin a systematic study of linear measurement until they are able to understand the conservation of length concept.

Measurement is an important part of science and mathematics when the youngster is ready for it (nine to ten years of age). There are many materials needed for experiences in measurement. These include balance scales, weights, rulers, yardsticks, tape measures, micrometers, protractors, compasses, stop watches, clocks, thermometers, trundle wheels (see page 316), and various-sized plastic containers.

Younger children may use balances of the following type:

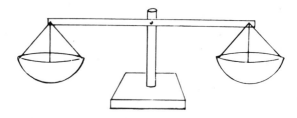

After the conservation concept has been mastered, older children will use the measuring instruments that are more precise.

Use of Commercial Materials

More expensive but also useful are various commercially prepared materials such as logic blocks, trundle wheels, stop watches, mathematical balances, Cuisenaire rods,[6] Dienes' Multibase Arithmetic Blocks,[7] Multimat,[8] and Number Blox[9]. Catalogs of descriptions and costs can be obtained from footnoted sources.

The Cuisenaire rods are wooden rods of different lengths. They allow children to explore number relationships by fitting the rods together. They serve as a concrete number line. For example, a rod three units long and another rod three units long is the same length as a rod six units long.

$$(3 + 3 = 6) \quad \text{or} \quad (2 \times 3 = 6)$$

The mathematical balance is also useful in developing the basic addition, subtraction, multiplication, and division facts. To solve $2 + 3 = \square$, represent $2 + 3$ as one weight on the 2 hook and one weight on the 3 hook. To balance, one weight must be placed on the 5 hook on the opposite side of the balance (see illustration on next page).

---

[6] Cuisenaire Co. of America, Mt. Vernon, N.Y.

[7] Distributed in U.S. by Herder and Herder, 232 Madison Ave., N.Y.; in England by Educational Supply Association, Harlow, Essex.

[8] Selective Educational Equipment, 3 Bridge St., Newton, Mass.; in England by Tiger Toys Limited.

[9] Creative Publications, P.O. Box 10328, Palo Alto, Calif. 94303.

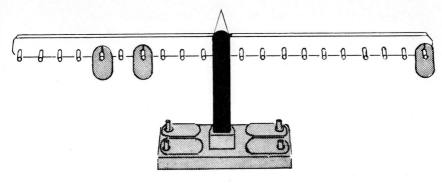

Invicta Mathematical Balance. (Distributed in U.S. by Selective Educational Equipment, Inc., Newton, Mass.)

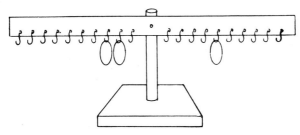

Homemade balance.

For a problem in subtraction (the inverse of addition), $2 + \square = 5$, if a weight is placed on 2 on one side of the balance and on 5 on the other side of the balance, then where must a weight be placed to balance?

For a multiplication such as $3 \times 2 = \square$, three weights are placed on the 2 hook. To balance, one weight must be placed on the 6 hook on the opposite side. For the problem, 4×3 or four weights on the 3 hook, a balance can be made by 2×6 or two weights on the 6 hook on the opposite side. For division, $3 \times \square = 6$, a weight is placed on 6, and three weights must be placed where on the opposite side to balance?

To explore geometric or spatial relationships, the geoboard is a very useful device. Rubber bands can be fitted on the pegs or nails to represent the various basic shapes, and such ideas as perimeter and area relations explored (see page 318).

A trundle wheel is useful for measuring long distances. It has a counter to determine number of rotations (see page 318).

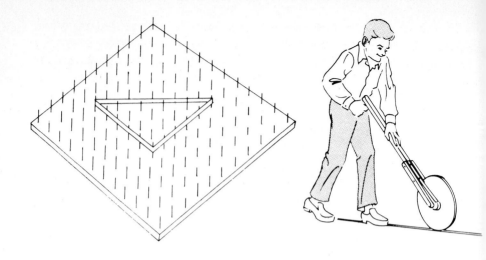

Care of Materials

The responsibility for the use of learning materials should be clearly defined.

Responsibilities of Teacher

1. Obtain and assemble the necessary materials.
2. Organize and label storage areas and containers.
3. When certain procedures are necessary, as in the use of delicate tools, introduce their use with great care.
4. Trust pupils to use materials. The teacher should not spend her time checking materials in and out.

Responsibilities of Pupils

1. Select appropriate material.
2. Use the material with care.
3. Return material to its proper storage space (chairman of group responsible).
4. Clean up working area.

Books

Textbooks are now much better than they used to be. The mathematical content is better. Also they are better organized, more attractively illustrated, and often related to the needs of the learner in terms of practical usage.

In the conventional classroom, there may be one graded textbook series through which the children proceed, page by page, lesson by lesson, with problem exercises for reinforcement. The teacher presents the idea, does some sample problems and the children then do other similar problems. Only one book may be used, but each child has a copy.

Many teachers, however, recognize the wide range in ability and achievement present in any group of the same chronological age. To remedy the problem, they may group children for instruction and use books written for different levels of achievement and ability. The trend toward the nongraded school is another way of attacking the problem. Such a procedure calls for a variety of books.

In the experience-centered math laboratory approach to learning, books are also necessary. Their use, however, is as a resource material, just like the other materials in the math laboratory. They are not the only basis for learning mathematics as they are in many classrooms.

Practice in computation is necessary but it should not be the whole mathematics program as it is in many schools. As the children attempt to solve a problem like "How many posts 4 feet apart will be needed to fence the playground?", they will need to find the perimeter of the playground and know that the necessary operation is division. They will also need to know the necessary multiplication facts. They will need practice in order to remember the basic multiplication facts and also to remember the division algorism.

It is more meaningful if such computational practice grows out of a need to solve a problem. If the children do not know the multiplication facts, they see quickly enough that the division problem becomes very laborious.

Practice with the multiplication and division operations, however, should come *after* experience with concrete materials. Otherwise, it may have little meaning. The adult reading this book probably learned multiplication facts from a "table" rather than developing them for himself using such materials as beans or blocks. Fraction problems are not understood by many adults because fractions were "taught" at the abstract level. For example, what problems in the physical world would be solved by the notations $3 \div \frac{1}{2}$ or $\frac{1}{2} \div 3$ or $\frac{1}{2} \div \frac{1}{3}$? Can you represent these notations with concrete materials (see Chap. 8)?

Books or worksheets of duplicated problems can serve as a reinforcement or practice material once the ideas have been abstracted from objects by children at the concrete operational level. Books are also an important source for problems to be used as reinforcement. Problems in a math lab learning situation are more often in the form of assignment cards.

A practical measurement activity book for children is *The Measurement Book* by Sohns and Buffington (Enrich Inc.).

ASSIGNMENT CARDS

In using a book as *the* learning material, assignments are in terms of pages or problems. In a laboratory situation, the material to be learned in a given concept area may be divided into "units." The units are in the form of "assignments," "jobs," or "work cards." The assignments or lessons are placed on individual cards or sheets of paper and kept in a pocket or card file. This allows for modifications, additions, or deletions from the file as the assignments are improved.

Examples of Assignment Cards

I

1. Put out two piles of money using both dimes and pennies in each pile (or use paper cutouts of money).
2. Make a column on your paper for dimes and one for pennies.

Dimes   Pennies

3. Write down the amount in each pile in the appropriate column.
4. Write down how much money there is in all. Can you represent this number with fewer coins? If so, how should it be written?
5. What is the best way of doing this kind of problem?
   What you have just done is called **addition**.

II

1. Using dimes and pennies, show 26 cents.
2. Double this number, first estimating what your answer will be.
3. Can you use fewer coins to represent your answer?
4. Write down what you did in solving the problem.

$$26$$
$$\times\ 2$$

5. Solve the following, first by using coins and then by writing the problem with numerals.

$$
\begin{array}{ccc}
13 & 912 & 14 \\
\times\ 4 & \times\ 5 & \times\ 3 \\
\hline
\end{array}
$$

III

1. Using dimes and pennies, show 32 cents.
2. Divide this amount equally between you and a friend.
3. How much will each have?
4. What you did can be expressed as $2\overline{)32}$. Write the answer above the line putting the number of dimes for each person over the number of dimes that there were altogether.
5. Now try some more division problems like this, beginning with a different amount of money.

IV

1. Get the bag of logic blocks and empty them in the place where you work.
2. Put them in sets so they are alike in some way. Write down how each set is alike.
3. Can you group them so they are alike in another way? Write how they are alike now.
4. Are there still other ways that they can be grouped so they are alike? If so, write the other ways they are alike.

The teacher should be available for discussion as the child records what he has done and to see if he has discovered the important patterns involved. When first using assignment cards, children may work through the assignment and miss the important ideas, feeling the game is to finish the assignments. If the child has not discovered the idea sought, the teacher should ask additional appropriate questions. After the child completes an assignment and records his result and conclusion, he moves on to the next assignment. It is a "doing" type of activity or assignment. The youngster solves problems for himself as a basis for learning, rather than having ideas "explained."

RECORDS

Records kept by children can be an important part of a learning experience, but it can also be a deadening one. Some experiences involve recording, others do not. The criteria should be whether recording enhances or detracts from the experience, which will be easy to observe in the behavior of the children as they make their records. Making records can be an enjoyable experience in the form of displays for other members of the class to see.

The first kind of recording by children is of a personal matter in the form of words in their individual diaries or workbooks. As their skill in writing develops, they love to write long rambling stories. If they have experiences of a mathematical sort, these will be included in their diaries.

The second type of recording will be in the form of displays—charts, graphs—for other members of the class to see (see illustration p. 326).

If assignment cards are used, a progress chart can be kept on the wall or in an ordinary exercise book. As a child completes an assignment, the date is recorded on the chart alongside his name in the proper assignment column.

The Nuffield Project material recommends that the teachers also keep a diary of the activities developed during the week—which succeed and which did not and why; which children excelled or failed and why. Also, individual cards or a notebook should be keep on each pupil. These individual records should include the dates on which assignments

A display recording made by children. (From *Beginnings*. Nuffield Junior Mathematics Project. Courtesy John Wiley and Sons, Inc., New York, N.Y.)

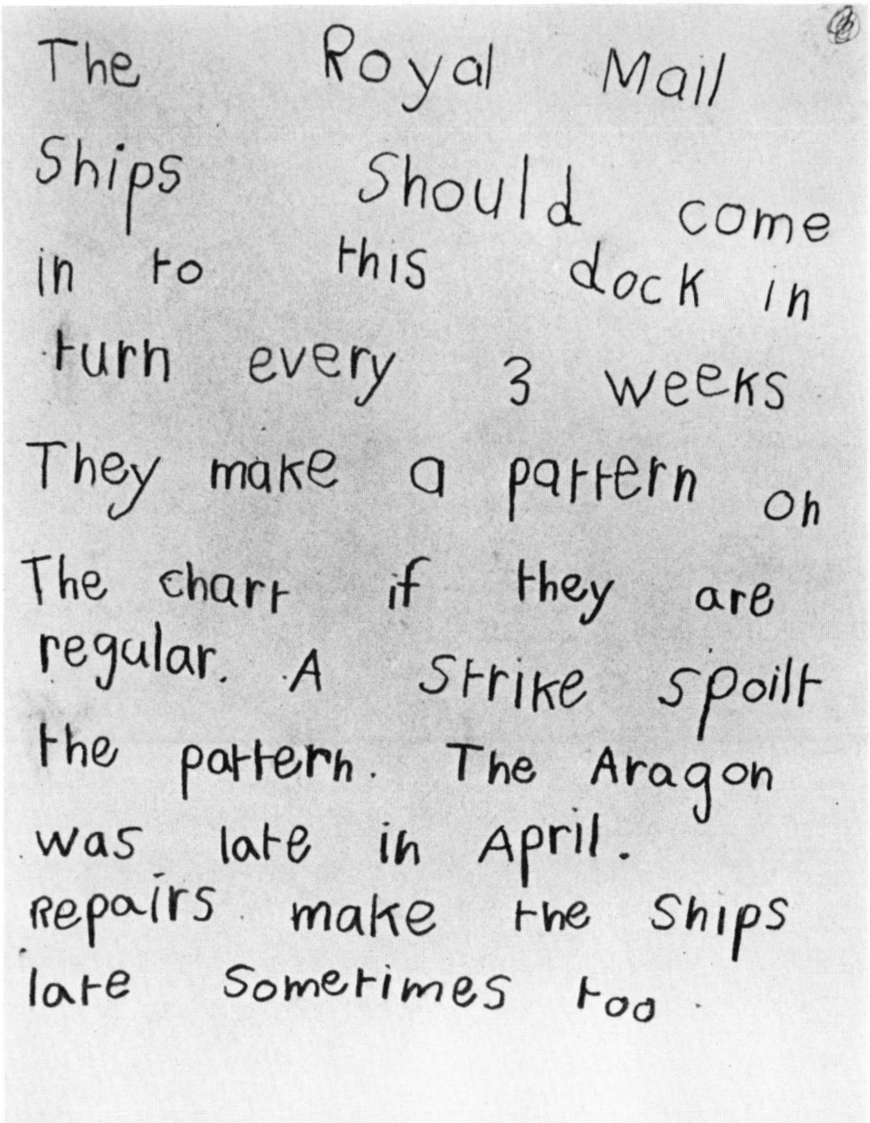

The Royal Mail
Ships Should come
in to this dock in
turn every 3 weeks
They make a pattern on
The chart if they are
regular. A strike spoilt
the pattern. The Aragon
was late in April.
Repairs make the ships
late Sometimes too.

Diary recording. (From *Beginnings.* Nuffield Junior Mathematics Project.
Courtesy John Wiley and Sons, Inc., New York, N.Y.)

are completed, achievements, and difficulties, including attitude toward mathematics.

The principal should keep a record of the general development of mathematics in the school. This can be a summary of the diaries kept by the classroom teachers. The second important record is of individual pupil progress, assessed at regular intervals (i.e., every six months or every year). Measures of individual progress in *concept development* are needed. This means individual testing of the child by an interviewer, using tests similar to the Piaget tests described throughout this book. A standardized achievement test in number manipulation is a mechanical process for the child and does not usually measure concept development.

SAMPLE ASSIGNMENTS FOR CHILDREN

Each assignment should involve:

1. Performing the experiment.
2. Expressing the results pictorially, if possible, such as with a graph or chart.
3. Writing down findings or conclusions.

Weight Relations

1. Using a pan balance, put a larger number of objects on one pan than on the other (shells, buttons, sand, and so forth). Estimate the weight relation and describe different ways of determining this relation.
2. Estimate the weight relations between the following pairs of objects (check estimates with a balance scale):
   (a) A toy car and a pencil.
   (b) A 2-inch and a 4-inch nail.
   (c) A large and a small object.
3. If two bags are the same size which is heavier?
   (a) A bag of beans or a bag of marbles?
   (b) A bag of shells or a bag of sand?
   Determine the weight relation using a balance.
4. What are the weight relations between a penny, nickel, dime, and quarter? Make a graph to show these relations. Write down your findings or conclusions.

Volume Relations

1. Using different shapes and sizes of containers, decide which ones hold more than the others.
2. Using a set of plastic containers of different sizes, find the volume relation between them. Make a chart or graph of your findings.
3. Using three drinking glasses of the same type and size, put different amounts of water in each until you get a musical scale. Test by striking glasses with a stick. Measure the volume of water in each glass. What is the mathematical relationship? Show with chart or graph.

Time Relations

1. Make a birthday graph for the children in your room. Show the number of children born each month. What are your conclusions?
2. Using a piece of string with a weight on one end as a pendulum, make a timing device. Experiment by shortening or lengthening the string. Can you graph your results? Write down your conclusions.
3. Make a graph of how you spend your time during a 24-hour day.

Size Relations

1. Draw an animal that would look large to a dog and also one that would look small. Express the size relationship between the objects. Can you graph this relationship? Write down your conclusions.
2. Using a piece of string, measure around your head, neck, waist, and knee. Can you make a graph showing the relationships? Compare these relations with those of a partner.
3. Measure with a piece of string the arm length or foot length of five children in your class and make a graph or chart to show the relationships.
4. Classify the children in class by height using 2-inch intervals. How many are there in each interval? Can you show this relation with a bar graph? What are your conclusions?
5. Classify a set of buttons, or dolls, by size and draw a graph of these relations.

My Day Graph. (Courtesy Miss Barbara Bittner, Henderson Laboratory School, Florida Atlantic University, Boca Raton, Florida.)

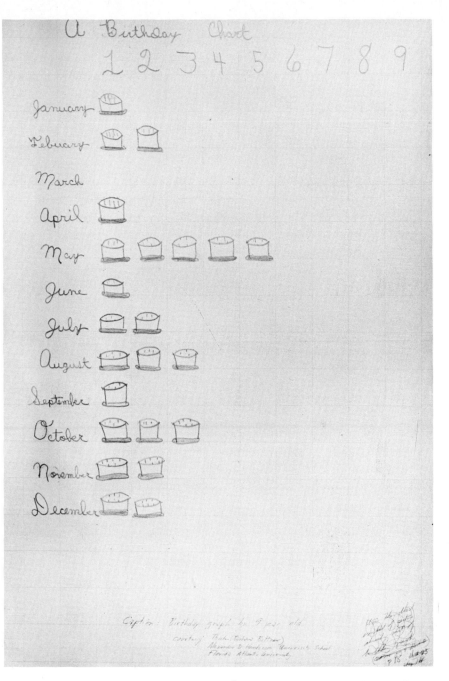

Birthday graph of class by nine-year-old. (Courtesy Miss Barbara Bittner, Henderson Laboratory School, Florida Atlantic University, Boca Raton, Florida.)

Shape Relations

1. Find how many models of triangles, squares, rectangles and circles there are in your room (such as the blackboard as a rectangle). Make a graph showing the number relation between these different shapes.
2. Draw a tent and describe the shapes you use. Write the relation of height to width and of width at the top to width at the bottom.
3. Look at a picture of, or draw, a boat or ship. What shapes are used to make a boat or ship? What is the number relationship between the different shapes used? Can you make a graph of these relations? Write your conclusions.

EXERCISES

Select and develop a set of concrete materials designed to teach a mathematical concept and prepare an assignment card or cards for the pupil to use in learning the concept.

INDEX

Centicube, 300–301
Centimeter, 294
Class inclusion, 41
Classification, 22–25
Closure property, 105–106
Commutative property
  addition, 63–66
  multiplication, 104–105
Concrete materials for teaching,
catalogs, 316*n*
Conservation
  of area, 290
  of distance, 287
  interview technique, 39–41
  of length, 286–87
  of number, 3, 12, 35–37
  of time, 259–60
Counting frame, 46
Cuisenaire rods, 316

Division, 116–33
  algorism, 123–32
  basic facts, 120–22
  error patterns, 132–33
  exercises, 120, 133, 193
  fractional numbers, 186–92
    invert and multiply rule (recipro-
    cal method), 190–92
    word or story problems, 189
  measurement, 117–20, 187–89
  in nondecimal bases, 154–57
  number line, 121
  partitive, 117–20, 187–89
  renaming, 125–28
  as repeated subtraction, 128–32
  by zero, 122–23
Drill and practice, 9
Duckworth, 12
Duration, 253–54

D

Decimal fractions, 194–208
  addition and subtraction, 197–99
  as a common fraction, 203
  division, 200–201
  introduction to, 195–97
  multiplication, 199–200
  per cent, 208–12
  proportion, 206–208
  ratio, 206–208
  scientific notation, 204
  types
    nonrepeating, 203
    nonterminating, 203
    repeating or periodic, 201–203
    terminating, 201–203
Development, stages of, 10
Developmental psychologists, 2
Dewey, 100
Diagnosing error patterns
  in addition, 76–78
  in division, 132–33
  in fractions, 175–76
  in multiplication, 114
  in subtraction, 92–94
Distributive property of multiplication,
106–108

E

Emotionally handicapped children, 236
Error patterns, diagnosing
  in addition, 76–78
  in division, 132–33
  in fractions, 175–76
  in multiplication, 114
  in subtraction, 92–94
Euclid, 261
Exceptional children, 231–51
  emotionally handicapped, 236
  exercises, 245
  gifted, 244–45
  learning disabled, 233–35
  materials for, 245–51
  mentally retarded, 235–36
  physically handicapped, 236–37
  strategies for teaching, 239–44
  suggested readings, 251
Exercises
  addition, 69, 76
  bases other than ten, 142, 149–50,
    157
  decimal fractions, 201, 206, 212–13
  developing math concepts, 19
  division, 120, 133
  exceptional children, 245

fractions, 176–77, 185–86, 193
geometry, 271, 279, 281–83
measurement, 292, 297–98
metric system, 297–98
multiplication, 115
number, 33, 51
problem solving, 221
subtraction, 87–88, 92
symmetry, 281–83
time, 260
Experience, role of, 17–18

F

Fractional numbers (fractions), 158–77, 178–93, 194–213
  addition, 161–71
  decimal, 194–208
    addition and subtraction, 197–99
    as a common fraction, 203
    division, 200–201
    introduction to, 195–97
    multiplication, 199–200
    per cent, 208–12
    per cent, word or story problems, 209–12
    proportion, 206–208
    ratio, 206–208
    scientific notation, 204
    types, 201–203
  division, 186–92
    reciprocal method, 190–92
    word or story problems, 189
  equivalent fractions, 169–70
  error patterns, 175–76
  exercises, 176–77, 185–86, 193, 201, 206, 212–13
  introduction, 159–61
  least common denominator, 166–68
    equivalence class, 167–68
    least common multiple, 168
  multiplication, 178–86
    unit regions, 182–83
    word or story problems, 183–84
  readiness, 158–59
  renaming, 168–69
  subtraction, 171–75
Fractions. *See* Fractional numbers

G

Gagné, 2, 5, 7, 8, 18, 19
Geoboard, 272–75, 317–18
Geometry, 261–85
  angles, 278–79
  children five to nine, 262–71
  curves, 267–68
  enclosure, 263
  exercises, 271, 279
  geoboard, 272
  golden rectangle, 279–80
  hexagon, 268
  horizontal, 270–71
  intersection, 277–78
  line segments, 276
  lines, 275–76
  order relation, 264
  parallelogram, 270
  pentagon, 268
  planes, 275–77
  polygons, 268
  Polyominoes, 273
  proximity, 262
  quadrilaterals, 269–70
  rays, 275–76
  rhombus, 270
  symmetry, 280–81
    axis of, 280–81
  tangrams, 283
    activities, 284–85
  trapezoid, 270
  triangles, 269–70
    union, 277–78
    vertical, 270–71
Gifted children, 244–45
Golden rectangle, 279–80
Gram, 294

H

Hand calculators, 222–30. *See* Calculators
Hands-on materials for teaching, catalogs, 316*n*
Horizontal concept, 270–71
Hundred chart, 49–50

Metric system, 293-302
   activities for children, 302-304
   centicube, 300-301
   considerations in teaching children,
      301-302
   conversions, 295
   introduction to, 298
   lesson on length for children, 299-
      300
   units of measure, 294
Milligram, 294
Milliliter, 294
Millimeter, 294
Montessori, 100
Motivation, 10
Multibase Arithmetic Blocks, 316
Multimat, 316
Multiplication, 95-115
   basic facts, 96-102
   Cartesian product, 102-104
   error patterns, 114
   exercises, 115
   fractional numbers, 178-86
      unit regions, 182-83
      word or story problems, 183-84
   in nondecimal bases, 150-53
      base five, 150-53
   number line, 101
   properties
      associative, 105
      closure, 105-106
      commutative, 104-105
      distributive, 106-108
      identity element, 106
   readiness, 96
Multiplicative inverse, 191-92
Multiplying, two-digit numbers, 109-
13

N

National Council of Teachers of Mathematics Agenda for Action in the 1980s,
214

Number
   cardinal, 34-44
   exercises, 33, 51
   and measurement, 288-89
   ordinal, 25-34
Number Blox, 316
Number line, 32-33, 61-62, 101, 121
   base five, 136-37
   fractions, 181
Numerals, learning to write, 42-44
   cursive, 43
   manuscript, 43

O

Ordering or succession, 253
Ordinal number, 25-34

P

Partitive division, 117-20
Per cent, 208-12
   word or story problems, 209-12
Philosophy, 18-19
Physically handicapped children, 236-
37
Piaget, 2-21, 26, 54, 57, 120-21, 217
   on multiplication, 120-21
Place value, 44-51, 228-29
Planes, 275-77
Pocket calculators, 222-30. *See also*
Calculators
Pocket chart, 46, 74
Polyominoes, 273
Problem solving, 214-21
   Agenda for Action, 214
   American Association for the Ad-
      vancement of Science, 216-17
   Bloom's taxonomy, 216
   exercises, 221
   Piaget, 217
   primary grades, 218-20
   upper elementary grades, 220-21

Proportion, 206–208
  time, 257–58
Psychologists
  behaviorists, 2
  developmental, 2
Pythagorus, 261

R

Ratio, 206–208
  and measurement, 291–92
Rays, 275–76
Readiness
  for addition, 54–57
  for equivalent fractions, 169–70
  for fractions, 158–59
  for measurement, 286–92
  for multiplication, 96
  for subtraction, 82–83
Rectangle, golden, 279–80
Renaming
  in addition, 71–76
  in division, 125–28
  in fractions, 168–69
  in multiplication, 110–12
Reversibility of thought, 3, 27, 36, 54

S

St. Augustine, 252
Sets, 53
Skinner, 2, 5
Smedslund, 4
Socialization, 15, 37–38
Stages
  concrete operational, 10, 11, 12
  formal operational, 10, 14
  of intellectual development, 10
  preoperational, 10, 11
  sensorimotor, 10
  in understanding fractions, 159
Stimulus-response, 5

Story problems
  fractions, 183–84, 189, 209–12
  per cent, 209–12
Strategies for teaching, 239–44
Subtracting
  three digits, 86–87
  two place numbers, 83–86
Subtraction, 79–94
  algorisms, 88–92
  basic facts, 79–81
  error patterns, 92–94
  exercises, 87–88, 92
  fractional numbers, 171–75
  methods (algorisms), 88–92
  models for, 81–82
    missing addend, 80–82
    subtract or take away, 79–81
  nondecimal bases, 143–49
  readiness for, 82–83
  renaming (borrowing), 84–86
Symmetry, 280–81
  axis of, 280–81
Synchronism, 254–56

T

Tangrams, 283
  activities, 284–85
Term projects, 19–21
Time, 252–60
  conservation of, 259–60
  duration, 253–54
  exercises, 260
  isochronism, 254
  ordering or succession, 253
  proportions, 257–58
  synchronism, 254–56
  time units, 256–57
Time units, construction of, 256–57
Transitivity, 27
  of length, 287–88
Trundle wheel, 317–18

U

Union of sets, 53, 277–78

V

Vertical concept, 270–71

W

Writing numerals, 42–44
    cursive, 43
    manuscript, 43

Z

Zero, division by, 122–23